THE SECRET HISTORY OF
THE NEW WORLD ORDER

HERBERT DORSEY

DENVER, COLORADO

Prologue

To write a history of secret conspiracies and agendas is usually not an easy task. However, the persons and organizations behind the "New World Order", in spite of their desire for secrecy, have left a discernable historical trail which the diligent researcher, with enough work, can follow.

There have been numerous insiders with a conscious and historians who have penetrated portions of the numerous plots to overthrow sovereign governments and create the super governments, like the Soviet Union, the European Union and the planned North American Union. These persons have authored, well documented books, on the subject. In my attempt to piece all the separate pieces of the puzzle together and create a coherent history of "The New World Order" I will make reference to these excellent books which will provide greater documentation and detail on the subject than I intend to provide herein.

The secret organizations behind the NWO have gone to great lengths to control the flow of information and in addition to gaining control of the news media, have set up foundations, publishing houses and schools to put forth a version of history that hides their own culpability in starting wars and insurrections to further their own goals. This book, to the best of my ability, will attempt to rectify that problem and give a truer version of history.

I touch on religion since it is a large component of mass control. From my own point, I follow no organized religion and consider myself a free thinker. I need no priest to commune with God within. I have studied most of the Religions and find the teachings of Jesus Christ to be divine wisdom. If we all could actually live by these teachings, Earth would be a paradise.

The three organized religions based on Abraham - Judaism, Christianity and Islam, I however find particularly reprehensive, in their long histories of soaking the earth in human blood in endless war. A truly spiritual person has more respect for the living creations of the Creator and would not engage in such profane and cruel activity as war. In fact, I consider war Satan's way of bringing hell to earth. Did not Christ say "Love thine enemy"?

So, the inevitable charges of "religious prejudice" brought against this book will probably be quite true. And, I will take no offence. I am but the messenger. The Truth is the Truth.

Table of Contents

1. A Short History of Empires 1

2. The Crusades 14

3. The Reformation, Counter Reformation and War....................23

4. Secret Societies 38

5. World Wars 64

6. Nation Destroying for the New World Order 155

7. Propaganda and Mind Control...193

8. Deep Underground Military Bases...215

9. The Extra-Terrestrial Presence 230

Conclusions..249

Bibliography 259

1

A Short History of Empires

The Neo-Assyrian Empire (911-605 BCE) was the most dominant power on earth and the largest empire in the World at the
time. This empire stretched from Cyprus in the west to central
Iran in the east, and from the Caucasus Mountains in the north
to Nubia, Egypt and Arabia in the south.

This empire fell in 605 BCE with the death of Ashur-uballit II after a period of internal strife followed by an attack by a coalition
of Babylonians, Medes, Scythians, Persians and Cimmerians led
by Nabopolassar, the Chaldean ruler of Babylon and Cyaxares of
Media/Persia. During the Neo-Assyrian Empire Mesopotamian
Aramaic became the lingua franca of the Empire.

Babylon had a flowering of power and influence under the
Chaldean dynasty which took over much of the empire. There
was a mystery religion in Babylon guided by the Chaldean
Magi. A religious Pontiff (meaning bridge maker) appointed by
the Sovereign ruled over a college of seventy two hierophants.
Religion was very important in Babylon. The Pontiff had almost
as much power as the king in ruling the kingdom.

In 539 BCE, Mesopotamia was invaded by the Persian Empire,

then ruled by Cyrus the Great. This brought to an end over 3,000 years of Semitic Mesopotamian dominance of the near east. The Persian wars caused the Chaldeans to flee to Pergamos (modern day Bergama in Turkey). At Pergamos, they carried out their Religious rites independent of any government and plotted with the Greeks against the Persians.

Then, in 330 BCE the Macedonian Greek emperor Alexander the Great overthrew the Persians and took control of Mesopotamia itself, bringing Hellenic influence to the region. Alexander the Great created a mighty empire that stretched from India to the lands around the Mediterranean Sea. The City of Alexandria, in Egypt, was made in his honor. A great library there held the collective knowledge of previous civilizations.

Later, Rome became the dominant empire which ruled much of the then known world. An important tool of ancient rule over people was religion. Both the early leaders of Rome and Alexander the Great knew it was better to allow conquered people to keep their religion as they would then be easier to rule. Rome's appointed ruler over Judea, Herod, even went so far as to rebuild King Solomon's Temple, which the Babylonians had earlier destroyed, to gain favor with the Jewish people.

Herod came from southern Judea near Egypt and adopted a version of the Jewish religion. He had successfully resisted being seduced by Cleopatra and later sided with Rome when Mark Anthony and Cleopatra tried to break with Rome. Thus, Rome trusted him to be their representative in Judea. However, the rebuilding of the Temple was part of Herod's plan to unify all the Jews of the Diaspora by recreating the Temple in Jerusalem as a place of pilgrimage, especially during Passover.

Rome acquired Pergamos by the decree of Attalus III. The

priesthood of Pergamos then moved to Italian peninsula and brought their Babylonian mystery religion with them. Rome's own religion contained a pantheon of Gods, each ruling over a different aspect of nature. The greatest god of Rome was Sol Invictus, God of the Sun and giver of life. The worship day of Sol Invictus was every Sunday and a particular annual celebration on December 25.

A new religion, Christianity, was emerging in Judea. Under Jesus's command, his elder brother James became the head of the Christian Church in Jerusalem. Paul went out to preach to the non-Jews or Gentiles in other lands. The first Christian council was convened when Paul returned to Jerusalem asking if Gentiles had to undergo circumcision in order to become Christians. James and the other Apostils decided that it wouldn't be necessary.

James the Just, as he was called, issued the first Apostolic Decree outlining the rules for the church. The early Christian priests didn't have to be celibate. In fact marriage was favored. If one had no experience as a father of a family, how could he be a good head of a church?

In fact, Jesus himself was married, as were most of his disciples including Peter. The wedding feast at Cana was Jesus's own wedding to Mary Magdalene. Jesus survived the crucifixion and lived for quite a while afterwards. Mary Magdalene bore Jesus three children, a daughter named Tamar, a son named Jesus Justis and a son named Joseph according to theological scholar, Barbara Thiering, in her book *Jesus the Man*.

Most Christians may not be aware of this because of the later censoring of the Scriptures. Also, for political reasons, some of the scriptures were written in coded "pershers." For example, some pershers would refer to Babylonian armies which were code for Roman armies. Another persher used Jerusalem (in the plural form) as Qumran. Another persher was "The word of God" actually meaning Jesus. These persher and many others were necessary because of the zealot movement in Judea that sought independence from Rome. The zealots at Qumran had to hide their activities from the Roman officials and Jesus had to be hidden from his enemies. More of the story of Jesus is being discovered all the time in ancient documents like the Nag Hammadi Scrolls, Dead Sea Scrolls and learning how to correctly interpret the script within by having a good knowledge of the contemporary realities on the ground in first century Judea.

The original teachings of Jesus were that all humans, like himself, were sons and daughters of God. His mission was to instruct mankind on the method of attaining this Godhood and overcoming the limitations and temptations of the material body and material world. "All these things I do, ye shall also do and even greater things" said Jesus. Some of his teachings were for the inner circle of Apostles and some, spoken in parables were for the masses. "Let him who has ears, hear." Jesus also talked about reincarnation, claiming that John the Baptist was the prophet Elijah reincarnated. If we don't evolve into Christ Consciousness in this lifetime, we are reincarnated until we do.

The early Gnostic Christian Churches, as created by Paul and Simon, carried on these traditions, teaching the importance of "going within" to find God and Heaven and the importance of a childlike heart, full of trusting love of God and God's creations. Through the "fall of man" we left our heavenly estate to incarnate on Earth. Also we would be tested by the legions of evil ones known as the Watchers or the Nephilim, who were fallen angles led by Satan. The idea was that through many reincarnations, our spirits would evolve until final mastery over the material world, Satan and death was gained and we would become like Christ.

The original Christian teachings were supposed to speed this process up. The heart was the gateway to the inner world and had to be purged of all hateful, prideful, lustful and other ungodly, impure impediments to realizing Godhood. This inner work was the responsibility of each person and not that of a priest - who could only show the way.

During the second century, the Christian religion, under Irenaeus, Justin, Tertullian and others started to modify these teachings to first gain congregations and then to gain more control over the Church congregations. At that time, there existed many religions whose hero was killed, and rose from death. Osiris, Indra, Mithra, Dionysus, and Apollonius of Tyana were the more well known. So, the death and resurrection of Christ was made the major Orthodox Christian Church dogma to appeal to the many who already believed in these things.

The idea that each person was a son or daughter of God was considered heresy and thrown out. Reincarnation was also thrown out for the same reason. "Heresy" comes from a Greek word meaning one who chooses or thinks for himself. The Orthodox Christians wanted rigidly held concepts – not free thinkers.

The Gnostic Christian Churches set up by Paul, Simon and others, were very loosely structured, allowing individual spiritual inspiration to play a role. The Gnostic Christian Churches initiated people into the "knowing" that would bring them to Christhood. The Gnostic Christian Churches allowed for women priests, the Orthodox Christian Churches did neither of these things. The Catholic Church later made even more changes to create a dependency on the Church and priests for "salvation."

For those interested in this subject, I recommend reading *The Orthodox Christian Conspiracy* by Joseph P. Macchio.

In 44AD, Mary Magdalene was in political danger and asked her friend Herod-Agrippa II, a Christian, for help. He arraigned for her and her children, Tamar and Jesus Justis to be moved to his estate in Gaul (near Provence in today's France). Later that year, She gave birth to a son. She named this "Grail Child" Joseph after his grandfather. Many ancient churches in southern France are dedicated to Saint Marie de Madeline in her honor. The Cathar religion as well many early French kings and the Grail legends evolved from this source.

In any case James – not Peter - led the first Christian Church in Jerusalem until his martyrdom in 62 AD. That year during Passover, the temple high priest, Ananus Demas, wanted James to stand on the wall of the temple and tell the multitudes that Christianity was a fraud. James saw his chance for an audience and agreed to speak. But, when on top of the Temple wall, instead he preached Christian principals to the crowd below. This angered the priests, who pushed James off the wall. The fall didn't kill James. But then, he was stoned to death by order of Ananus Demas.

After James' martyrdom, Jesus's cousin, Simeon son of Clopas, becomes the head of the Christian Church in Jerusalem. In 64 AD, Nero blames the Christians for the burning of Rome and starts persecuting them.

In 66 AD a fierce revolt in Jerusalem begins which successfully drives the Romans out. However within a few years, General Titus counter attacks with fresh legions from all over the Roman Empire. In AD 70, in retaliation for the Jewish revolt, Roman General Titus had the temple destroyed as foretold by Jesus.

Many Jews were killed or captured and sold into slavery. Many other Jews, including the Christian Jews, fled to Pella and other lands.

In 131 AD, a second Jewish rebellion, led by Simon Bar Kokhba, occurs against the Romans. By 136 AD, the rebellion is crushed by Roman forces and Jews are forbidden to live in Jerusalem. This effectively ends the nation of Israel.

Around 160 AD the Gospel of Mary Magdalene was written. Around 200 AD the Gospel of Phillip was written with some references to Mary Magdalene.

The early Christian churches were largely persecuted by Romans. Christians wouldn't worship Roman gods, make sacrifices to them or join in Roman celebrations and holidays to their gods. This persecution reached a climax under Emperor Diocletian for a ten year period from 303 to 313 AD.

During this time, Diocletian had many documents of early Christian history destroyed. This is probably why the Nag Hammadi Scrolls and others, yet to be discovered, of the early Christian Church were hidden away.

At the time of Emperor Constantine, things started to change. Constantine's mother was a devout Christian. Constantine passed a law in 313 AD known as the Edict of Milan which guaranteed tolerance towards Christians. Constantine traveled to Jerusalem with his mother and under her guidance had the Church of the Holy Sepulchre constructed. Other Churches were also created at Bethlehem and Nazareth under her guidance.

Constantine was considering making Christianity the official religion of Rome but was troubled by the many different sects of

Christianity that had evolved since the time of Jesus. There was Arian Christianity, Gnostic Christianity, Orthodox Christianity and other versions.

Also, Constantine being a political pragmatist decided to merge many pagan beliefs with Christianity to make it more acceptable to the Citizens of Rome. The primary God of Rome was Sol Invictus and his day of worship was on Sunday. With the help of Pope Sylvester, Constantine had the Christian Church in Rome changed its day of worship from the Sabbath on Saturday to the first day of the week or Sunday - directly disobeying God's commandment to keep the Sabbath Holy. Such was the arrogance of the Caesars and Popes of Rome.

Constantine decided to convene a Council at Nicaea in AD 325, to determine the "true" form of Christianity. After this council of learned elders duly deliberated, a universal (Catholic) version of Christianity was approved by a majority vote. Soon after, Catholic Christianity was made the official religion of Rome. Religious groups that did not follow the Nicaean creed of Catholicism were charged with heresy and were often put to death. Do you think that Jesus would have approved of that policy?

The actual birthdate of Jesus Christ was unknown to the Romans. In 345 AD, Pope Julius decides that Christ's birthday was on December 25, the main celebration day of Sol Invictus. Later, the Council of Laodicea, convened from Ad 363 to AD 364, determined which gospels would be incorporated in the Bible. Notably, more gospels were rejected than accepted. In 381 AD, Christianity is made the State religion of the Roman Empire by Emperor Theodosius.

In 391 AD, because of the thrall of Catholicism, Emperor

Theodosius abolishes all non-Catholic Churches. Much looting and destruction occurs, including the destruction of the Library of Alexandria in Egypt. Much of the knowledge and history of ancient civilizations was lost. Churches practicing true Christianity were forced to practice in secret.

In 431 AD, the council of Ephesus created the Cult of the Virgin Mary, mother of God. This was incorporated to emulate Isis worship. Jesus never said to worship his mother. The Holy Communion largely mimicked the Egyptian ceremony of the resurrection of Osiris. The worship and prayer before statues in the church was reminiscent of idol worship, also forbidden by God. Many of these Pagan beliefs and ceremonies incorporated into the Church had their origins in Babylon. (1)

The leaders of the Christian Churches in each large city were called Bishops. Rome was the most important City in the empire. So, the Bishop of Rome was considered the papa of all Bishops, or the Pope. Before long, the Catholic Church invested new powers in the Pope of the Church of Rome.

The original claim was that the Pope was the representative or vicar of Peter. This claim was based on the false belief that Peter was the first head of the Christian Church. In actuality, it was James - not Peter. There is no archeological or scriptural evidence that Peter was ever in Rome. Peter's tomb as well as James' tomb have both been discovered in Jerusalem. Paul - not Peter - was the apostle that brought Christianity to Rome.

Later, the claim was made that the Pope was *Vicarvs Fili Dei,* the vicar or representative of Christ, the Son of God, on Earth. As such, the Pope held the keys to Heaven and Hell. Many actually believed this patent absurdity.

Out of fear of eternal damnation many were very careful not cross the Pope or be excommunicated from the Church of Rome. More practices of the Babylonian mystery religion were incorporated into the Catholic Church. The Popes developed a college of seventy Cardinals with the power to elect new Popes and rule over Bishops and also took on an additional title, Pontiff Maximus (the greatest bridge builder). In the original Babylonian mystery religion, the Pontiff ruled over a college of seventy two hierophants.

One has to wonder what Christ has to say about his pretended vicar – the Pope. Actually, when Christ was alive on Earth, he voiced the following warning; "Many shall come in my name, doing the works of Satan." The long, cruel, bloody history and the fraudulent deceptions of the Church of Rome certainly bring this warning to mind.

In any case, the original Christian religion was severely altered and perverted, first by the Orthodox Christians and then by the influence of the Roman Popes and Caesars. The Decline of the Roman Empire quickly followed the creation of the Church of Rome. Soon, Roman legions had to be recalled from the outlying regions of the Roman Empire to defend Rome itself as the Barbarians were raiding and pillaging that great city.

By AD 476, the last Roman Emperor, Romulus Augustus's, was deposed by the barbarian general, Odoacer, who then ruled Italy. This barbarian rule allowed the Christian religion to continue unmolested. The church organizations already in place actually became a de-facto government of sorts, passing out grain from church properties to feed the people, keeping records, converting barbarians to Christianity and so forth. The Catholic Church became even more influential and powerful after the fall of Rome.

The Curia of the Vatican realized that it was only a matter of time before they would lose their grip on the holy city of Jerusalem which they greatly coveted. They decided on a plan that would help them keep control of Jerusalem and the holy land:

In the Arabian Peninsula, the Augustine order of the Catholic Church had a number of missions. A wealthy, Arab woman, named Khadijah, donated most of her wealth to the Catholic mission and retired to a Convent after the death of her second husband. But, while in the Convent, she was given a strange assignment. She was to go back into the world and marry Mohammed.

She hired Mohammed, who had a good reputation for honesty, to do a trade caravan to Syria for her. After his return from this profitable caravan, Khadijah asked one of her maids to tell Mohammed that she was interested in marrying him. She was still good looking at 40 years of age and Mohammed was 20 at the time. Mohammed agreed to the marriage. She married Mohammed in AD 595. Her cousin, Waraquah was also a devout Catholic who later developed considerable influence over Mohammed.

His wife's remaining wealth gave Mohammed the free time to meditate in a cave on a mountain near his residence, sometimes for days at a time. He would return home claiming to have received teachings from Arc Angel Gabriel. Waraquah would help Mohammed interpret these visions of Gabriel. At first the interpretations were memorized and recited to others. Quran means recital in Arabic. Later, the recital was committed to writing in a book called the Quran (Koran).

Waraquah also instilled a hatred of the Jews in Mohammed and had inserted some untruths into the Koran. For example, In the Koran, Abraham was supposed to sacrifice Ishmael – not Isaac

– on the temple mount. Worship of the Virgin Mary was also included. Under Waraquah's teachings Mohammed was also informed that the Catholics were the only true Christians and the other sects of Christianity were evil imposters.

The plan of the Vatican was to use their financial and other influence over Mohammed to create a new religion suitable to Arabs. This religion would inspire an army in Arabia, using Vatican financing, that would eventually invade the holy land. In return for the Vatican's assistance to Mohammed, he would agree to make war on the non –Catholic Christians and Jews, protect the Augustinian Missions and Roman Catholics, invade and turn the holy land over to the Church of Rome. (2)

Well, after several setbacks, Mohammed's armies with Vatican financing, finally prevailed. The Muslim religion and armies were sweeping Arabia and moving into other areas. While Jewish and non-Catholic churches were pillaged, the Catholic Churches and people were left unharmed.

In AD 632 Mohammed died and Abu Bakr became the new Caliph. In Ad 636 Abu Bakr's armies invaded Judea. Abu Bakr felt that their armies were so strong that they no longer needed the Vatican's assistance and that they did not have to live up to Mohammed's agreements with the Vatican. So, they kept control of the holy land for themselves.

Under Muslim rule, the Jews were allowed to return to Jerusalem, from where they had been exiled by Rome after the Bar Kokhba revolt. The Muslims also allowed Christian Pilgrims to continue to visit the holy land.

After the decline of the Roman Empire, the Church of Rome held its influence over much of the western portion of the former

Roman Empire. This was particularly true in Gaul, land of the Franks. From this land would raise King Clovis, a devout Catholic whose armies would defend the Church and its fiefdoms.

Another Frankish King, Pepin embarked on an ambitious program to expand his power. He reformed the legislation of the Franks and continued the ecclesiastical reforms of Pope Boniface. Pepin also intervened in favor of the Papacy of Stephen II against the Lombards in Italy. He was able to secure several cities, which he then gave to the Pope as part of the Donation of Pepin. This formed the legal basis for the Papal States in the middle Ages

Later, Charlemagne, Pepin's son, also a devout Catholic, would increase the following of the Catholic Church. The people that his armies conquered had a simple choice - convert to Christianity or be put to death. In 800 AD, Pope Leo III Crowned Charlemagne the Emperor of the Holy Roman Empire.

One fraudulent device invented by the Vatican was the "Donation of Constantine" which purported to be Constantine's will, in which Constantine granted all of the Western Roman Empire to the Catholic Church. The Donation of Constantine was used to strengthen the Church's claims of dominion over that area.

The many kingdoms that formed the Holy Roman Empire gave fealty to the Pope. Kings that did not "toe the Church line" ran the risk of excommunication and eternal damnation. This Empire, that lasted about 1,000 years, was not ruled by the Pope's armies. It was ruled by Kings who were ruled by the power of belief in the Pope and the Catholic Church.

2 | The Crusades

After stability settled about the Holy Roman Empire, many knights became restive and a certain amount of infighting between kingdoms would happen. Another problem was that the Muslims were now invading former western Christian lands held by Rome, notably the land now known as Spain. The biggest problem however was the Seljuk Turks. They had taken control of the holy land and put a stop to Christian pilgrimages to the holy sites. Also, they had begun invading the Byzantine Empire. The Byzantine Emperor, Alexis I, requested help from the Western European kingdoms.

The Vatican Curia decided that a crusade to regain the Holy Land would give the knights a quest to expend their energies on elsewhere and a crusade would help to create a more unified Holy Roman Empire. In 1095 AD, Pope Urban II proclaimed the First Crusade with the stated goal of gaining Christian access to the holy places in and around Jerusalem. The Pope proclaimed that any soldier joining the Crusade would be guaranteed a place in heaven.

The Crusaders pillaged the countries in transit, living off the land, as did all transiting armies of the time. The First Crusade resulted in the massacre of 8,000 Jews in the Rhineland in the first of Europe's pogroms.

In 1099 AD, the crusaders invaded Jerusalem under the leadership of Godfrey de Bouillon. The First Crusade also resulted in the slaughter of a purported 70,000 citizens in the fall of Jerusalem.

Thus, started the era of the Crusades. Many crusades would follow. And, not all of them were against Muslims! Where previously the Catholic Church had killed heretics that represented a small percentage of the population. A new era of wholesale slaughter by the Holy Roman Empire, led by the Pope, had begun. There followed 6 more major Crusades to control the holy land in a 2 century struggle that ended in failure after the fall of Acre, the last Christian stronghold in the holy land, in 1291.

The forth Crusade from 1202 to 1204 AD, was hijacked by the merchants of Venice. The Crusaders needed their ships to transport their army to the holy land. The merchants of Venice wanted to eliminate their largest competitor in the Mediterranean Sea, Constantinople. The merchants made a deal with the Crusaders. If they would first invade Constantinople and sack that city, the Crusaders could keep all the loot and then the merchants would transport the Crusaders to the holy land.

Up to this time the Vatican had been influencing Alexis IV, the Byzantine Emperor in Constantinople to yield to the Catholic Church. But, Alexis IV had just been killed by agents of the Eastern Orthodox Christians who were very much opposed to the idea. So, Pope Innocent III also agreed to the sacking of Constantinople and the Crusaders, with the Pope's nod, agreed with the merchants of Venice terms.

But, after sacking Constantinople, the Crusaders were war weary and were content to return home with their looted treasures. So, no attempt to regain the Holy Land occurred with this crusade. Fierce antagonism has existed between the Catholic and Eastern Orthodox Christian Churches ever since.

When Mary Magdalene came to Southern Gaul in 44 AD, she brought her 2 Children, Tamar and Jesus Justis with her. Soon after her arrival, she gave birth to Joseph. Later, Jesus Justice joined his father Jesus Christ in Rome. They most likely perished in Nero's anti-Christian pogroms in Rome. The Roman Caesars had been hunting down Dosposyni (Greek for the descendants of Jesus), since this bloodline could create a messiah over the Jews and potentially cause more trouble for Rome.

Joseph, carrying the bloodline of Jesus and King David survived in hiding and sired the Merovingian linage of Kings in Southern Gaul. This linage also carried the secrets of King Solomon's treasure buried under the now destroyed Herod's temple. When the Merovingian line was usurped by the Carolingians, the 'bloodline' was preserved in secret and became the French noble House of Lorraine.

After Christian fighters captured Jerusalem during the First Crusade, groups of pilgrims from across Western Europe began visiting the Holy Land. Many were killed while crossing through Muslim-controlled territory during their journey. Godfrey of Bouillon, through the intervention of secret preservers of his lineage through the House of Lorraine, became the first King of Jerusalem. These secret backers of Godfrey were established in an abbey or priory on Mount Zion and were later known as the Priory de Sion. They went on to engineer the Order of Knights Templar with Hugues de Payens in 1118 AD, allegedly to protect the pilgrims to the holy land.

In reality the Knights Templar, at first, protected no pilgrims to the holy land. The Priory de Scion had the Knights Templar excavate under the remains of the old Jewish Temple in Jerusalem, to find the lost treasure of King Solomon.

In 1867, Captain Wilson, Lieutenant Warren and a team of Royal Engineers had re-excavated the area and uncovered tunnels extending vertically, for some 25 meters, before fanning out under the Dome of the Rock, which is generally thought to be the site of King Solomon's temple. Crusader artifacts found in these tunnels attest to Templar involvement.

More recently, a team of Israeli archaeologists, intrigued by the Warren and Wilson discovery, reinvestigated the passage and concluded that the Templars did in fact excavate beneath the Temple. The Templars may have discovered texts that had been hidden beneath the site prior to its destruction by the Roman invasion in 70 AD.

In spite of not protecting the pilgrims the Knights Templar were given rave reviews back in Rome by the members of the Priory de Scion. Soon the donations to the Knights Templers started flowing. Also, knights were lining up to become members of the Templars. Whether or not they actually discovered the lost treasure, the legend lives on that they actually did and secreted it back to Southern France.

The Templars learned from certain "initiates of the East", a Jewish doctrine which was attributed to St. John the Apostle. These Christians of St. John were known as Johannites. In Public the Templars professed Catholicism while in secret they were actually Johannites.

Later, numbering in the thousands, the Templars established

new chapters throughout Western Europe. They developed a reputation as fierce warriors during key battles of the Crusades, driven by religious fervor and forbidden from retreating unless vastly outnumbered. They also set up a network of banks that enabled religious pilgrims to deposit assets in their home countries and withdraw funds in the Holy Land. Along with their donated fortune and various business ventures, this system gave the Knights Templar enormous financial sway. At the height of their influence, they boasted a sizeable fleet of ships, owned the island of Cyprus and served as a primary lender to European monarchs and nobles.

The Cathar religion basically descended from the churches created by Mary Magdalene who had fled Jerusalem with the children of Jesus, and settled in Sothern France in the Languedoc region. The Cathar religion actually practiced the teachings of Christ by loving their God with all their heart and their neighbors as themselves.

The Cathars observed the offensive amount of pomp and ceremony exhibited by the Catholic bishops and priests and consequently had little respect for the Pope or his representatives. Dominic De Guzman, a Catholic Priest, had spent 10 years trying to convert the Cathars to the Catholic faith but met with very little success.

Count Raymond VI of Toulouse was allowing the Cathar heresy to spread throughout his domain. . In 1207 Pope Innocent III appointed Peter de Castelnau, as apostolic legate and inquisitor to lead an expedition against the Cathars and particularly to obtain the recantation of Count Raymond VI of Toulouse. Having urged him from 1205 to stamp out the heretics with no success, Peter now excommunicated Raymond, placing the Languedoc region under interdict.

Peter's campaign on behalf of Innocent III ended in disaster. He was assassinated, supposedly at Raymond's instigation. After the murder of the papal legate, Pope Innocent III declared a crusade against Languedoc in southern France. He offered the lands of the Cathar heretics to any French nobleman or knight willing to take up arms.

All the men, women and children in whole cities and villages in Sothern France were put to death in this crusade. Toulouse was ravaged and its inhabitants, Cathar and non-Cathar alike, were massacred. Notably, in spite of the Pope's offer of lands, the Knights Templar had no part of the Crusade against the Cathars. In fact some Cathars were given sanctuary at Templar bases.

Dominic De Guzman was to become renown by the Vatican because of his zeal in overseeing the slaying of Cathar heretics there. He later formed the Dominican Order.

Then, there were the Northern Crusades, which finished the work started by Charlemagne in converting northern Europeans pagans to Christianity at the point of the sword.

Even before the start of the Crusades, another military operation of the Holy Roman Empire was the Reconquista, which sought to retake Spain from the Muslim invaders. The Reconquista lasted from AD 718 to 1492.

Under Muslim rule in Spain, Jews were allowed to live in peace with the Muslims. But, when the Catholic armies re-conquered Spain, Muslims and Jews faced expulsion or conversion to Catholism. If they choose expulsion, they had to forfeit all their property to the Catholic Church. Naturally, under those conditions, many Jews and Muslims chose to convert.

The Tribunal of the Holy Office of the Inquisition, commonly known as the Spanish Inquisition was established in 1478 by Catholic Monarchs Ferdinand II of Aragon and Isabella I of Castile. This Inquisition was created because it was suspected that some of the converts were only faking it and secretly were still practicing their former religion. The suspects were charged with heresy and, if found guilty, were burned at the stake and all their property confiscated by the Church. Eventually, the Inquisition was placed in charge of the Dominican order, founded by Dominic De Guzman, because of his previous zeal in combating the heresy of the Cathars.

Jacques de Molay, Grand Master of the Knights Templar, had been called to Poitiers, France, for the purpose of discussing with the new pope a new crusade to retake the Holy Land. For almost two years, he shuttled back and forth between the pope and King Phillip IV, essentially stamping out various diplomatic fires, such as the proposal to merge all the Papal military orders.

In June 1307, de Molay rode into Paris at the head of a column of his knights, with a dozen horses laden with gold and silver, to begin the financing of the new Crusade. For the next several months, Phillip treated the aging Grand Master with interest and diplomacy.

King Philip IV of France, had borrowed considerable amounts of money from the Knight Templars to finance his wars against England. Soon, he became so deeply in debt that he decided the only way out was to have the Knights Templars outlawed.

King Philip IV engineered the election of the pope and the relocation of the papal court to Avignon, France. The King of France also held Pope Clement V's brother hostage, not to be released until the Templars were outlawed by the Pope. On Friday,

October 13, 1307, many of the Order's members in France were arrested, tortured into giving false confessions, and then burned at the stake.

Apparently, members of the Priory de Scion had tipped off the Templars that the mass arrests were coming.

When the Templar depositories were raided all the money was missing. Also the Templar fleet at La Salle was missing along with many of the Templars most valiant knights. The Templar fleet sailed, with the Templar wealth and fighters, around Ireland and landed in Scotland where they joined forces with Robert the Bruce.

The Templars had chosen Scotland because they knew they would be immune from attack from the Catholic Church there. King Robert the Bruce, and the whole Scottish nation, had been excommunicated for taking up arms against King Edward II of England.

In 1312, Pope Clement V finally decided to end the situation at a council in Vienna. Just to make certain the decision went the way he intended, Phillip IV stationed his army on the outskirts of the city. The pliant Pope Clement V officially dissolved the Order of the Knight Templars, without formally condemning it.

All Templar remaining possessions were handed over to the Knights Hospitaller, and many Templars who freely confessed were set free and assigned to other Orders. Those who did not confess were sent to the stake. Phillip, soothed his loss of the Templars' treasure by demanding a yearly fee from the Hospitallers to defray his costs of prosecuting the Templars.

Later, according to John J. Robinson, in his book *Born in the Blood: the lost secrets of Freemasonry*, the outlawed Templars in all countries of Europe went underground and secretly evolved into the Freemasons.

3

The Reformation, Counter Reformation and War

The Holy Roman Empire arrived at its greatest power in the fifteenth century. The Catholic Church had amassed great wealth by many methods:

There were donations to the Church. There was confiscated property of heretics. Many would will their property to the Church. There was the sale of indulgences, which would forgive the sins of the purchaser. And there was the outright sale of the ecclesiastic offices of the church. In the Vatican, pomp and corruption was rampant. The Vatican had all the appearances of a giant corporation disguised as a religion!

But, a new problem arose for the Catholic Church. In 1453, Constantinople, which never fully recovered from the Fourth Crusade, was overrun by the Muslims. Many priests of the Eastern Orthodox Church took valuable church records with them as they fled into Germany. Some of these records, which included original scriptures of the Bible written in Greek, found their way into the University of Wittenberg in Germany, where Martin Luther was a Doctor of Theology, around 1512.

In 1516, Johann Tetzel, a Dominican friar and papal commissioner for indulgences, was sent to Germany by the Roman Catholic Church to sell indulgences to raise money to rebuild St. Peter's Basilica in Rome. On 31 October 1517, Luther wrote to his bishop, Albert of Mainz, protesting the sale of indulgences. He enclosed in his letter a copy of his "Disputation of Martin Luther on the Power and Efficacy of Indulgences," which came to be known as *The Ninety-Five Theses*.

In 1518 friends of Luther translated the *95 Theses* from Latin into German, printed, and widely copied, making the controversy one of the first in history to be aided by the printing press. Within two weeks, copies of the theses had spread throughout Germany; within two months throughout Europe.

Archbishop Albrecht of Mainz did not reply to Luther's letter containing the 95 Theses. He had the theses checked for heresy and in December 1517 forwarded them to Rome.

After careful deliberation, on 15 June 1520, the Pope warned Luther with the papal bull *Exsurge Domine* that he risked excommunication unless he recanted 41 sentences drawn from his writings, including the 95 Theses, within 60 days. Luther responded by publicly burning the papal bull.

ON April 1521, Luther was ordered to appear before The Diet of Worms. This was a general assembly of the estates of the Holy Roman Empire that took place in Worms, a town on the Rhine. It was conducted from January 28 to May25, 1521, with Holy Roman Emperor Charles V presiding.

The Emperor presented the final draft of the Diet of Worms on 25 May 1521, declaring Luther an outlaw, banning his literature, and requiring his arrest: "We want him to be apprehended and punished as a notorious heretic." It also made it a crime for anyone in Germany to give Luther food or shelter. It permitted anyone to kill Luther without legal consequence.

However, Prince Frederick III, Elector of Saxony and admirer of Luther, had obtained a safe conduct for Luther to and from the Diet of Worms. So, it was assumed that Luther would be arrested after his return home.

Frederick III had him intercepted on his way home in the forest near Wittenberg by masked horsemen who were made to appear as armed highwaymen. They escorted Luther to the security of the Wartburg Castle at Eisenach. During his stay at Wartburg, Luther requested the Greek scriptures from the University of Wittenberg. He translated the New Testament from Greek into German and poured out other doctrinal and polemical writings. These writings were smuggled back into Wittenberg and publicly printed by Luther's friends.

The Catholic Church now had two problems, Martin Luther and the printing press. When people had access to the actual scriptures in their own language they could decide for themselves whether or not the Catholic Church was legitimate or it was just inventing things for its own worldly gain. Even though Martin Luther was excommunicated he had powerful friends in Germany that agreed with him.

To make a long story short, Luther started the Protestant Reformation which spread from Germany to Switzerland and into France. Another Protestant leader was Calvin who stated that that the Popes claim to be the representative of the son of God was preposterous. Another Protestant demonstrated that the numeric value of the Vatican's name for the Pope, *Vicarvs Fili Dei,* added up to 666, the number of the Beast, warned about in Revelations. Luther himself said that the "Whore of

Babylon that fornicated with the kings of the earth", described in Revelations was the Church of Rome. This seemed like a fairly accurate historical assessment of the Catholic Church at that time in history, but it would even become truer, in the future.

In England, Henry VIII was advised to start his own Church because the Catholic Church would not allow him to divorce his wife. So, with the creation of the Anglican Church, England was also joining the Protestant revolution against the Holy Roman Empire.

Ignatius of Loyola was the main creator of the Society of Jesus also known as the Jesuits. He was very vigorous in opposing the Protestant Reformation and promoting the following Counter-Reformation. He had developed a plan to combat the Protestants and all heretics (non-Catholics) which he presented to Pope Paul III in 1540.

The formation of the Society of Jesus was approved by Francis Borja, Duke of Grandia, grandson of Pope Alexander VI and the patron of Ignatius of Loyola. Francis Borja was the principle financier and architect in the formalization of the Jesuits into the first dedicated military order of monks of the Catholic Church. He was also responsible for securing the Papal Bull Regimini militantis (September 27, 1540) from Borja family friend Alessandro Farnese Pope Paul III which first gave the Jesuits official status as an order.

Ignatius of Loyola first came to the attention of the young Duke of Grandia by 1529 after Ignatius was again arrested by the Inquisition for practicing extreme religious devotion. Borja saw potential in the extreme military based devotion being preached by Ignatius of Loyola and his desire to establish an order of military monks. It was the young Borja who saved the life of Ignatius from the Inquisition.

After careful consideration of Loyola's plan, Paul III passed a bull incorporating the Society of Jesus into the Catholic Church. Loyola was granted *cart blanche* to make the constitution and rules of the society and to change them. Also, Loyola was made the First Jesuit General.

The first move by Pope Paul III was to convene the Council of Trent from 1545 to 1563. This council tackled the problems of Church Corruption and the sale of Indulgences. It's primary purpose however, was to develop strategies to counter the Protestant inroads into the Holy Roman Empire. The Pope used a member of the Society of Jesus as his theological advisor in this council. This advisor performed so well that the Jesuits became highly favored at the Vatican. Later, the Jesuits became the Vatican's favorite order and, because of their zeal combating heresy, they were placed in charge of the Inquisition in place of the Dominicans.

Meanwhile, the Jesuits were developing their own strategy: Loyola had shown the Society of Jesus' constitution to Pope Paul III and the society had been approved. This constitution allowed; Jesuits to take on any guise or appearance, legicide (the destruction of laws), regicide (murder of kings), usury, murder, vendetta, insurrection and treason if it furthered the cause of the Society of Jesus and Pope.

Naturally, the Jesuit Constitution was kept quite secret. The Jesuits would themselves only be shown sections of the constitution appropriate to their level of initiation. Another item of great secrecy (but now available at many websites including Amazon.com) was the *Secreta Monita Societatis Jesu*, which was an instruction manual for the Jesuits, laying down methods

---

for increasing the influence, power and wealth of the order.

The organization of the Jesuits was like a military order with a strict chain of command. Not only the will of the Jesuit, but also reasoning and even moral scruple, must be sacrificed to the primordial virtue of obedience to the superior. The primary mission of the Jesuits was to place all kings and political leaders in the world under the rule of the Pope and the Church of Rome and to wage unceasing war against all heretics.

At the death of Ignatius in 1557, Francis Borja was expected to be the second Superior General. However, his ambitions were hampered firstly by arch-enemy Giovanni Pietro Carafa as Pope Paul IV (1555-1559). Carafa had been one of the greatest enemies of Borja. Pope Alexander VI and immediately nominated Diego Laynez (James Lainez) as Superior General.

Pope Paul IV died in August of 1559 and was replaced by Giovanni Angelo de' Medici (Pope Pius IV). In both cases, Jesuit Superior General Diego Laynez aligned himself closely making him virtually untouchable.

However, after Pope Pius IV rounded up and tortured and murdered Benedetto Accolti and other members of Papal families in an alleged failed plot, Cardinal Borja made his move and Pius IV was poisoned to death on December 9, 1565. A few days later, Superior General Diego Laynez suffered the same fate and soon after Cardinal Francis Borja was unanimously elected the third Superior General.

The Jesuits created schools and colleges to educate young men with the view of countering the education of the Protestants. They started foreign missions to convert heathens and other religious groups to Catholism. Borja secured a Papal Bull from

Pope Paul III in 1545 permitting the Jesuits to preach, hear confession, dispense the sacraments and say mass without having to refer to a bishop- effectively placing them outside the control of the regional clergy.

These confessionals were supposed to be confidential, but if influential people were involved, sometimes records of the confession were made to be used for intelligence or blackmail. All interesting intelligence was forwarded to the Jesuit General in what amounted to a global spy network!

Borja strengthened the already substantial powers of the Jesuit Superior General to be greater than any other Order in the history of the Catholic Church. While technically monks, the Constitution of the Order was unique in that it exempted priests from the cloisted rule (i.e. living in monasteries). Instead, Jesuit monks were to live "in the world". Only the Dominican Priests who were the chief torturers of the Inquisition and the Catholic Church at the time had anything like such freedoms. However, the Jesuit Constitution from the very beginning went even further in that it permitted and even encouraged the priests not to wear the habit (traditional monk dress) so that they would "blend in" to the world.

In addition, Borja amended the Constitution of the Jesuit Military Order even further when he bestowed powers to the office of the Superior General of the Jesuits second only to the Pope. By its own constitution from 1565, the Superior General can absolve priests and new recruits of all their sins, even the sin of heresy and schism, the falsification of apostolic writings. Further, the Superior Generals from the time of Borja onwards had the "official" power by Papal Bull and its by-laws to reverse sentences of excommunication, suspension or interdict and even absolve Jesuit priests guilty of murder and bigamy.

But one of the most stunning victories of Superior General Borja was in the year he died, when he secured under Pope Gregory XIII in 1572 the rights of the Jesuits to deal in commerce and banking - a right that had not been granted to any religious order of the Catholic Church since the Knights Templars four hundred years earlier.

In the Americas, they set up missions, and created communistic "reductions" in Paraguay where housing clothing and food was provided to the natives who in return were put to work producing products which could be sold in Europe at considerable profit for the Jesuits.

Jesuit General Claudio Acquaviva in 1580, ordered Jesuit, Father Vilela to purchase of the port of Nagasaki from a local Japanese warlord. Acquaviva then sent Jesuit, Alessandro Valignano back to manage the new commercial mission. The Jesuits promoted heavily the growth of their wholly owned port of Nagasaki, to one of the most profitable trading ports in the world. Jesuit ownership of the port of Nagasaki gave the Society a concrete monopoly in taxation over all imported goods coming into Japan.

General Claudio Acquaviva formed an alliance in 1595 with the Dutch in supporting their merchant ships and trade. In response to the new alliance, the English Parliament issued a charter granting a monopoly on the pirate trade alliance of the East India Company in 1600.

In 1602, General Claudio Acquaviva assisted the Jesuit merchants to gain a 21 year charter of monopoly from the States-General of the Netherlands to form the Dutch East India Company. Using the exclusive powers of the Jesuits to conduct banking and commerce, the Dutch East India Company represented one of the most profitable companies of history thanks to its control of spices, drugs and plantations.

Jesuit General Peter Claver was instrumental in the development of the slave trade from Africa to South America to be used in the gold mines. Up to half a million slaves were shipped and arrived under the watch of Peter Claver.

When King Henry VIII broke with Rome and started his own Church, he used the theory that God placed kings into power and that kings ruled by divine right – not because they were ordained by the Pope. King James I also promoted the divine rights of kings. Divine rights staunchest opponent was the Jesuit Cardinal Robert Bellarmine, private theologian to Pope Clement VIII. Bellarmine's book *Controversiae* caused dismay among the Protestants. His ideas were logically well thought out and contained the precursors to liberation theology.

However Bellarmine's logic was purely based on scriptural doctrine. In the area of Science, Bellarmine's logic fell short. He served as one of the judges at the trial of Giordano Bruno, and concurred in the decision which condemned Bruno to be burned at the stake as a heretic for claiming that the Earth revolved around the Sun. He was more lenient with Galileo who had had improved on Bruno's calculations and observations. Galileo was sentenced to permanent house arrest and forbidden from teaching while his books were banned.

In places where Catholics and Protestants lived together, from the Catholic Pulpits, Jesuit Priests would exhort Catholics to slay the Protestants, claiming that it was no sin to slay a heretic. The Jesuits did this in Ireland, which led to a great massacre of Protestants which was only stopped when Cromwell landed his forces in Ireland and put a stop to the slaughter. The same tactics led to the massacre of the Protestant Hugonauts in France. (3)

The Jesuits were confessors to Princes and Kings and used their influence to instigate the Thirty Years War. Henry Garnet, the superior of the Jesuits in England along with other Jesuits, one who was confessor to Guy Falks, were found guilty in planning the infamous "Gunpowder Plot", in which the Jesuits planned to blow up King James I and the entire British Parliament. (4)

In 1717, the Freemasons in England decided it was safe enough to come out of hiding and openly proclaimed their existence. Soon, Freemason lodges were appearing on the continent. Many influential people became members. The Freemasons developed into a secret power behind the scenes as princes and members of government became members of the Freemasons.

The Jesuits, recognizing the secret power of the Freemasons, started infiltrating these lodges with the plan of taking over their leadership. In one of the Jesuit Universities, Claremont College in France, higher orders of Freemasonry were written, so that the Jesuits could penetrate and more easily control the Freemasons through these higher orders.

The considerable amount of criminal activity, including inciting insurrection, political assassination, outright fraud and treason on the part of the Jesuits caused the Kings of Europe to demand the Pope outlaw the Society of Jesus.

Clement XIII, elected on the 6th of July 1758, had resisted a long time the pressing requests of several nations demanding the Jesuits' suppression. He was about to yield and had already arranged a consistory for the 3rd of February 1769 at which he was to tell the cardinals about his resolution to comply with the wishes of these nations; on the night before that particular day, he suddenly felt ill as he was going to bed and cried out: "I am dying... It is a very dangerous thing to attack the Jesuits!" He was the victim of the Jesuits "poison cup."

A conclave assembled and went on for three months. At last, cardinal Ganganelli put on the miter and took the name of Clement XIV. The nations which had banished the Jesuits kept on asking for the total suppression of the Society of Jesus. But, the Pope was in no hurry and studied all the court records against the Jesuits. Four years passed before Clement XIV, convinced of validity of the courts charges against the Jesuits, at last signed the Bull of dissolution: "Dominus ac Redemptor" on July 21, 1773. Ricci, the Order's general, was even imprisoned at the castle of Saint-Ange. Clement XIV died of poisoning on September 22, 1774.

Interestingly, the castle of Saint-Ange had a tunnel that connected with the Vatican, allowing the imprisoned Jesuit General to visit with the Pope. Later, Ricci also died. But, some historians, like Tupper Saussy, suggest that Ricci faked his own death and funeral and slipped away to the American colonies where he appeared as the "mysterious stranger" at the signing of the Declaration of Independence and later at the Constitutional convention.

Jesuit General Ricci himself may well have planned the dissolution of Jesuits as part of his global strategy. All of the officials in the various countries expelling the Jesuits were Freemasons. The Jesuits were by that time in history were notorious and feared everywhere much like the CIA is today. A more secretive organization, the Freemasons was already in existence and used as a tool of the Jesuits.

The English colonies in America had very few Catholics with the exception of Maryland. These colonies had laws which prohibited Catholics from taking public office. The Jesuit General, Ricci, first through Canadian Jesuits, instigated the French Indian War and then, through their control of the English Freemasons, the American Revolution. The Freemasons in England influenced the king to pass onerous laws like the stamp act, a tax on tea Etc. to anger the Colonies, while the Colonial Freemasons were organizing acts of rebellion like the Boston Tea Party which finally escalated into in the Revolution.

The resulting United States was created whose constitution guaranteed freedom of religion and separation of Church and State. This allowed the Jesuits to operate freely in the United States. Some of the ideas in the U.S. Constitution were identical to Jesuit Cardinal Robert Bellarmine's liberation theology. (5)

One of the Wealthiest families in the Colonies was the Catholic Carroll family in Maryland. After the Boston Tea Party, Jesuit John Carroll organized the Catholics in Maryland, northern Virginia and Pennsylvania into joining the independence movement. After the Revolution, John Carroll was made the Bishop of Baltimore and was the direct representative to the Pope for the whole United States.

So, by directing the U.S. Revolutionary War, the Jesuits with their control of the Freemasons, was able to punish heretical England by separating one of her colonies while gaining a substantial foothold in the Protestant United States. And, much of this was done while they were outlawed by the Church of Rome. It would be a grave error to underestimate the Jesuits!

Later, land owned by the Carroll family around rock creek would be turned into the District of Columbia. John Carroll's brother, Daniel Carroll, presented the silver plaque to President Washington that was placed under the cornerstone of the United States Capitol building. In 1789, Bishop John Carroll established Georgetown University, the oldest Jesuit College in the United States where many U.S. statesmen and military leaders were educated.

Four hours before George Washington's death, Jesuit priest, Lenard Neale was called to Mount Vernon from Saint Mary's Mission nearby. George Washington, like Constantine, converted to Catholicism on his death bed.

Like the city state of London and the Vatican, a third city state was officially created in 1790. That city state is called the District of Columbia and located on ten square miles of land in the heart of Washington. The District of Columbia flies its own flag, and has its own independent constitution. The constitution for the District of Columbia operates under a tyrannical Roman law known as Lex Fori which has no resemblance to the U.S. Constitution. The flag of Washington's District of Columbia has three red stars, one for each city state in this three city empire.

Although geographically separate, today, the city states of London, the Vatican, and the District of Columbia are one interlocking empire called Empire of the City. These three City State CORPORATIONS control the world economically, through the City of London Corporation, Militarily, through Washington DC and Spiritually, through The Vatican

- They pay no taxes
- Are under no National Authority
- Have their own Independent Flag
- Have their own Separate Laws
- Have their own Police Force
- They have totally Independent Identities from the rest of the world.

The City of London Inc. Became a Sovereign State in 1694, when King William III of Orange privatized and turned the Bank of England over to the Private Bankers. By 1812, Nathan Rothschild crashed the English stock market by creating the rumor that Napoleon had won the battle of Waterloo and thereby gained control of the Bank of England from the great profits from this stock market manipulation.

Today, the City State of London is the world's financial Power Center and the wealthiest square mile on the planet. It houses; the Rothschild controlled 'Bank of England', Lloyds of London, The London Stock Exchange, All British Banks, The Branch offices of 384 Foreign Banks of which are70 USA Banks, Fleet Streets Newspaper and Publishing Monopolies, Headquarters for Worldwide Freemasonry, Headquarters for the worldwide money cartel known as 'THE CROWN.' It is not part of London or England or the British Commonwealth.

The Vatican Inc., which colossal wealth includes enormous investments with the Rothschilds in Britain, France and the USA and with giant oil and weapons corporations like Shell, British Petroleum, Raytheon, Lockheed and General Electric. The Vatican's' SOLID GOLD BULLION worth Billions, is stored with the Rothschild controlled 'Bank of England' and the USA 'Federal Reserve Bank'.

The Catholic Church is the biggest financial power, wealth accumulator and property owner in existence, possessing more material wealth than any Bank, Corporation, Giant Trust or Government anywhere on the globe. The Pope, who is the visible ruler of this colossal global wealth, virtually is one of the richest Men on earth.

While two thirds of the world earns less than $2 a day and one fifth of the world is underfed or starving to death, the Vatican hoards the worlds wealth, profits from it on the stock market and at the same time preaches about giving. During World War II, The Vatican was criticized for supporting Hitler and his Nazi regime. To this day, the Vatican is still under investigation for plundering Nazi Gold from the Swiss Bank accounts of Jewish Holocaust victims.

4

Secret Societies

In 1750, Mayer Amschel Bauer purchased his father's banking business in Frankfurt, Germany. Since the bank had a red shield over its door, he changed last name to Rothschild (red shield in German). Mayer married and had five sons and 5 daughters. His son's names were Amshel, Salamon, Nathan, Kalmann, and Jacob.

The Rothschilds became the bankers of Prince William IX of Hess Hanau, with whom he was known to have attended Freemason meetings in Germany. This prince derived his fortunes from renting out his mercenary Hessian army to England. This same army would fight against George Washington at Valley Forge.

Prince William IX had to flee to Denmark because of political problems and left the mercenary army pay roll of six hundred British pounds with Mayer Rothschild for safe keeping. This money was sent to London with Nathan Rothschild to start a bank there.

Gold was purchased from the East India Co. for security on paper money issued from the bank. Fourfold profits were made by loaning money to the Duke of Wellington's army and later on from selling the gold that was the security on the paper money. This was the start of the great fortune of the Rothschilds.

An international banking operation was set up by sending each of Mayer's sons to a different country to set up a bank; Amshel to in Berlin, Salamon in Vienna, Jacob in Paris, and Kalamann in Naples.

The Rothschilds did so well that their banking operations attracted the attention of the Jesuits. The Jesuits devised a secret plan to make the Rothschilds the guardians of the Vatican Treasury. They knew that Mayer Rothschild was a Freemason and could be controlled. Who would suspect that Jews were in charge of the Vatican's wealth? The Rothschilds had proven their ability to secure wealth and make good profits. The Catholics weren't supposed to charge interest but the Jews could. In 1769, The Rothschilds were made the guardians of the Vatican treasury.

The Catholic Church is the biggest financial power, wealth accumulator, and property owner in existence, possessing more material wealth than any bank, corporation, giant trust, or government anywhere on the globe.

So, imagine the financial power, being the guardian of the Vatican treasury, would give a person.

The Crown is not the Royal Family or the British Monarch. The Crown is the private corporate city state of London. It has a council of twelve members who rule the corporation under a mayor called the Lord Mayor. The Lord Mayor and his twelve member council serve representatives for thirteen of the world's wealthiest, most powerful banking families. This ring of thirteen ruling families includes the Rothschild family, the Warburg family, the Oppenheimer family, and the Schiff family.

These families and their descendants run the Crown Corporation of London. The British Parliament and the British Prime Minister serve as a public front for these ruling crown families. The Crown Corporation holds the title to worldwide Crown land in Crown colonies like Canada, Australia, and New Zealand. So now we see the link between the Vatican, the Rothschilds, the Bank of England and the British Crown.

After the 1773 Papal Bull dissolving the Society of Jesus, it appeared that the Jesuits were closing shop. But, an organization that powerful and wealthy doesn't simply go away. Many Jesuits simply moved to non- Catholic countries, where the Papal Bull dissolving the Society of Jesus had no legal effect, like England, Prussia, Lutheran Controlled Bavaria, Russia and the United States.

Frederick of Prussia recognizing the value of the Jesuits as educators refused to promulgate the Bull. So, too, Catherine II of Russia forbade its promulgation for the some of the same reasons. At first, some Jesuits became parish priests and continued to teach in the Jesuit Colleges as before.

In Catholic countries, their society simply went underground. On May 1,1776 Adam Wieshaupt, a Jesuit Professor of Cannon Law, at the Bavarian University of Ingolstadt, inaugurated the secret order of the Illuminati, which in many ways was patterned after the Society of Jesus. The stated goals of the Illuminati was " to do away with the monarchs of Europe and the Church and return man to his natural happy state."

The Illuminati was organized like a pyramid with secret cells, lower level members knew who their superior was but had no idea who their superior's superior was. The grand master's identity was kept secret from all but those directly below him.

Also, borrowing from the Jesuits, a system of spying and reporting was developed so that the strengths and weaknesses of Illuminati members, who were called Patriarchs, could be evaluated. This policy insured that each Patriarch was placed in positions where his talents could best be used. Blackmail could also be used to control a Patriarch who might decide to leave the order and reveal Illuminati secrets.

Weishaupt recruited the most intelligent in the fields of education, writing, industry and finance. He planned to use, among other things, money and sex bribery to obtain control of people in high places. Once they succumbed, black mail could be used to control these unfortunate leaders. Also, adept Illuminati Patriarchs could be used as advisors to political leaders and persuade them to adapt policies that further the Illuminati agenda much as the Jesuits had been doing before.

The famous French Orator, the Marquis de Mirabeau, whose excessive penchant for the good life left him heavily in debt, was befriended by Illuminati Patriarch, Moses Mendelssohn who introduced him to the beautiful wife of Hertz. Soon she was seeing more of Mirabeau than her own husband. Now, blackmail combined with indebtedness kept Mirabeau under control.

Next, Mirabeau was introduced to Illuminism. Weishaupt then used Mirabeau's fame to get introduced to Talleyrand and the grandmaster of the Paris Freemason lodge, the Duc D'Orleans.

Later, Weishaupt, under great secrecy, promised the Duc D'Orleans that if he would help in overthrowing the French monarch that the Illuminati would make him the next monarch of France.

The Order of the Illuminati was given a huge boost at the Masonic

Congress of Wilhelmsbad held at Meyer Amschel Rothschild's castle on the 16th of July 16, 1782. This meeting included representatives of all of the secret societies such as the Martinists, the Freemasons, and the Illuminati which now numbered no less than three million members all over the World. This enabled the Illuminati to solidify their control over the Freemasonry Lodges of Europe and to be viewed as the undisputed Leaders of the occult One World Movement

One order of business was to allow Jews to become members, at a time when Jews had few rights and were still prosecuted in Europe. The fact that the expenses of the Congress were paid by the Rothschilds might have had something to do with this decision.

All present were sworn to secrecy. But, when Freemason Comte de Virieu was asked what events transpired there, he replied; "I will not confide them to you. I can only tell you that all this is much more serious than you think. The conspiracy which has been woven is so well thought out that that it will be, so to speak, impossible for the monarchy and the church to escape from it."

Another one present, Count de Saint Germain, later warned his dear friend Marie Antoinette, of the murderous plot to overthrow the French monarchy. Unfortunately, Marie Antoinette warned her husband but, her warning was not heeded.

The French revolution soon followed with Jesuit Cardinal Robert Bellarmine's ideas enshrined in the slogan "Liberty, Equality and Brotherhood". After the stability of the French government was destroyed the "reign of terror" followed. The Duc D'Orleans was not made the next monarch of France but, was one of many beheaded in the guillotine. Thus, demonstrating that the

Illuminati absolutely cannot be trusted.

Some subversive secrets started leaking from the Illuminati and by October 11, 1785, the Bavarian Elector ordered a raid on the home of Weishaupt's chief assistant, Herr Von Zwack. Many documents were recovered which outlined the Illuminati's plan for worldwide revolution.

The Bavarian Elector decided to have the papers published as the "Original Writings of the Order and Sect of the Illuminati". These papers were widely distributed as a warning to the European Monarchies.

Wieshaupt was dismissed from his professorship at the University of Ingolstadt and went into hiding with another Illuminati member, the Duke of Saxe Gotha. Allowing people to believe the lie that the Illuminati had been dissolved, the order continued to exist under other names. One secret order was the Order of Skull and Bones, from which a branch was, in 1832, transplanted to Yale University in the United States. Skull and Bones would play a role in causing the Civil War and all the wars afterwards. Some of the other Illuminati secret orders were the League of the Just, and the Carbonari.

The French revolution itself did not at first advance the cause of the Jesuits to see their reinstatement. Instead, it gave renewed confidence to their ability to topple even the oldest of monarchies and so gave rise to the audacious plan to capture the Pope and the wealth of the Catholic Church.

In one of the great misdirection of history, loyal Jesuit agent La Fayette did not simply abandon his loyal troops and influence to hide in the obscure Belgium region of Liège where he was conveniently held "prisoner" for 5 years. Instead, La Fayette was tasked by the Jesuits to take the vast gold reserves of France to America. In New York, the stolen French gold was placed in the care of the Bank of New York (founded 1784) and the newly formed Bank of the Manhattan Company (now JP Morgan Chase Bank).

Jesuit agent Antoine Christophe Saliceti had carefully groomed the career of fellow Corsican Napoleon Bonaparte for several years. In 1795, whilst serving in Paris, Napoleon succeeded in crushing a rebellion of royalists and counter-revolutionaries and was promoted by the new regime leader Paul François Jean Nicolas, vicomte de Barras (Paul Barras).

After his marriage to Josephine de Beauharnais, Saliceti ensured Napoleon was given command of the French Army of Italy in March 1796 and ordered to invade Italy, specifically to capture the Pope in Rome. At the same time, the Jesuits through Switzerland formed the private banks Darier Hentsch & Cie and Lombard Odier Darier Hentsch as custodians for all gold, treasure and contracts seized during the campaign.

The Holy Roman Empire known also as the "First Reich" had survived over a thousand years, when it was finally destroyed by Napoleon with his defeat of Holy Roman Emperor, Francis II. This was part of the Illuminati's war against the Church of Rome for dissolving the Society of Jesus. After the French invasion of Italy, Napoleon had the Pope Pius VI arrested. Napoleon also Invaded Malta to subjugate the Pope's other army, the Knights of Malta.

At the death of Pius VI in August 1799 as a French prisoner, Cardinal Count Barnaba Chiaramonti was eventually elected as Pope Pius VII on March 14, 1800. While initially on acceptable terms with Napoleon having secured a Concordant in 1801 and attending his coronation in 1804. However, by 1808, he was a prisoner of France, not by Jesuit intrigue but by Napoleon now running his own program.

After the disastrous Russian campaign had sufficiently weakened the power of Napoleon, Jesuit leader Tadeusz Brzozowski (first Superior General after restoration) met with Pope Pius VII at his prison in Jan/Feb 1814 and secured an agreement with Pope Pius VII to fully restore the Jesuit Order and grant it new lands and rights in Asia upon the agreement: (1) That the Jesuits would arrange for the safe release of the Pope upon the arrest of Napoleon (which occurred in April 1814); (2) That the Jesuits would not undertake any more actions against any more Popes and restate their pledge of loyalty; (3) That the Pope get back control of the Papal territories and (4) That some of the funds of the Catholic church controlled by the Vatican would be returned.

After five years of imprisonment in France, Pius VII agreed and was released. After his return to Rome he reinstated the Society of Jesus by the Bull "Solicitudo omnium ecclesiarum" on August 7, 1814.

So, now the Jesuits were reinstated by the Church of Rome and the Jesuits gained control over the Knights of Malta. From then on, the Jesuit General would be the real power behind the Church of Rome and the Pope, a figure head.

After being betrayed by his Jesuit masters and imprisoned in St. Helena Island in the middle of the South Atlantic, Napoleon had this to say:

"The Jesuits are a military organization, not a religious order. Their chief is a general of an army, not the mere father abbot of a monastery. And the aim of this organization is power. Power in its most despotic exercise. Absolute power, universal power, power to control the world by the volition of a single man…"

The Jesuits also incorporated an army of secular volunteers called "Jesuits of the Short Robe." These people were not priests and could continue in their usual trade but had to promise for a period of time (in France it was 5 years) to render all possible service to the order and obey its instructions. In return they were promised a ready promotion of their worldly views and interests and absolution and indulgence of all sins and transgressions.

Since the Jesuits possessed so much secret worldly power they could keep their promise more readily than any corporation, fraternity or secular power. For this reason the Jesuits had no trouble enlisting Jesuits of the Short Robe to carry out their work.

After the restoration of the Jesuits, the execution of the secret Treaty of Verona was placed in their hands. One provision of this treaty was the Jesuit's well laid plans to destroy popular governments in the Americas. Thomas Jefferson was informed of this and warned President Monroe. Monroe countered this threat by declaring the Monroe Doctrine.

After Adam Weishaupt's death in 1830, an Italian revolutionary leader, Giusseppe Mazzini (1805-1872), a 33rd degree Mason, was selected by the Illuminati to head their worldwide operations in 1834. Mazzini also founded the Mafia in 1860. Because of Mazzini's revolutionary activities in Europe, the Bavarian government cracked down on the Illuminati and other secret societies for plotting the overthrow of monarchies.

During his leadership, Mazzini enticed Albert Pike into the Illuminati. Pike was fascinated by the idea of a one world government, and when asked by Mazzini, readily agreed to write a ritual tome that guided the transition from average high-ranking mason into a top-ranking Illuminati mason (33rd degree).

Albert Pike, became the Grandmaster of Scottish Rite Freemasonry in the United States. Albert Pike had been a Brigadier General in the Confederate army and later an organizer of the Ku Klux Clan. He has a temple dedicated to him in Washington D.C., the only Confederate military leader to have one there.

An interesting letter from Albert Pike to Giuseppe Mazzini dated August 15, 1871 contained a plan for world conquest using three world wars:

"The First World War must be brought about in order to permit the Illuminati to overthrow the power of the Czars in Russia and of making that country a fortress of atheistic Communism. The divergences caused by the "agentur" (agents) of the Illuminati between the British and Germanic Empires will be used to foment this war. At the end of the war, Communism will be built and used in order to destroy the other governments and in order to weaken the religions."

"The Second World War must be fomented by taking advantage of the differences between the Fascists and the political Zionists. This war must be brought about so that Nazism is destroyed and that the political Zionism be strong enough to institute a sovereign state of Israel in Palestine. During the Second World War, International Communism must become strong enough in order to balance Christendom, which would be then restrained and held in check until the time when we would need it for the final social cataclysm."

"The Third World War must be fomented by taking advantage of the differences caused by the "agentur" of the "Illuminati" between the political Zionists and the leaders of Islamic World. The war must be conducted in such a way that Islam and political Zionism mutually destroy each other. Meanwhile the other nations, once more divided on this issue will be constrained to fight to the point of complete physical, moral, spiritual and economical exhaustion…We shall unleash the Nihilists and the atheists, and we shall provoke a formidable social cataclysm which in all its horror will show clearly to the nations the effect of absolute atheism, origin of savagery and of the most bloody turmoil. Then everywhere, the citizens, obliged to defend themselves against the world minority of revolutionaries, will exterminate those destroyers of civilization, and the multitude, disillusioned with Christianity, whose deistic spirits will from that moment be without compass or direction, anxious for an ideal, but without knowing where to render its adoration, will receive the true light through the universal manifestation of the pure doctrine of Lucifer, brought finally out in the public view. This manifestation will result from the general reactionary movement which will follow the destruction of Christianity and atheism, both conquered and exterminated at the same time."

For a short time, this letter was on display in the British Museum Library in London, and it was copied by William Guy Carr, former Intelligence Officer in the Royal Canadian Navy in his book *Pawns in the Game.*

Quite prophetic I would say! Perhaps, the third war is going on right now (2014) with the destruction of Iraq, Libya and Syria. At any rate, it shows the Illuminati's ability to make long range plans.

The Illuminati "League of the Just" commissioned Carl Marx to write the *Communist Manifesto*. The money came from Engels who owned a factory that underpaid its employees, demonstrating the hypocrisy of the Illuminati. The book was planned to be widely published for the planned world revolution of 1848. That revolution was not totally successful because many still remembered the horrors of the French Revolution and refused to participate.

For the purpose of creating a breach between the Czarist regime and the Jewish owned Royal Dutch Shell, a notorious forged document titled the *Protocols of the Learned Elders of Zion* was written by a Jesuit and given to Russian Professor S. Nilus around 1910. Professor Nilus had them published in Russian under the title *"The Jewish Peril"*. The publication was a falsified translation derived from Adam Wieshaupt's strategy for world control and disguised to look Jewish in origin. The Jesuit authors of these protocols were so astute at disguising the plan for global control as a Jewish plot, that even intelligent people like industrialist, Henry Ford were fooled.

Later, Victor Marsden translated the document in 1921, under the original title the *Protocols of the Learned Elders of Zion*. The Jesuits, whenever possible, liked to scapegoat Jews and make them take the blame for their own terrible deeds. Later, Hitler would use the *Protocols of the Learned Elders of Zion* to justify his anti-Jewish program. Interestingly, it seems that these protocols describe what is happening in the United States and elsewhere.

These protocols are available on the internet and from book stores like Amazon.com. So, I won't write them here.

But, I might use excerpts from the protocols to show how recent history corresponds to this Illuminati plan.

The secret "Order of Skull and Bones", Chapter 322 was founded at Yale University in 1833 by William Huntington Russell and Alphonso Taft. Both men had just returned from Germany where they had been initiated into the Illuminati. This order was incorporated as the Russell Trust in 1856, financed by money from Russell and Company, one of the great opium syndicates.

Yale was the favorite northern college of the southern, slave holding aristocracy. John C. Calhoun, the famous defender of slavery, and Judah P. Benjamin, the secretary of state for the confederacy, both attended Yale.

Each year, 15 Influential seniors at Yale would be inducted into the Order of Skull and Bones. During their senior year they would be called Knights and after graduation, they would be called Patriarchs for life. Patriarchs of Skull and Bones get considerable support from the order. William Russell became a member of the Connecticut State legislature in 1846 and a general in the Connecticut National Guard. Alphonso Taft became Secretary of War in the Grant Administration in 1876, U.S. Attorney General in 1876 and U.S. Ambassador to Russia in 1884. His Son became Chief Justice and later President of the United States.

According to historian, Anthony Sutton, in his book, *America's Secret Establishment* Patriarchs of Skull and Bones represent ultimate power and influence in the United States. The candidates for Skull and Bones were always white, male, Protestants and usually from wealthy or influential families. Catholics weren't invited into this order, but they had other opportunities in the Society of Jesus, Knights of Columbus and Knights of Malta.

The Order of Skull and Bones played a role in in causing the Civil War. Henry Roots Jackson, initiated into Skull and Bones in

1839 (S&B 1839), was a leader of the 1861 Georgia Secession Committee. John Perkins Jr. (S&B 1840), was a leader in the Louisiana secession convention. William Terry Sullivan (S&B 1841), was chairman of the Mississippi secession convention. (6)

The Jesuits were worried that the United States was becoming too independent and powerful after the war of 1812 and the Monroe Doctrine, so they planned to destroy the United States via the Civil War. Their plan was multifaceted:

They would stir up the Slavery issue and other differences between Northern and Southern States to cause the Confederacy to form. A Catholic General of the Confederacy would fire on Yankee Ft. Sumter to get the shooting war started. The French Monarch and Freemason, Napoleon III would send Maximillian to Invade Mexico and take over that country. After conquering Mexico, Maximillian's forces would then join the Confederate forces. Then, after the Union army had been weakened sufficiently, an invasion from Canada would finish off the United States.

Well, the plan didn't go as expected. Lincoln sent a letter to France to withdraw their forces from Mexico or risk war with the U.S. Maximilian was shot dead on June 18, 1867 by Juarez's forces. The Union Army, which was badly out maneuvered in the early part of the war, finally won a decisive victory at Gettysburg. The Catholic General Mead however, allowed General Lee to retreat without capturing his army. Consequently the War drug on for another 2 years. But for the Confederates, it was only a matter of time before their ultimate defeat after that. The Union army was never weakened sufficiently to realistically mount an invasion from Canada.

The Pope decidedly was on the side of the Confederacy. Before the battle of Gettysburg, the Cardinal of New York instigated the Irish Catholics into a violent anti-draft riot. General Mead was ordered to send a third of his army to New York to put down the riots. Later the Pope sent a letter to Jefferson Davis praising his efforts to resist Union tyranny. The letter was widely published causing many Irish Catholics in the Union army to dessert. President Lincoln knew of the Vatican's plans to destroy the Union and broke off diplomatic relations with the Vatican.

Failing in the war plan, the Jesuits planned to decapitate the Union government. The simultaneous plot to assassinate, President Lincoln, Vice President Andrew Johnson, Secretary of State Seward, and General Grant was formulated in great secrecy.

This was not an unusual policy of the Jesuits, who were behind the poisoning of President William Harrison in 1841 and the poisoning of President Zachery Taylor in 1850. In Fact, all of President Harrison's 8 children except 1 were also poisoned about the same time he was.

An unsuccessful attempt to poison President Buchanan had also occurred. He was having his usual dinner at the National Hotel in Washington D.C., which was the favorite dining place for political figures. He had a large table reserved for himself and his many compatriots. Buchanan was known to love tea and in general northerners preferred tea while the southerners preferred coffee. Someone sprinkled arsenic in the tea pot that was set at Buchanan's table and 38 of the about 50 people sitting at that table that night, died of poisoning. Buchanan nearly succumbed but, realizing what had happened, told his doctor to give him the antidote for arsenic and was saved. Not a single southerner sitting at that table died that night.

The plotters to decapitate the Union government were members of Knights of the Golden Circle (KGC), founded by George Bickley, who also wanted to Join Mexico and some Caribbean Nations with the Confederacy. The KGC was later infiltrated and taken over by the Jesuits. The assassins, chosen by a drawing of lots, were; John Wilkes Booth for the President Lincoln, George Atzerodt for the Vice President, Johnson, Louis Payne for the Secretary of State, Seward and Michael O'Laughlin for General Grant.

The conspirators would often meet in Mary E. Surratt's boarding house in Washington D.C. The Surratts were all ardent secessionists and fanatical Roman Catholics. Mary Surratt's rule was that no heretical Protestants were allowed at her boarding house.

The plot was partially successful as only Lincoln was killed. The newspaper had stated that Lincoln and General Grant would both be at Ford's Theater the night of the assassination, but Grant had a change of plans in order to visit an ailing relative and wasn't present. Vice President Andrew Johnson's intended assassin, George Atzerodt, at the last minute, became fearful and didn't perform his assigned task, but later confessed to the conspiracy. Lewis Payne forced his way into Seward's residence where Seward was lying in bed, convalescing from a riding accident, and proceeded to stab him. Payne was finally stopped by others in the house and fled away. Seward eventually recovered from his multiple stab wounds. (7)

After the Civil War, the United States was in a terrible financial condition. Congress agreed to a Rothschild plan in exchange for financial assistance. When Congress passed the Act of 1871 it created a separate corporate government for the District of Columbia. This treasonous act allowed the District of Columbia to operate as a corporation called THE UNITED STATES, outside the original constitution of the United States and outside of the best interest of U.S. citizens.

Then, the fourteenth amendment was passed, which created the UNITED STATES Citizen. This citizen had certain privileges called civil rights which could be removed at will by THE UNITED STATES corporation - unlike the God given inalienable rights in the Constitution guaranteed to State Citizens. One being a citizen of a corporation called THE UNITED STATES located in Washington D.C or its U.S. territories. - the other being a citizen of the state of residence in the United States. It sounds complicated and was meant to be by the Rothschilds so as to fool the common man. One automatically becomes a Corporate U.S. citizen when one receives a social security number.

Holy Roman Empire cannon law of the seas is known as Admiralty law. There are few Constitutional Courts in the United States today. Most courts are Admiralty Courts and can be recognized by the golden fringe around the American flag in the courtroom. So, don't be assured that you will get your Constitutional rights upheld in Admiralty Courts. It is a good idea to hire a common law lawyer if you want your rights upheld, because they know "the score", where most lawyers, who are members of the bar, do not.

To demonstrate the Jesuit's ability to penetrate any country, a good example would be Cecil Rhodes in Protestant England. As a student at the Jesuit controlled Oxford College, Cecil Rhodes was a mediocre student and probably would not have qualified for a Rhodes scholarship. But, according to his Biographer, Sara Millin, "The government of the world was Rhodes simple desire."

While at Oxford Rhodes was initiated into Freemasonry at the Apollo University Lodge No. 357. And in 1877 was raised to Master Mason at the same lodge. He also joined the Scottish Rite Lodge at Oxford called the Prince Rose Croix Lodge No. 30. Later, he revealed some secrets of the 33 degree, indicating that he had become a 33 degree Scottish Rite Freemason.

Later Rhodes went to Southern Africa and made his fortune in gold and diamond mining. He became Prime Minister of the Cape Colony, Africa from 1890 to 1896. The country of Rhodesia (now divided into Zambia and Zimbabwe) was named after him. Rhodes traveled back and forth to England during this time and formed the "Round Table" with William T Stead, a famous journalist and Lord Esher, friend and confidant of Queen Victoria.

The "Round Table" was the British equivalent of the Bavarian Illuminati or the United States Skull and Bones. Early members of the Round Table included Rudyard Kipling, Lord Author Balfour, Lord Rothschild and H.G. Wells.

One goal of this secret society was to bring the United States back in to the English Empire. According to instructions by Rhodes the constitution of this secret society was identical to the Jesuit Constitution except the words "the English Empire" would replace the words "Roman Catholic Religion." Could it be that the actual goal was to bring the U.S. into the Roman Catholic religion?

Also, Rhodes set up 6 different wills between 1877 and 1899. Cecil Rhodes collaborator and mentor was the well-known Journalist William Thomas Stead. Rhodes, Stead and other collaborators worked to create a secret society that could be made presentable to the public without revealing its secret purpose. According to Stead, the method was incorporated in the wills made by Rhodes. In particular, the first will which creates secret societies and the last will which created the Rhodes Scholarship Fund.

Carroll Quigley a Jesuit professor at Georgetown, in his book *The Anglo American Establishment* writes that the sixth will creating the Rhodes scholarship at Oxford is well known but what is not well known is that the other 5 wills were used for creating a secret society with Rhode's principal trustee, Lord Milner and that secret society is still operating today.

The Rhodes scholarship has given us one U.S. President, Bill Clinton, three Supreme Court Justices; John Marshall Harlan, Byron White, and David Souter and other influential world figures.

Quigley also stated that the Rhodes scholarship was merely a façade to conceal the secret society or one of the instruments to carry out the secret society's purpose. Rhodes purpose in setting up the Scholarship in his words was "nothing less than a scheme to take the governments of the whole world." This is totally identical to the Jesuit agenda.

Quigley also states that the following institutions evolved from the Rhodes- Milner secret scheme:

The New York Times, the Bilderberg Group, Bohemian Grove Club, Club of Rome, Council on Foreign Relations, Nerucam International, the Round Table, Royal Institute of International Affairs, Trilateral Commission and the United Nations.

Not mentioned by Quigley was the Pilgrim Society which also evolved from the Round Table just after Rhodes death when his wills were executed. The patron of the Pilgrim Society is the

Queen of England, Elizabeth II.

Notable Pilgrim members included J.P Morgan, George F. Baker, John D. Rockefeller, Jacob Schiff, Winston Churchill, Tony Blair and Henry Kissinger among others. The Pilgrim Society runs Barclays, National Westminster, HSBC Bank Group and Standard Charter Bank Group among others. The John Birch Society was also a Pilgrim Society creation.

Toward the end of the nineteenth century, the Rothschild banks, as guardians of the Vatican Treasury, started a campaign to gain control of the rich United States economy. The Rothschild bank financed J.P. Morgan Co., the Bank of Kuhn Loeb and Co., John D. Rockefeller' Standard Oil Co., Edward Harriman's railroads and Andrew Carnegie's steel mills.

The first Protocol of the Elders of Zion (in reality a Jesuit protocol) stresses the importance of gaining control of money to gain control of a nation:

"...Whether a state exhausts itself in its own convulsions, whether its internal discord brings it under the power of external foes – in any case it can be counted irretrievably lost: It is in our power. The despotism of capital, which is entirely in our hands, reaches out to it, a straw that the state, wily-nilly must take hold of: If not, it goes to the bottom..."

Rothschild agents, Paul Warburg and Jacob Schiff, worked at Khun Loeb Bank and started a campaign to create a central bank in the United States. They helped to manipulate the financial panic of 1907, which was later used by Paul Warburg, as an argument for the need for a central bank before the Banking and Currency Committee.

However there were influential millionaires in the U.S. opposed to the idea of a central bank and would be able to block the idea. These included Benjamin Guggenheim, Isador Strauss, head of Macy's Department stores, and John Jacob Astor.

The White Star shipping line, owned by J.P. Morgan was making two sister ships, the Olympic and the Titanic, in Belfast, Ireland. The Olympic was launched first. Under the command of Captain Edward Smith the Olympic soon had a collision with HMS Hawke, causing extensive damage to both the Olympic and the HMS Hawke. The Olympic was returned to the Belfast yard for repairs. A board of inquiry by the Royal Navy Admiralty decided that the accident was the fault of the Olympic and therefore no insurance damages were awarded to the White Star line. This resulted in about $800,000 in losses.

After the Olympic had repairs, it was decided to secretly change the name plates and different carpeting between the two otherwise identical ships during a two week work break in the ship yard. Only select workers sworn to secrecy did the work of changing the identities between the Titanic and the Olympic.

The reason for this change was that the Olympic (now the Titanic) was going to be sacrificed and the Ship owners wanted to recover insurance. The Jesuit General had decided that the three millionaires that would oppose the planned central bank in the United States would have to die. They were invited to join the maiden voyage of the "Titanic" and they accepted.

The Captain of the Titanic, Edward Smith, was a Jesuit of the short robe and took orders from Jesuit Francis Brown, the Jesuit superior of Ireland who took orders from Franz Xavier Wernz, the Jesuit General in Rome. To the Jesuits, the Jesuit General is like God himself and is absolutely obeyed without question.

Also, Smith, an older gentleman, would have no future any way, after being involved in two shipping disasters, no one would ever hire him again. So, His own death may not have been that important to him.

J.P. Morgan had another of his ships, the Californian standing by the scene of the accident. The only cargo on the Californian was 3,000 blankets and 3,000 woolen jumpers. But, Captain Stanley Lord of the Californian was 12 miles off course.

The rest is known history. Captain Smith ordered the Titanic to proceed at full speed through the dangerous ice field at night, a thing that no experienced Captain would ever do. But, he had a special secret mission and was oath bound to follow his orders.

The Titanic struck an iceberg and sunk. Of the 2,224 Passengers and crew aboard Titanic about 1,500 perished in the icy waters that night, including Benjamin Guggenheim, Isador Strauss and John Jacob Astor, the men opposed to a central bank in the U.S. Captain Stanley Lord took the blame for the 1,500 deaths for not getting the Californian to the scene of the accident in time. White Star Shipping Line collected $12.5 million insurance damages.

When the "Titanic" wreck was finally discovered on the ocean floor, places where the black paint had chipped away on the hull showed a grey undercoat. The Olympics' hull had a grey under coat whereas the Titanic hull was only painted black, proving that the ships were indeed switched.

The Federal Reserve Act was the idea of Baron Alfred Rothschild of London. The final version of the Act was determined at a secret meeting at Jekyll Island, Georgia, which was owned by J.P. Morgan. Attending this meeting were; A. Piatt Andrew, assistant secretary to the treasury, Senator Nelson Aldrich, Frank Vanderlip, president of Kuhn Loeb Bank, Henry Davidson , senior partner of J.P. Morgan Bank, Charles Norton, President of Morgan's First National Bank of New York, Paul Warburg, Partner in Kuhn Loeb Bank and Benjamin Strong, President of Morgan's Bankers Trust.

The Federal Reserve Act was passed during Christmas vacation of 1913 when most congressmen were at home. Pierre Jay, initiated in Skull and Bones in 1892, became the first chairman of the New Your Federal Reserve Bank. Many members of the Federal Reserve Bank are linked to Skull and Bones.

The Federal Reserve Bank is a consortium of private banks operating for profit. The Class A stockholders of the Federal Reserve Bank originally were:

1. Rothschild Banks of London and Berlin.
2. Lazard Brothers Bank of Paris.
3. Israel Moses Seif Bank of Italy.
4. Warburg Bank of Hamburg and Amsterdam.
5. Lehman Bank of New York.
6. Kuhn Loeb Bank of New York.
7. Chase Manhattan Bank of New York.
8. Goldman Sachs Bank of New York.

The Federal Reserve Bank creates money by merely ordering it from the U.S. Mint and paying the printing costs. It then lends the money to the U.S. government at interest, creating the National Debt. It is quite a racket and totally unconstitutional since Article 1, Section 8 of the U.S. Constitution states that Congress shall have the power "to coin money, regulate the value thereof." The immense profits from interest on the national debt are distributed to the member banks of the Federal

Reserve Bank and their shareholders. It is probably the largest racket on the planet.

As stated in Jon Phelp's *Vatican Assassins III*, Goldman Sachs is nothing more than an international banking house for the Jesuit papacy. Several notorious Knights of Malta have been the true power brokers of Goldman, including Geoffrey T. Boisi. Boisi is also a member of Rome's Trilateral Commission, a former CEO of JPMorgan Chase, a member of the Board of Directors for Freddie Mac, an overseer of the Wharton School (which Papal Knight Donald Trump attended), a trustee of Jesuit Boston College and was honored by Pope John Paul II becoming a "Steward of St. Peter."

The Federal Bureau of Investigation (FBI) first incarnated in 1896, as the National Bureau of Criminal Identification. The Bureau of Investigation (BOI) was created on July 26, 1908. In 1933 it was linked to the Bureau of Prohibition and rechristened the Division of Investigation (DOI) before finally becoming an independent service within the Department of Justice in 1935. In the same year, its name was officially changed from the Division of Investigation to the present-day Federal Bureau of Investigation, or FBI. The Director of the BOI, Knight of Malta J. Edgar Hoover, served from 1924–1972, a combined 48 years with the BOI, DOI, and FBI.

All these incarnations of the FBI were, in addition to investigating crime, used as an intelligence gathering agency for the Vatican. Hoover was notorious for investigating political leaders and keeping files on them. Few politicians were willing to go up against Hoover for fear of blackmail.

Starting in 1943, a joint US/UK code-breaking effort with which the FBI was heavily involved—broke Soviet diplomatic and intelligence communications codes, allowing the US and British governments to read Soviet communications. This effort confirmed the existence of Americans working in the United States for Soviet intelligence.

Hoover was administering this project but failed to notify the CIA until 1952. Hoover disliked the CIA and felt that there should be only one intelligence gathering agency. The discovery of Soviet spies operating in the US allowed Hoover to pursue his longstanding obsession with the threat he perceived from the American Left, ranging from Communist Party of the United States of America (CPUSA), union organizers to American liberals.

During the Vietnam war, the FBI became known to infiltrate leftist anti-war groups like the Students for a Democratic Society (SDS) and act as agent provocateurs in anti-war demonstrations. In March 1971, the residential office of an FBI agent in Media, Pennsylvania was robbed; the thieves took secret files which detailed the FBI's extensive COINTELPRO program. These files which, were given to local newspapers, revealed the FBI's spying on and disrupting lawful groups that were pro civil rights, pro-union or anti-war.

When President John F. Kennedy was shot and killed, the jurisdiction fell to the local police departments until President Lyndon B. Johnson directed the FBI to take over the investigation. Later, Congress passed a law that put investigations of deaths of federal officials within FBI jurisdiction. After Hoover's death, Congress passed legislation that limited the tenure of future FBI Directors to ten years.

The Second Protocol stresses the need to control the press:

"...in the hands of the states of today there is a great force that creates the movement of thought in the people, and that is the press..."

These days the entertainment media, particularly music, movies and T.V. also have an effect on our thoughts and feelings.

As Art Kunkin, editor of the Los Angeles Free Press, once said, "The only way to have a free press is to own it."

The House of Rothschild bought Reuters news service in the 1800's. Later, Reuters bought the Associated Press. Now the elite own the two largest wire services in the world, where most newspapers get their news. The New York Times had 6 Rhodes Scholars on its board of Directors. The Rothschilds have control of all three U.S. Networks, plus other aspects of the recording and mass media industry according to research by Eustice Mullins in his book *Who Owns the TV Networks*.

The six corporations that collectively control U.S. media today are Time Warner, Walt Disney, Viacom, Rupert Murdoch's News Corp., CBS Corporation and NBC Universal. Since the Rothschilds are intimately connected with the Illuminati, it follows that we have a controlled news and entertainment media which is controlled by the Jesuits.

Since the Society of Jesus was reinstated in 1814, the Jesuits were the real power at the Vatican – not the Pope. The Jesuits were playing one European power against the other as in a giant global chess game. The Church of Rome, always the enemy of the Eastern Orthodox Christian, was secretly plotting against Serbia and Russia where that religion prevailed. After instigating the Civil War in the United States, the Vatican instigated the Crimean War and set the stage for World War I.

5

World Wars

The Vatican was at a low point in history, having lost the Papal States in 1860 to the newly formed republic of Italy, and by 1870, reduced to the 108.6 acre plot in Rome known as Vatican City, which only existed with the permission of the Italian government. Anti-Catholic sentiment was sweeping Europe as the age of rationality and liberalism set in.

Pope Pius IX, in an effort to shore up the religious institution, convened the First Vatican Council. The primary result of this council was to proclaim the infallibility of the Pope, all Bishops worldwide were to be appointed by the Pope and that all Church doctrine would be strictly directed from the Vatican.

A powerful contingent within the Austro-Hungarian government advocated war with Serbia long before the war began. Prominent members of this group included Leopold von Berchtold, Alexander von Hoyos, and Johann von Forgách, all of which were under the influence of the Jesuits. Austria-Hungary hoped for a limited war against Serbia and that strong German support would force Russia to keep out of the war and weaken its Balkan prestige. There is little doubt that Austria-Hungary played a large role in starting World War I.

Besides extirpating Eastern Orthodox Christian heretics, the Jesuits had much larger long range plans, as indicated in Albert Pike's letter to Giuseppe Mazzini. Plans were already in place to overthrow the Czar of Russia. Germany was antagonistic towards France ever since Napoleon, and in fierce economic competition with England. So, Germany and Austria- Hungary and the Ottoman Turks were forming an alliance, known as "The Second Reich", against Serbia, Russia, France and England. The Jesuits would cause these nations to clash in a giant upheaval.

The Black Hand was a secret society in Serbia. Its leader was Colonial Dragutin Dimitrijevic who also was the chief of intelligence of the Serbian Government and a member of the Jesuits' Illuminati. A certain Bosnian Serb, Danilo Ilic was recruited into The Black Hand in 1913 in Belgrade. Ilic returned to Sarajevo in 1914 and became a member of Mlada Bosna (Young Bosna) and became a journalist at a local Serb newspaper. Among his comrades in Mlada Bosna , he recruited Gavrilo Princip, Nedeljko Cabrinovic, Vaso Cabrinovic, Trifko Grabez, Muhamed Mehmedbasic, and Cvjetko Popovic to assassinate Archduke Franz Ferdinand of Austria in Sarajevo. This was the Jesuit engineered event that set off World War I, by giving a good excuse for Austria to invade Serbia.

The Pope, in his hatred of the Orthodox Church, continually incited Emperor Franz Joseph of Austria-Hungary to eliminate the Serbs. After the events of Sarajevo, Baron Ritter, the Bavarian representative in the Vatican, wrote to his government: "The Pope approves of Austria's harsh treatment of Serbia. He has no great opinion of the armies of Russia and France in the event of a war against Germany. The cardinal secretary of state (Rafael Merry del Val) did not see when Austria could make war if she does not decide to do so now."

Austria-Hungary delivered to Serbia the July Ultimatum, a series of ten demands intentionally made unacceptable, intending to provoke a war with Serbia. When Serbia agreed to only eight of the ten demands, Austria-Hungary declared war on 28 July 1914. The Austrian attack on Serbia quickly escalated as various allied nations became involved, leading to World War I.

In England, the State of Israel was being planned during World War I. The leader of the Masonic Jewish Labor Zionists was Theodor Herzl, who led the fight to found a new Jewish State in historic Palestine to be a rebirth of the historic nation of Israel. The Jesuit's covert purpose for the establishment of a Jewish homeland was to revive the Latin Kingdom of Jerusalem (AD 1099-1291) for the benefit of the Pope – not the Jewish people. Theodore Hertzel had already gained the support of the Rothschilds for the Zionist cause.

On November 17, 1917, Lord Arthur James Balfour wrote a significant letter to an international banker who had been elevated to a Lord of the realm:

> Dear Lord Rothschild,
>
> I have much pleasure in conveying to you in behalf of his majesty's government the following declaration of sympathy with Jewish Zionist aspirations, which have been submitted to and approved by the cabinet.
> His majesty's government views with favor the establishment in Palestine of a national home for the Jewish people and will use their best endeavors to facilitate the achievement of this object, it being clearly understood that nothing shall be done which may prejudice the civil and

religious rights of existing non-Jewish communities in Palestine or the rights and political status enjoyed by Jews in any other country.

I should be grateful if you would bring this declaration to the knowledge of the Zionist Federation.

Yours Sincerely,
Arthur James Balfour

At the time of this letter, Turkey still held Palestine and England was doing very poorly in the war against Germany and Turkey. Nevertheless, one nation was promising land held by another nation to the people without a nation. The *Quid pro quo* was that in return, the Rothschilds would use their influence in the United States to get the isolationist United States to join the War on the side of England. As already mentioned the Rothschilds were the guardians of the Vatican treasury and via Freemasonry, were knowingly or not, under the influence of the Jesuits.

This letter became known as the Balfour Declaration. The Zionist headquarters in Berlin was moved to New York under the leadership of Justice Louis D. Brandeis. The Zionist Transfer Department was used to finance the Zionist cause where ever needed.

Other agents of the Rothschild bankers were Edward House and Bernard Baruch. Edward House, the son of a millionaire banker, who had made his fortune running guns during the Civil War, was to become the closest advisor to President Wilson and basically selected his entire cabinet! There is little doubt that President Wilson became a puppet of the Rothschilds, via their agent Edward House, in backing war against Germany and signing the unconstitutional Federal Reserve act of 1913.

Benard Baruch made a fortune investing in the sugar market and became the best known financier on Wall Street by 1910. In 1916, Baruch left Wall Street and became an advisor to President Wilson on National Defense. In 1918, Baruch became Chairman of the War Industries Board.

After the War, Baruch joined Edward House at the Paris Peace Conference to help write the treaty of Versailles and express support for the League of Nations. World War I proved very profitable for Benard Baruch, whose net worth went from about one million dollars before the, war to about two hundred million after the war as a result of his leadership of the War Industries Board. England became a protectorate of Palestine and allowed Jews settle there. However, life in Palestine was harsh and most Jews preferred to stay where they were.

In the 1920s and 30s, Baruch expressed his concern that the United States needed to be prepared for the possibility of another world war. He wanted a more powerful version of the War Industries Board, which he saw as the only way to ensure maximum coordination between civilian business and military needs. He would eventually become a prominent head of the "Military Industrial Complex" During World War II.

At the Paris Peace conference of 1919, Edward House called together the dedicated individuals of President Wilson's "Brain Trust" (which House had created) including John and Allen Dulles, Christian Herter and Tasker Bliss to form a group to study international affairs. The resulting Council on Foreign Relations was incorporated as the American branch in New York on July 29, 1921. Founding members included Colonel House, and such potentates of international banking as J.P. Morgan, John D. Rockefeller, Paul Warburg, Otto Kahn, and Jacob Schiff... the same clique which had engineered the establishment of the

Federal Reserve System. The British, sister organization was the Royal Institute of International Affairs (RIIA). The CFR in the future would virtually direct all U.S. foreign policy.

After World War I, Edward House influenced President Wilson to speak before Congress to approve the League of Nations, which was a part of the Illuminati plan for world government. The proposal failed because the Senate realized that the United States would give up much of its sovereignty if the League of Nations treaty was ratified and voted it down.

Another Freemason order was set up in New York that was only comprised of Jews, called B'nai B'rith (Children of the Covenant). Its official purpose was to render aid to Jews in distress. Later, it evolved into a powerful political organization and created the Anti-Defamation League (ADL). The ADL openly works to prevent anti-Semitism while secretly operating a spy network.

On December 10, 1992 and April 8, 1993 the building of the ADL of the "B'nai B'rith" in San Francisco and Los Angeles were simultaneously searched by FBI agents; many documents prove that ADL, through its section of documentary research (Fact Finding Division) directed by Irwin Svall since 1962, has been a wide network of espionage. Such network of espionage has been established thanks to the friends of ADL among policemen, sheriffs and even FBI agents. The power of the Jewish community is such that the ADL building in Los Angeles had to be searched by the San Francisco police, because the local police refused to cooperate directly with the inquest. The Attorney General of San Francisco, Arlo Smith, said that it was 'the biggest network of espionage working on a national scale'.

In 1966 B'nai B'rith held secret meetings with Cardinal Bea, representing the Vatican. The January issue of Look magazine ran an article on the meeting. The seemingly strange historical disparity between the Vatican and a Jewish organization meeting is explained by the Masonic nature of B'nai B'rith Nothing of great importance happens in New York City without the direction or the permission of New York Archbishops. Thus, the Jewish/Israeli businesses in New York are resident at the permission of Rome, and their businessmen are usually high-level Jewish Freemasons connected to the Black Pope's Masonic B'nai B'rith. The Winnipeg Free Press is owned by two Jewish Freemasons members of B'nai Brith, Bob Silver and Ron Stern.

In 1916, at a secret B'nai B'rith meeting in New York, Jacob Schiff, President of Kuhn Loeb Bank, was appointed chairman of the committee on the Revolutionary Movement in Russia. On January 13, 1917 Leon Trotsky arrived in New York and received a U.S. Passport. He was frequently seen entering the palatial residence of Jacob Schiff.

Jacob Schiff financed the training of Trotsky's rebel band, comprised mainly of Jews from the East Side, on Rockefeller's Standard Oil Land in New Jersey. When sufficiently trained in the tactics of guerrilla war, Trotsky's band of revolutionaries departed to Russia with twenty million dollars of gold on the ship S.S. Kristianiafjord, all supplied by Jacob Schiff.

According to the French Secret Service, Jacob Schiff had also donated twelve million dollars to the Russian Revolutionaries in proceeding years. Other financiers of the Russian Revolution were Felix Warburg, Otto Kahn, Mortimer Schiff, Jerome Hanauer and Max Breitung in the U.S. and Max Warburg, Olauf Aschburg and Jivtovsky in Europe.

The bloody massacre of millions of Russians that followed did not seem to trouble the conscious of these bankers. According to the Russian Imperial Ambassador to the U.S., Bakhmetiev, after the Bolshevik victory, 600 million rubles in gold was transferred from Russia to Khun Loeb Bank in New York between 1918 and 1922. The Russian Revolution finally delivered Russia into the hands of the Illuminati, as planned by Albert Pike in his 1871 letter to Mazzini.

The Market crash of 1929 and ensuing depression was caused by agents of the Federal Reserve Bank. The 1920's had been a time of economic expansion. It was commonly thought that the way to become wealthy was to invest in the stock market as stock prices continued to go up.

People would even borrow money to buy stocks. Lenders had offered 24-hour broker call loans, which meant that if the lenders called you up to pay back your loan, you had 24 hours to pay it back. For many, this meant selling their stock to get the money to repay the loan.

First, the Federal Reserve raised the prime interest rate. Then later, all the lenders, in coordination, called in their 24 hour call loans at the same time. This caused a massive sell off of stocks leading to the "Black Friday" stock market collapse. These two tactics by the international bankers lead to the following depression which was felt worldwide.

World War I did little to advance the Vatican agenda. In1917, during the First World War, the Papal Nuncio in Munich, Eugenio Pacelli, had secretly negotiated with the Central Powers to accomplish the Pope's *Peace without Victory* In order to save the Vatican's client states, Germany and Austria-Hungry from total defeat, eventually leading to the Ceasefire on November 11, 1918.

Even before the Cease fire, on October 28 1918, Czechoslovakia and the next day on October 29, Yugoslavia both declared their Independence from the Austrian-Hungarian Empire. Yugoslavia with two thirds of the population being Eastern Orthodox Christians, in particular, represented a huge obstacle to the Vatican's strategy to eliminate the Eastern Orthodox Christians. No sooner than Yugoslavia came into existence, did the Vatican start plotting against it.

The Croatia section of Yugoslavia was predominantly Catholic, so the Vatican worked to promote Catholic politicians into positions of secular power with the aim of eventually having political control over the Orthodox Christians. Also, the plan was eventually to separate Croatia from Yugoslavia.

Ante Pavelic became the primary proponent of a separate Croatia. He was a raciest, a fascist and a Catholic. Also, Ante Pavelic was head of the Ustashi, a fanatical Catholic terrorist organization. Ante Pavelic was supported by the Archbishop of Croatia, A. Stepinac. Both Hitler and Mussolini saw Ante Pavelic and Stepinac as allies in their expansionistic agendas in that region.

The Vatican was also helping Franco come into power in Spain, Mussolini come into power in Italy and Hitler to come into power in Germany. This was an attempt to bring the Catholic nations of central and Eastern Europe together into a pan-German federation and re-create the Holy Roman Empire or The Third Reich.

When Mussolini came into power, as *Quid Pro Quo*, he created a sovereign state for the Vatican in Rome with the Lateran Treaty of 1929, which allowed the Vatican to operate independently of Italy and made Catholism the sole recognized religion in Italy.

The Vatican was also awarded $85 million for properties seized from the Church. In return, the Vatican agreed to stay out of Italian Politics.

Cardinal Secretary of State, Eugenio. Pacelli presided over the signing of a concordat, which he had spent years in negotiations, between the Vatican and the Nazi party on July 20, 1933. Like in Italy, the Concordant kept the Catholic Church out of German Politics while strengthening the Vatican's control over German Catholics. Also the Catholic Center Party was disbanded on orders from Pacelli. This was the only Party left opposing the Nazis.

Pope Pius XI, after observing their actions, started disapproving of the Fascists in Italy and Germany. But, he died of a heart attack on February 10, 1939. Some believe he was murdered, based on the fact that his primary physician was Dr. Francesco Petacci, father of Claretta Petacci, Mussolini's mistress. Perhaps, the Jesuits also had influence on the Doctor.

Other German Catholic priests and bishops didn't like Hitler or his policies. But, the Concordant kept them under strict control from the Vatican. In 1939, Eugenio Pacelli would become Pope Pius XII. Papal Nuncio, Von Papen became Germany's vice Chancellor, second only to Chancellor Hitler. Hitler's book *Mien Campf* was actually ghost written by the Jesuit, Father Staempfle. The Jesuit, Himmler designed the Nazi SS closely after the Society of Jesus. Pacelli had promoted the group Catholic Action in Germany in the late 1920's. Catholic Action used radio and cinema to unite Catholic laypersons with the Roman hierarchy. Catholic Action also formed a fifth column in France and Czechoslovakia which allowed the Nazi armies to more easily invade those countries.

So, we see collusion between some of the Catholics and the Nazis.

The Illuminati Bankers Financed both the Soviet Union and Germany. This was the Hegelian concept of creating two sides and bring them together into conflict. Out of the conflict would raise a new order more favorable to the Illuminati.

The International Barnsdall Co., controlled by Patriarchs of Skull and Bones, sent much needed drilling equipment to the Baku oil fields in the Caucasus region of Russia after the Bolsheviks came into power. Patriarch, Averell Harriman's company, Georgian Manganese Co. spent $4 million on improving Russia's' Manganese mines and associated railroads.

Guaranty Trust bank, founded by Patriarchs of Skull and Bones, in 1922 made joint banking agreements with Ruskombank in Russia and placed Patriarch Max May in as vice President of Ruskombank. This was at a time when U.S. laws forbid lending money to Bolshevik Russia. Rockefeller's Standard Oil built a refinery in Russia in 1927. Then, Standard Oil concluded a deal to market Russian oil in Europe and floated a loan of $75 million to the Bolsheviks. Apparently U.S. law doesn't apply to large corporations.

After the world depression, German industry was on the brink of collapse. Fritz Thyssen, the German steel baron, openly joined the Nazi party and threw his support behind Hitler. The flow of funds to rearm Germany went through the Bank Voor Handel, which controlled the Union Bank in New York.

The Union Bank was a joint Thyssen - Harriman operation. William Averell Harriman (S&B 1913), his brother Rowland Harriman (S&B 1917), E.S. James(S&B 1917) and Knight

---

Woolly(S&B 1917) all had major holdings in Union Bank. In 1932, of the 8 directors of Union Bank 4 were Patriarchs of Skull and Bones and 2 were Nazis.

George Walker (President Bush senior's grandfather) was the president of the Harriman Fifteen Company. George Walker, Prescott Bush (S&B 1917) and Averell Harriman were the sole directors of the company. One company of the Harriman Fifteen Corporation was the Hamburg Amrika Shipping line.

Remington Arms shipped a great number of Thompson submachine guns and revolvers on Hamburg Amrika Shipping line, to assist Hitler's rise to power at a time when the treaty of Versailles prohibited rearming Germany.

By 1936, more than 100 United States companies, including General Motors, Ford, International Harvester, and DuPont had subsidiaries or cooperative agreements in Germany helping to build its war machine.

World War II was virtually assured by the terms of the Treaty of Versailles. The war reparation payments demanded of Germany kept that nation in desperate financial straits. That and the world depression made things intolerable for the German worker. In that situation it was easy for Hitler's National Socialism to have appeal to the people of Germany. Hitler promised to create full employment and to resist Communism.

The depression paved the way for the man Wall Street had groomed for the presidency, Franklin Delano Roosevelt. Portrayed as a "man of the little people", the reality was that Roosevelt's family had been involved in New York banking since the eighteenth century. Frederic Delano, FDR's uncle, served on the original Federal Reserve Board. FDR attended Groton and

Harvard, and in the 1920's worked on Wall Street, sitting on the board of directors of eleven different corporations. Roosevelt was also a Freemason.

Roosevelt was a New York State Senator from 1911 to 1913, Assistant Secretary of the Navy from 1913 to 1920 and Governor of New York from 1929 to 1932. President Roosevelt was made the first Honorary Grand Master of the Order of DeMolay on April 13, 1934 at the White House.

The economy of the U.S. was in a shambles when Franklin Delano Roosevelt took office. Roosevelt immediately declared a bank holiday to stop runs on the banks. A number of measures known as the "New Deal" were put into action to assist the working class and poor.

By the summer of 1933, shortly after Roosevelt's "First 100 Days," America's richest businessmen were in a panic. It was clear that Roosevelt intended to conduct a massive redistribution of wealth from the rich to the poor. Roosevelt had to be stopped at all costs.

The answer was a military coup. It was to be secretly financed and organized by leading officers of the Morgan and Du Pont empires. This included some of America's richest and most famous names of the time:

Irenee Du Pont - Right-wing chemical industrialist and founder of the American Liberty League, the organization assigned to execute the plot.

Grayson Murphy - Director of Goodyear, Bethlehem Steel and a group of J.P. Morgan banks.

William Doyle - Former state commander of the American Legion and a central plotter of the coup.

John Davis - Former Democratic presidential candidate and a senior attorney for J.P. Morgan.

Al Smith - Roosevelt's bitter political foe from New York. Smith was a former governor of New York and a codirector of the American Liberty League.

John J. Raskob - A high-ranking Du Pont officer and a former chairman of the Democratic Party. In later years, Raskob would become a Knight of Malta.

Robert Clark - One of Wall Street's richest bankers and stockbrokers.

Gerald MacGuire - Bond salesman for Clark, and a former commander of the Connecticut American Legion. MacGuire was the key recruiter to General Butler.

The plotters attempted to recruit General Smedley Butler to lead the coup. They selected him because he was a war hero who was popular with the troops. The plotters felt his good reputation was important to make the troops feel confident that they were doing the right thing by overthrowing a democratically elected president. However, this was a mistake: Butler was popular with the troops because he identified with them. That is, he was a man of the people, not the elite. When the plotters approached General Butler with their proposal to lead the coup, he pretended to go along with the plan at first, secretly deciding to betray it to Congress at the right moment.

What the businessmen proposed was dramatic: they wanted

General Butler to deliver an ultimatum to Roosevelt. Roosevelt would pretend to become sick and incapacitated from his polio, and allow a newly created cabinet officer, a "Secretary of General Affairs," to run things in his stead. The secretary, of course, would be carrying out the orders of Wall Street. If Roosevelt refused, then General Butler would force him out with an army of 500,000 war veterans from the American Legion. MacGuire assured Butler the cover story would work: "You know the American people will swallow that. We have got the newspapers. We will start a campaign that the President's health is failing. Everyone can tell that by looking at him, and the dumb American people will fall for it in a second..."

And what type of government would replace Roosevelt's New Deal? MacGuire was perfectly candid to Paul French, a reporter friend of General Butler's: "We need a fascist government in this country... to save the nation from the communists who want to tear it down and wreck all that we have built in America. The only men who have the patriotism to do it are the soldiers, and Smedley Butler is the ideal leader. He could organize a million men overnight."

In 1933, the crimes of fascism were still mostly in the future, and its dangers were largely unknown, even to its supporters. But in the early days, many businessmen openly admired Mussolini because he had used a strong hand to deal with labor unions, put out social unrest, and get the economy working again, if only at the point of a gun. Many famous millionaires back then who initially admired Hitler and Mussolini: Henry Ford, John D. Rockefeller Jr., John and Allen Dulles, and other millionaires only changed their minds (at least publically) when the atrocities of fascism became widely known.

The plot fell apart when Butler went public. The general revealed the details of the coup before the McCormack-Dickstein Committee, which would later become the notorious House Un-American Activities Committee. The Committee heard the testimony of Butler and French, but failed to call in any of the coup plotters for questioning, other than MacGuire. In fact, the Committee whitewashed the public version of its final report, deleting the names of powerful businessmen whose reputations they sought to protect.

The press tried to pass off the whole military coup story as a hoax. However this letter dated 1936, from William Dodd, the U.S. Ambassador to Germany, to President Roosevelt states: "A clique of U.S. industrialists is hell-bent to bring a fascist state to supplant our democratic government and is working closely with the fascist regime in Germany and Italy. I have had plenty of opportunity in my post in Berlin to witness how close some of our American ruling families are to the Nazi regime.... A prominent executive of one of the largest corporations told me point blank that he would be ready to take definite action to bring fascism into America if President Roosevelt continued his progressive policies."

It is also instructive to note that American Liberty League, that was to execute the plot, would oppose all of Roosevelt's New Deal policies, including Social Security, in the near future.

Taking America off the gold standard in 1934, FDR opened the way to unrestrained money supply expansion, decades of inflation–and credit revenues for banks. Raising gold prices from $20 an ounce to $35, FDR and Treasury Secretary Henry Morgenthau, Jr. (son of a founding CFR member), gave international bankers huge profits.

FDR's most remembered program, the New Deal, could only

be financed through heavy borrowing. In effect, those who had caused the Depression loaned America the money to recover from it. Then, through the National Recovery Administration (NRA), proposed by Bernard Baruch in 1930, they were put in charge of regulating the economy

FDR appointed Baruch disciple Hugh Johnson to run the NRA, assisted by CFR member Gerard Swope. With broad powers to regulate wages, prices, and working conditions, it was, as Herbert Hoover wrote in his memoirs: "…pure fascism;…merely a remaking of Mussolini's 'corporate state'…" The Supreme Court eventually ruled the NRA unconstitutional.

During the FDR years, the Council on Foreign Relations captured the political life of the U.S. Besides Treasury Secretary Morgenthau, other CFR members included Secretary of State Edward Stettinus, War Secretary Henry Stimson, and Assistant Secretary of State Sumner Welles. Since 1934 almost every United States Secretary of State has been a CFR member; and all Secretaries of War or Defense, from Henry L. Stimson through Richard Cheney. Since President Truman, virtually all presidential candidates have been members of the CFR.

Publically, President Roosevelt stated to the American people, "Your boys are not going to be sent to any foreign wars." He would not have been reelected in 1940 on a war platform. But, the U.S. along with Briton, China and Holland had already placed a trade embargo on Japan, which is an act of war in itself.

The Philippines had just won their independence from the United States after a long protracted guerilla war. The 1934 Philippine Independence Act created in the following year, 1935, the Commonwealth of the Philippines, a limited form of independence, and established a process that would, in several years, end in full Philippine independence. After this, the Philippine government started releasing U.S. prisoners of war.

By order of President Roosevelt, these U.S. prisoners of war were blocked from returning to the U.S. They were refused passports and travel documents that would allow their return. Roosevelt and Churchill agreed to this plan to allow these U.S. citizens to be recaptured by the Japanese during the Japanese invasion of the Philippines and be placed into cruel Japanese POW camps to cause outrage of the U.S. public at the Japanese.

Top U.S. government officials had plenty of forewarning of the Japanese planned attack on Pearl Harbor. On January 27, 1941, U.S. Ambassador to Tokyo, Joseph Grew wrote a letter to Roosevelt's State Department warning, "In the event of trouble breaking out between the U.S. and Japan, the Japanese intended on making an attack on Pearl Harbor." On August 1941, Congressman Dies personally submitted evidence to Roosevelt of Japan's planned attack on Pearl Harbor, including a map prepared by the Japanese Imperial Military Intelligence Department. Dies was told not to release this information to the public.

Even worse, no preparations were made at Pearl Harbor for an attack. Ammunition for anti-aircraft guns was stored in ware houses - not besides the guns where it was needed for immediate response to an air attack. Air Craft were parked in circles with their propellers pointing to the center of the circle so that the planes had to be pushed backward by hand before they could take off. This would make the planes "sitting ducks" in an air attack. It was reported that these unusual circumstances were ordered by President Roosevelt "to prevent sabotage."

On November 28, 1941 Roosevelt sent a war ultimatum to Japan, "Withdraw all troops from Indochina and Manchuria – or else." Most Asian experts agree that that this ultimatum left Japan no choice but to attack the U.S. Naval fleet at Pearl Harbor.

The Japanese Purple Code had already been broken with deciphering machines that were supplied to all important commanders - except Admiral Kimmel at Pearl Harbor. By early morning December 7,1941, messages were intercepted and decoded, indicating that the Japanese attack was impending. At 9:30 AM EST Admiral Stark met with General George C. Marshall. Stark wanted to radio a warning to Kimmel. Marshall replied that the Japanese might intercept a radio message and complicate matters and that he would personally wire a message to Kimmel. Marshall's warning to Kimmel was sufficiently delayed that the bombs were already falling on Pearl Harbor when Kimmel received it.

The Japanese attack on Pearl Harbor caused a declaration of War to be declared against Japan and her ally Germany by the United States. When the United States entered World War II, President Roosevelt appointed Bernard Baruch as a special adviser to the director of the Office of War Mobilization. He supported what was known as a "work or fight" bill. Baruch advocated the creation of a permanent superagency similar to his old War Industries Board. His theory enhanced the role of civilian businessmen and industrialists in determining what was needed and who would produce it. Baruch's ideas were largely adopted, with James Byrnes appointed to carry them out. During World War II, Baruch remained a trusted advisor to President Roosevelt.

The war caused one figure to make great progress in his career.

Dwight D. Eisenhower had the rank of Lt. Colonial when the U.S. got into the war. In three months, he was promoted to full Colonial and three months later to Chief of Staff of the U.S. Third Army. In another three months he was made a Brigadier General, proving it is not what you know, but who you know that counts. Eisenhower was a personal friend of Bernard Baruch! Eisenhower was called to Washington by General Marshall and brought into war planning at the highest level. Following this, Eisenhower enjoyed a series of promotions until on December 24, 1942, he was made the Supreme Allied Commander of Europe.

It was decided to attack Italy before Invading France. After the German army was pushed out of Rome, General Mark Clark stated, "After the fall of Rome, Kesselring's army could have been destroyed if we had been allowed to shoot the works in a final offensive." The Allies could then have easily advanced across the Adriatic into Yugoslavia and then into Vienna, Budapest and Prague.

But, Mark Clark's army was halted and then weakened by removing men for the planned invasion of Normandy. This tactic probably prolonged the war for about a year, caused the Allies an unnecessary loss of about 100,000 men and drastically changed the political nature of Eastern Europe in the following decades.

To understand why, it must be understood that Roosevelt, Marshall, Eisenhower, Stalin and Churchill were Illuminati insiders. The division of Europe between the Soviets and the West had already been decided by the "Big Three", Roosevelt, Churchill and Stalin, at the Soviet Embassy in Teheran, Iran from November 28, to December 1, 1943 and at the Quebec Conference of the Allies called by General George Marshall in

1943. Nobody bothered to ask the people of Eastern Europe what they thought about the idea.

Harry Hopkins became the head of "Lend Lease" a U.S. program which gave military aid first to England and later, after Germany invaded Russia, to Russia. Major Racey Jordan was appointed liaison officer with the Soviets at an air base in Great Falls, Montana, which was a transshipment point on the Alaskan-Siberian air rout.

Major Racy Jordan was surprised that Russian Colonial, Anatoli Kotikov had considerable influence with Harry Hopkins. Whenever he couldn't get items the Russians needed, Kotikov would call Harry Hopkins and get results. Often supplies needed by our own forces in the battlefield were diverted to Russia!

In one incident, Racey Jordan inspected a diplomatic pouch, over the objections of the Russians. It contained a list of materials on the plane bound for Russia. The list included papers describing atomic fission and two pounds of refined uranium. Jordan at the time, didn't realize the significance of what he saw because atomic research was top secret. Major Jordan kept diaries with detailed notes of all that he observed at the Lend Lease operation. (8)

Not only did the Vatican not use their considerable influence to protest the Nazi death camps, the Vatican was operating their own holocaust in Croatia, overseen by Arch Bishop Stepinac and Ante Pavelic, head of the Ustashi terrorists. During the existence of Croatia as an independent Catholic State, 700,000 persons had been exterminated by a Catholic militia. Many were tortured, mutilated, died of starvation, were burned alive or buried alive. Franciscan Catholic priests were operating the death camps. Most of the victims were Eastern Orthodox Christians and some Jews and Gypsies. So the Jesuits were still carrying out their mission of exterminating heretics, even during the supposedly enlightened twentieth century. (9)

Commander George Earl, former American Minister to Austria from 1935 to 1939 and to Bulgaria from 1940 to 1942, was Roosevelt's personal naval attaché to Istanbul in 1943. In Istanbul, Earl was approached by the head of the German Secret Service, Admiral Wilhelm Canaris, with a proposal of the Surrender of Germany. Canaris had a more realistic view of the war than Hitler, and wanted a truce with the U.S. and England so that they could mount a defense against the Russians. He also proposed turning Hitler over to the Allies. Later, Fritz Von Papen, now the German ambassador, made a similar proposal to George Earl. Earl promptly sent a coded message via diplomatic pouch to Roosevelt. These proposals of surrender were ignored by Roosevelt.

Not only were the Germans not allowed to surrender, neither were the Japanese. The Japanese issued a formal offer of unconditional surrender on March, 1945. Their offer was ignored. The firebombing of Tokyo proceeded next, destroying 16 square miles of Tokyo and leaving millions homeless. Then, came the use of Atomic bombs on Nagasaki and Hiroshima. The only reason the U.S. leaders have not been charged with war crimes is that we haven't been militarily defeated.

The massive rebuilding of Germany and Japan following the war was a source of astronomical profits for the Illuminati bankers that helped cause the war. The Council on Foreign Relations (CFR) was considerably strengthened by the war and along with other affiliate groups that sprang up, like Institute of the Pacific Rim (IPR) and the Foreign Policy Association (FPA) which virtually ran all U.S. Foreign policy. The IPR policies handed mainland

China over to the Communists, under the guidance of General George Marshall, who ordered the disarming of the Nationalist Chinese army. The IPR later handled our Vietnam Policy.

International organizations like the United Nations was created by the CFR during the war and was first heard of by the public when the news stated that the invasion of Normandy was a United Nations operation. Rockefeller donated land in New York for the United Nations Building. The Illuminati finally got the start of their desired world government after failing with the League of Nations idea.

The Vatican, which brought the fascist governments of Hitler and Mussolini into power, assisted Nazi war criminals to escape justice after the war, through the "Nazi Rat Lines". Considering the concentration of Catholic power in the Pope, Eugenio Pacelli, Pope Pius XII, was the man ultimately in charge of the Nazi Ratlines. Pius XII "preferred to see fascist war criminals on board ships sailing to the New World rather than seeing them rotting in POW camps in zonal Germany"

After the end of the war in Italy, Alois Hudal became active in ministering to German-speaking prisoners of war and internees then held in camps throughout Italy

Hudal was appointed a representative to the German-speaking civil internees in Italy and used this position to aid the escape of wanted Nazi war criminals, including Franz Stangl, commanding officer of Treblinka, Gustav Wagner, commanding officer of Sobibor, Alois Brunner, responsible for the Drancy internment camp near Paris and in charge of deportations in Slovakia to German concentration camps, and Adolf Eichmann, a fact about which he was later unashamedly open. Some of these wanted men were being held in internment camps: generally without identity papers, they would be enrolled in camp registers under false names. Other Nazis were in hiding in Italy, and sought Hudal out as his role in assisting escapes became known on the Nazi grapevine.

According to Mark Aarons and John Loftus in their book *Unholy Trinitity,* Hudal was the first Catholic priest to dedicate himself to establishing escape routes. But, many others would do the same.

Many questions are brought up about World Wars I and II. Why would Jewish bankers finance the Bolshevik revolution in Russia when the Vatican was opposed to communism, if the Vatican controlled these banks? Why would Jewish bankers, like the Rothschild's finance Hitler who would then wage a holocaust against the Jews?

The Jesuits, at least the leadership of the Jesuits, who were once outlawed by the Pope, felt that they owed no real loyalty to the Pope. They had their own agenda for world control through the Illuminati and their other secret societies. They would work with the Pope when their goals were parallel and eliminate the Pope when they weren't.

The Jesuits financed the Bolsheviks through their control over the Masonic Jewish bankers like Jacob Schiff, to carry out their agenda as outlined in Albert Pike's letter to Mazzini. In the case of financing Hitler, the Jesuits never liked Jews to begin with and wanted to make life so intolerable for them in Europe, that they would be willing to migrate to Israel and create that Nation as also outlined in Pikes letter.

The Knights of Malta, whose members swear an oath of loyalty to the Pope that supersedes all other oaths, like upholding the U.S.

Constitution, are actually under the control of the "Black Pope" or the Jesuit General. Knights of Malta, William Donovan, and Allen Dulles both served in the Office of Special Services (OSS). In 1943, Donovan worked with the Catholic Church in Rome to be the center of Anglo-American spy operations in Fascist Italy. This would prove to be one of America's most enduring intelligence alliances in the Cold War, giving U.S. leaders "intelligence" that the Vatican wanted them to believe.

While other American agencies were hunting down Nazi war criminals for arrest, the Joint Intelligence Objectives Agency (JIOA) at the Pentagon, in "Operation Paperclip", was bringing them into America, unpunished, for their use against the Soviets. The JIOA created Operation Paperclip in 1946 to bring in German scientists to advance U.S. military and civilian technology and intelligence agents like Gehlen to advance our spying capabilities. The problem was that the U.S. State Department wasn't about to allow Nazis into the United States.

The JIOA expunged from the public record the scientists' Nazi Party memberships and régime affiliations. Once "cleaned" of their Nazism, the scientists were granted security clearances by the U.S. government to work in the United States. Paperclip, the project's operational name, derived from the paperclips used to attach the scientists' new political personae to their "US Government Scientist" JIOA personnel files.

The most important of these Paperclip Nazis was Reinhard Gehlen, Hitler's master spy who had built up an intelligence network in the Soviet Union. With full U.S. blessing, he creates the "Gehlen Organization," a band of refugee Nazi spies who reactivate their networks in Russia. These include SS intelligence officers Alfred Six and Emil Augsburg (who massacred Jews in the Holocaust), Klaus Barbie (the "Butcher of Lyon"),

Otto von Bolschwing (the Holocaust mastermind who worked with Eichmann) and SS Colonel Otto Skorzeny (a personal friend and bodyguard of Hitler's).

After the war, Truman disbanded the OSS. However some were concerned that U.S. leaders lacked sufficient information to properly direct foreign policy. England, which previously supplied intelligence to the U.S., had also cut back considerably on its intelligence budget after the war, as a cost cutting measure. U.S. military intelligence was not properly shared between the services because of inter-service rivalry. It seemed that a centralized intelligence agency that would correlate all information from the different sources and would provide a condensed report to the president was badly needed.

In 1946, General Vandenberg recruited Allen Dulles, then a Republican lawyer at Sullivan and Cromwell in New York, "to draft proposals for the shape and organization of what was to become the Central Intelligence Agency in 1947." Dulles promptly formed an advisory group of six men, all but one of whom were Wall Street investment bankers or lawyers. Allen Dulles and two of the six, William H. Jackson and Frank Wisner, would later join the CIA.

On June 27, 1947 a congressional committee held secret hearings. Allen Dulles was selected to hold a secret intelligence seminar. Room 1501 of the Longworth Office Building was sealed off by armed guards and everyone inside was sworn to secrecy. Dulles gave a reassuring speech to those present claiming that the CIA should only need a few hundred good men. He never said what he really wanted – to resurrect the wartime OSS.

The National Security Act of July 26, 1947 created a separate Air Force and the Central Intelligence Agency (CIA) with emphasis on the word "central" in its title.

Knight of Malta agents of the Vatican, Bill Donovan former head of OSS and Allen Dulles were primary organizers of the CIA. The agency was supposed to become the unifying organization that would distill and write up all available intelligence, and offer it to political leaders in a manageable form. From the very beginning, the Agency failed to do what President Truman expected of it, turning at once to covert projects that were clearly beyond its mandate and considered illegal by many since Congress knew little of these covert actions and did not sanction them.

From its inception the CIA has labored under two contradictory conceptions of what it was supposed to be doing, and no president ever succeeded in correcting or resolving this situation. Espionage and intelligence analysis seek to know the world as it is. Covert action seeks to change the world.

When Allen Dulles became director of CIA, he proceeded to orchestrate policies, such as the overthrow of the socialist Arbenz regime in Guatemala that he had previously promoted in New York at the Council on Foreign Relations meeting.

This overthrow was at the request of United Fruit Company because Arbenez was instituting a land reform program, buying up United Fruit company land at its tax assessed value. For years before, the assessed value of the land was considerably lowered under its market value by company brought assessors to reduce United Fruit Company land tax payments.

In November 1952 CIA officials began planning to involve CIA in the efforts of MI6 and the oil companies in Iran. Operation TP/AJAX was devised to overthrow Iran's democratically elected

Mossadeq government because he had nationalized the British oil companies. Operation AJAX was not finally approved by Eisenhower until July 22, 1953. Much of CIA policy ever since, has been to promote big business interests in other countries. That is probably why the CIA is known as "the company."

To bypass government regulation of the CIA, much of its operations were out sourced to private contractors.

Booz Allen (BA), one of the oldest and largest of the "cleared contractors," has been intertwined with the CIA's covert operations since Allen Dulles became CIA Director in 1953. Only recently has Booze Allen come into public awareness because it was NSA whistleblower Snowden's employer.

The most important CIA-Booz Allen cooperation may have been in Egypt. In March 1953 Miles Copeland, having resigned from the CIA to join Booz-Allen, returned to Cairo under what was, for all practical purposes, a joint CIA-BA mission. In addition to offering management advice to the Egyptian government in general, Miles also gave Nasser advice on establishing his Mukhabarat intelligence service and soon became his closest Western advisors as well as his top channel to the U.S. Government, more important than either the local U.S. ambassador or CIA station chief.

By 1964, the CIA's covert actions were consuming close to two-thirds of its budget and 90% of the director's time. Former OSS operative, Frank Wisner was head of covert operations under the, harmless sounding, Office of Policy Coordination (OPC).

In the late 1940s the CIA begins recruiting American news organizations and journalists to become spies and disseminators of propaganda in Operation Mockingbird. The effort was headed by Frank Wisner, Allan Dulles, Richard Helms and Philip Graham. Graham is publisher of *The Washington Post,* which becomes a major CIA player. Eventually, the CIA's media assets will include ABC, NBC, CBS, *Time, Newsweek,* Associated Press, United Press International, Reuters, Hearst Newspapers, Scripps-Howard, Copley News Service and more. By the CIA's own admission, at least 25 organizations and 400 journalists will become CIA assets.

The deal Gehlen struck with the Americans was not, for obvious reasons, released to the news media. The German general took his entire apparatus, "unpurged and without interruption, into the service of the American superpower." Allen Dulles funneled an aggregate of $200 million in CIA funds to the Gehlen Organization as it became known. Directing operations from a fortress-like nerve center in Bavaria, Gehlen reactivated his network inside Russia.

"Intelligence" provided by the Vatican and these Paperclip Nazis at CIA, particularly Gehlhen, directed attention away from the Vatican's guilt in causing World II and towards the "Russian menace." Soon, former allies were now enemies and former enemies were allies. And, the "Cold War" started - all being managed by the Illuminati secret societies, whose ultimate leader is the Jesuit General or the "Black Pope".

The Gehlen Organization supplied the U.S. with its only intelligence on the Soviet Union for ten years after its creation. However, much of the "intelligence" the former Nazis provide was bogus. Gehlen inflated Soviet military capabilitiesat a time when Russia was still rebuilding its devestated society to inflate his own importance to the Americans.

In 1948, Gehlen almost convinces the Americans that war was

imminent, and the West should make a preemptive strike. In the 50s he produces a fictitious "missile gap." To make matters worse, the Russians have thoroughly penetrated the Gehlen Organization with double agents, undermining the very American security that Gehlen was supposed to protect.

One estimate was that at one time, about half of CIA employees were Paperclip Nazis. Other Paperclip Nazis were hired by defense contractors. The space program was initially operated by the military and used the Paperclip Nazis to manage the program. These Nazis sabotaged the program to the extent that the Russians were the first to place the satellite, Sputnik into orbit. After that, they were given the ultimatum to "get with the program" or be replaced. Later, when NASA was formed, Paperclip Nazi, Werner Von Braun was placed in charge

So essentially, even though the German army was defeated after World War II, the Nazis, a creation of the Vatican, were not. The Nazis never signed a surrender document. And, Knights of Malta agents of the Vatican helped Nazi war criminals escape justice and created the CIA which assisted in bringing the Nazis into the U.S. and provided employment for them. Wow!

Higher level Jesuits in the know, celebrated the Creation of the CIA saying, "now we have an organization where we can legally do that which was before illegal." Besides spying, covert operations, and political assassinations, many of which violated international laws and treaties, the CIA got involved with illegal narcotics trafficking. Not all people working at CIA know about these illegal practices because the CIA, like so many Illuminati organizations, is compartmentalized into cells, with one cell not knowing what the other cell is doing.

By December 14, 1947 the NSA issued its first top secret orders to CIA - defeat the Italian Communist party in the upcoming Italian elections. It was an illegal operation not sanctioned by Congress. CIA station Chief at Rome and Knight of Malta, James J. Angleton who had bragged that he had penetrated the Italian secret service so deeply that he practically ran it, estimated that $10 million would be needed to sway the election away from the Communists.

The money came from the Exchange Stabilization Fund and was deposited into certain Italian U.S. citizen's bank accounts. These citizens would then donate the money to certain CIA front organizations, Italian politicians and priests of Catholic Action, the Vatican's political arm. The Christian Democrats won the election by a comfortable margin.

The Marshall plan offered billions of dollars to repair nations destroyed by the war and create an economic and political barrier to the spread of Communism. The plan which Marshall presented had already been outlined in the proposals of a CFR study group of 1946 headed by the lawyer Charles M. Spofford and David Rockefeller, entitled 'Reconstruction in Western Europe'; and the specific proposal for unifying the Western European coal and steel basin as a bulwark against the USSR was made by John Foster Dulles in January 1947. Allen Dulles served as a consultant to this plan and made sure the CIA could skim uncounted millions of this money and conduct political warfare by placing certain codes in the plan.

Bob Edwards, a member of British Parliament and Kenneth Dunne, presented documentary evidence that Allen Dulles had carried on secret conferences with representatives of Hitler's SS Security Office in February and March 1943. Official Washington knew Martin Bormann, Deputy Fuhrer of Hitler's Germany, master-minded the international 'Die Spinne' (Spider) underground organization which is planning to revive Nazism. Allen Dulles had seemed unconcerned.

By 1952, Klaus Barbie had arrived in Bolivia via a stop in Argentina. He had been spirited out of Germany by the CIA, with a hand from the Vatican. Soon he teamed up with SS Major Otto Skorzeny, who now was affiliated with the CIA. Fritz Thyssen and Gustav Krupp bankrolled Skorzeny from the start. Skorzeny's father-in-law was Hjalmar Schacht, president of Hitler's Reichsbank. Schacht guided Onassis' shipyards in rebuilding the German and Japanese war fleets prior to World War II.

Nicolae Malaxa had belonged to Otto von Bolschwing's Gestapo network and had escaped from Europe with over $200 million in U.S. dollars. Upon arrival in New York, he picked up another $200 million from Chase Manhattan Bank. The legal path for his entry was smoothed by the Sullivan & Cromwell law offices, the Dulles brothers firm.

Undersecretary of State Adolph Berle personally testified on Malaxa's behalf before a congressional subcommittee on immigration. In 1951 Senator Nixon introduced a private bill to allow Malaxa permanent residence. Later in 1952, Malaxa went to Argentina where he linked up with Juan Peron and Otto Skorzeny.

Barbie and Skorzeny were soon forming death squads such as the Angels of Death in Bolivia, the Anti-Communist Alliance in Argentina, and in Spain, with Stephen Della Chiaie, the Guerrillas of Christ the King. He also went to Egypt to train the Muslim Brotherhood fighters. Otto Skorzeny also organized Odessa, a continuation of the Nazi government in secret. Odessa virtually ran the governments of Paraguay and Uruguay from behind the scenes.

The United States CIA had joint operations between Argentina, Bolivia, Brazil, Chile, Paraguay and Uruguay. The joint operations were known as Operation Condor. These are special teams used to carry out 'sanctions,' the killing of enemies. Assassination teams are centered in Colonia Dignidad, Chile, founded by Nazis from Hitler's SS, headed by Franz Pfeiffer Richter.

After World War II, the UK and the US decided to create "stay-behind" paramilitary organizations, with the official aim of countering a possible Soviet invasion through sabotage and guerrilla warfare behind enemy lines. This idea was modeled after a concept of England's Prime Minister, Winston Churchill, who created the secret stay-behind army Special Operations Executive (SOE) which assisted resistance movements and subversive operations in enemy held territory after 1940. "Operation Gladio" is an umbrella name used by commentators and historians to refer to actions taken by these secret armies. Gladio was the name for Italy's secret army.

In Germany, for example, Gladio had as a central focus the Gehlen Organization. Its clandestine "cells" were to stay behind in enemy-controlled territory and to act as resistance movements, conducting sabotage, guerrilla warfare and assassinations. They consisted of a mixture of volunteers, ex-military men, spies of various state intelligence organizations and, ultimately, terrorists.

In 1947, President Harry Truman creates the National Security Council (NSC) and the Central Intelligence Agency (CIA). The covert action branch of the CIA, the Office of Policy Coordination (OPC) under Frank Wisner sets up stay-behind armies in Western

Europe. CIA director Allen Dulles was one of the key people in instituting Operation Gladio, and after 1947, most of Gladio's operations were financed by the CIA.

After the creation of NATO, these secret armies were originally set up in most NATO countries and became a joint NATO – CIA operation. Arms caches were hidden, escape routes prepared, and loyal members recruited: i.e., mainly hardline anticommunists, including many ex-Nazis or former fascists, whether in Italy or in other European countries. So, Nazi type secret armies and intelligence agencies were organized after the defeat of Germany by secret organizations like the CIA, largely created by Agents of the Vatican like Knights of Malta, William Donovan and Allen Dulles.

The problem was that these secret armies were being used for other purposes than fighting a hypothetical Russian invasion of Western Europe. In France, Prime Minister, De Gaulle was trying to give colonial Algeria independence from France. Some members of the French military were opposed to an independent Algeria and created the Organisation Armée Secrète (OAS) which merged with the French version of Gladio. Members of the OAS made several assassination attempts of De Gaulle. After French investigations revealed the complicity of NATO in these attempts of De Gaulle's life, NATO was forced to leave French soil. (18, 19)

By 1972, with the prospect of a Soviet invasion receding, a decision was taken to "make a pre-emptive attack" on the Italian communist party which was gaining popularity. There immediately followed a series of bomb outrages signaling the beginning of a "strategy of tension," designed to shift Italian politics sharply to the right. These terror attacks were blamed on the Red Brigade communists.

However, The attacks actually were done by Gladio and directed by the fascist P-2 or Propaganda Due masonic lodge. P-2 was headed by Licio Gelli - known as the "Puppet-master." During the war, Gelli had been a member of Mussolini's notorious "Black shirts," and later acted as liaison officer to the Hermann Goering SS division.

In 1974, Gelli met secretly with Knight of Malta, Alexander Haig. Formerly, the NATO Supreme Commander, Haig had meanwhile become President Nixon's White House Chief of Staff. The secret meeting was held in the US Embassy in Rome. Receiving the blessing of US National Security Adviser Henry Kissinger, Gelli left the meeting with a promise of continued financial support for the Gladio network Later, Gelli was sentenced to prison by an Itialian Court but disappeared. P-2 was outlawed by the same court.

Previously, any member of the Catholic church who was found to be a Freemason was automatically ex-communicated. Despite this, Itialian court investigations discovered many members of the Vatican's Curia were covert members of P-2. Subsequently, in 1983, a new Canon Law announced that this would cease. Thereafter, members of the Roman Catholic Church were free to become Freemasons.

Gladio terrorist attacks were happening throughout Europe whenever democratically elected governments leaned too far to the left. So, Operation Gladio started being illegally used for political purposes instead of defensive purposes. Also, the Gladio concept was extended to Briton and the U.S. for political purposes.

Harold Wilson's Labor government was the target of a Gladio type campaign. Wilson's surprise resignation has been credited to a dirty tricks campaign operated by British intelligence at the behest of the US. Known as operation "Clockwork Orange" Army psyops personnel began "fabricating" evidence that showed that senior members of the Wilson Cabinet, including the Prime Minister himself, were Soviet dupes. The Kennedy assassination was a Gladio operation so that the Vietnam war could be escalated and generate more profits for the Military Industrial Complex.

In 1955, by pre-arrangement, the Gehlen Organization was transferred to the West German Government, becoming its first intelligence arm, the BND. The BND became a Siamese twin of the CIA, a global operation. Gehlen pioneered the setting up of dummy fronts and cover companies to support his far flung covert operations

Another group that the CIA befriended was an affiliate group of the Nazis – The Muslim Brotherhood. It was founded in 1928 by Hassan al-Banna in Egypt. The founder of the Muslim brotherhood became an admirer of Adolph Hitler when he came into power. Later, Hassan al-Banna traveled to Germany and met with Hitler and was sent into Czechoslovakia to help with the German invasion of that country.

After the war, Hassan al-Banna was wanted for war crimes and fled back to Egypt, where he enlarged the Muslim Brotherhood. Otto Szartenzy, Hitler's favorite commando, Joined Hassan al-Banna in Egypt to train the Muslim Brotherhood's fighters in guerrilla war tactics.

In 1952, when the Brotherhood was sufficiently trained and supplied, they worked with Gamal Abdel Nasser and staged a coup against the King of Egypt. They installed Muhammad Naguib as President and Nasser as Deputy Prime Minister. In

1953, Nasser introduced far-reaching land reforms and gained popularity. For whatever reason, the Brotherhood attempted to assassinate Nasser in 1954. After the failed attempt on his life, Nasser placed President Muhammad Naguib under house arrest and assumed the executive office. Then, he exiled the Muslim Brotherhood from Egypt.

The CIA helped the Muslim Brotherhood to move their base of operations to Saudi Arabia. In the 1980s, the CIA would use the fighters of the Muslim Brotherhood first to cause the Soviet occupation of Afghanistan, and later, to fight the Russian occupation. In the 1990s fighters of the Muslim Brotherhood were used in Serbia to fight Eastern Orthodox Christians, and more recently to fight against Libya and Syria. It would seem that the Muslim Brotherhood is the CIA's favorite terrorist organization.

Many of the directors of the CIA were Knights of Malta, like Allen Dulles, John McCone, William Casey, William E. Colby and George Tenant and others were Patriarchs of Skull and Bones like George Bush Senior. So, we have a secret government agency headed by members of other secret agencies whose loyalties are to a foreign power, the Vatican, controlled by Jesuits.

CIA operations follow the same recurring script. First, American business interests abroad are threatened by a popular or democratically elected leader. The people support their leader because he intends to conduct land reform, strengthen unions, redistribute wealth, nationalize foreign-owned industry, and regulate business to protect workers, consumers and the environment. So, on behalf of American business, and often with their help, the CIA mobilizes the opposition.

First it identifies right-wing groups within the country (usually the military), and offers them a deal: "We'll put you in power if you maintain a favorable business climate for us." The Agency then hires, trains and works with them to overthrow the existing government (usually a democracy). It uses every trick in the book: propaganda, stuffed ballot boxes, purchased elections, extortion, blackmail, sexual intrigue, false stories about opponents in the local media, infiltration and disruption of opposing political parties, kidnapping, beating, torture, intimidation, economic sabotage, death squads and even assassination.

These efforts culminate in a military *coup*, which installs a right-wing dictator. The CIA trains the dictator's security apparatus to crack down on the traditional enemies of big business, using interrogation, torture and murder. The victims are said to be "communists," but almost always they are just peasants, liberals, moderates, labor union leaders, political opponents and advocates of free speech and democracy. Widespread human rights abuses follow. This scenario was repeated in Iran, Most of Latin America, South East Asia, Indonesia, and Africa.

This scenario has been repeated so many times that the CIA actually teaches it in a special school, the notorious "School of the Americas." (It opened in Panama but later moved to Fort Benning, Georgia.) Critics have nicknamed it the "School of the Dictators" and "School of the Assassins." Here, the CIA trains Latin American military officers how to conduct coups, including the use of interrogation, torture and murder. The Association for Responsible Dissent estimates that by 1987, 6 million people had died as a result of CIA covert operations.

Former State Department official William Blum correctly calls this an "American Holocaust."

Another organization, started after World War II, was the

Bilderberg Group. Knight of Malta, Joseph Retinger, the CIA's primary liaison to the Vatican, met with Prince Bernard of the Netherlands, the Prime Minister of Italy, Sir Collin Grubbin, who was also director of SOE, a British spy agency, and CIA director Walter Bedell Smith. This group formed a "think tank" which met at the Hotel de Bilderberg in Oosterbeek in 1954. This was the beginning of the Bilderberg group. Prince Bernard was made the first director. The Bilderberg Group comprised of world leaders in government, finance, news media and other form of influence would become a primary planning group for the New World Order. They meet secretly every year to plan their strategy and next moves.

One of the first major plans of the Bilderberg Group was to create a European Union. To trace the origin of the movement for European unification, however, requires that we go back to May 8 1946 and an address given at Chatham House (RIIA) by Joseph Retinger. In this talk he outlined a plan for a federal Europe in which the states would relinquish part of their sovereignty. At the time, Retinger was secretary general of the Independent League for European Co-operation (ILEC), run by the Belgian Prime Minister Paul van Zeeland. During the war, Retinger worked closely with van Zeeland and other exile leaders who would become prominent in the Bilderberg network.

In the U.S there was considerable approval of the plan among financiers, businessmen and politicians. Mr. Leffingwell, senior partner in J. P. Morgan, Nelson and David Rockefeller, Alfred Sloan (chairman of General Motors), Charles Hook, President of the American Rolling Mills Company, Sir William Wiseman, (British SIS) and partner in Kuhn Loeb bank, and CFR members, George Franklin and Adolf Berle Jr. were all in favor, and Berle agreed to lead the American section (of ILEC). John Foster Dulles also agreed to help

Thus was formed the European Movement (whose first congress at the Hague in 1948 is- the origin of the Council of Europe), which received substantial contributions from US government secret funds as well as private sources via the American Committee for a United Europe (ACUE). The names mentioned above are significant in the present context: Leffingwell preceded John McCloy and David Rockefeller as CFR chairman, 1946-53, and had been a CFR director since 1927, while Franklin was executive director of the CFR 1953-7 and was later a Trilateral Commission Co-coordinator: also, incidentally an in-law of the Rockefellers.

As for ACUE, its chairman was William Donovan and its vice-chairman was Allen Dulles (who was a leading figure in the CFR War and Peace Study Group during the early part of the war, and later the director of the CIA); and it was run in Europe by another CIA executive, Thomas W. Braden.

So here we see Knight of Malta agents of the Vatican and members of the Pilgrim secret societies RIIA and CFR, setup by Rhodes, organizing to create the Fourth Reich, as the European Union, after the defeat of the Third Reich. Many capitalists and industrialists supported fascism before and after World II. These same organizations are working to create the North American Union.

The Vietnam War was a distinct policy of the Vatican, which desired to create a Catholic country in South Vietnam. Vietnam was a French colony until 1954 when the French army was defeated by Nationalist Ho Chi Minh's Viet Minh army. The 1954 peace deal between the French and the Viet Minh, known as the Geneva Accords, involved a partition of the country into northern and southern zones. The accords called for an election in 1956 that would reunite North and South Vietnam under a common leader.

Bao Dai, the French appointed leader of Vietnam moved to Paris, but remained "Head of State" of South Vietnam, appointing Ngo Dình Diem as his prime minister. In 1955, Diem called for a referendum to remove Bao Dai and establish a republic with Diem as president. The Vatican wholly approved, as Diem was a staunch Catholic while Bao Dai was viewed by the Vietnamese people as a playboy puppet of the French.

There were many Catholics in both North and South Vietnam. After Vietnam was divided, the Vatican through Bishop of Hanoi, Trin Nhu Khue, started a propaganda program in the North. Even though Ho Chi Minh's constitution for Vietnam was modeled after the U.S. Constitution, guaranteeing religious freedom, Catholics in the North were told by their priests that Ho Chi Minh was a Communist and would persecute the Catholics and they should move to South Viet Nam for their own safety. They were also informed that they would get land from the South Vietnamese government.

At the same time, CFR member and Secretary of State, John Foster Dulles placed provisions in the Geneva Accords to move the Catholic North Vietnamese to the South. Then, Cardinal Spellman, who had a direct link to Pope Pious XII at the Vatican, used the U.S. Catholic lobby to pressure President Eisenhower to use the U.S. Navy, under the command of Knight of Columbus and secretary of the Navy, Francis Matthews to transport Catholic North Vietnamese to South Vietnam. About 1,100,000 North Vietnamese, many destitute, were moved south where a government barely existed.

Also, Cardinal Spellman influenced Eisenhower to not allow the Vietnam election of 1956. This was because the Vatican wanted Vietnam to stay divided. Spellman also influenced the U.S. News Media through, Skull and Bones Patriarch and Knight of Malta, Henry R. Luce, creator of Time, Life, and Fortune magazines which provided pro Vietnam War propaganda to the American people.

When Ho Chi Minh, whom everyone knew would win the election, realized that the western powers would not live up to their agreements and allow the elections to take place, he started his military campaign to reunite Vietnam.

Ngo Dình Diem became a problem for the U.S. To keep promises to give land to the Northern Catholic Vietnamese who came south, Diem confiscated land from the Buddhists and placed the disposed Buddhist farmers into hamlets. Being a staunch Catholic, Diem also started many anti-Buddhist policies in South Vietnam. The situation escalated when the Buddhists started demonstrating in Saigon. Diem started attacking Buddhist temples, and had some demonstrators shot, using U.S. Supplied military aid. Diem's terrorizing of the Buddhists was assisted by his two Catholic brothers, Chief of the Secret Police, Ngo Dinh Nhu, and the Archbishop of Hue, Ngo Dinh Thuc.

Much of the South Vietnamese army was comprised of Buddhists who started wondering why they should help a government that was oppressing them. When fighting against the Viet Minh, many Buddhist South Vietnamese regulars would simply dessert into the jungle. (10)

By then, the Catholic President, John F. Kennedy was Commander in Chief. At first, the inexperienced Kennedy, who was a great admirer of Eisenhower, went along with the former President's policies, which included the planned Bay of Pigs invasion of Cuba and the Vietnam policy. Later, when he became more aware of the true situation on the ground in Vietnam, he decided that Diem had to be replaced and ordered the CIA to assassinate Diem. Kennedy also withdrew military aid and advisors from Saigon, effectively abandoning Diem.

Diem and his brother Nhu fled to the sanctuary of the Jesuit Church of St. Frances Xavier in Saigon for protection.

But, they both were turned over to Buddhist Generals and were promptly executed to prevent any political comebacks. After this event, South Vietnam fell into more chaos requiring even more U.S. Military involvement.

Kennedy also ordered the CIA to assassinate Fidel Castro, in Cuba and Rafael Trujillo, the military strongman in the Dominican Republic. I suspect that the reason the many attempts by the CIA to assassinate Fidel Castro failed, was that he was protected by the Jesuits who originally helped Castro and the Cuban Revolution with arms and financing.

After, Diem was replaced, the South Vietnamese army was still doing poorly against the Viet Minh. Kennedy realized that the U.S. was in an unwinnable situation and was going to withdraw U.S. military advisors from South Vietnam.

After the Bay of Pigs fiasco, Kennedy realized that the CIA had fed him bogus intelligence on Cuba. He was told that that once a beachhead was established that the local people would join the Anti-Castro Forces and help to defeat Castro. He was also told by CIA director of operations Bissell that the invasion of Cuba would be disguised to look like a Cuban Exile force and that the U.S. was to use no official military forces in the operation so as to maintain plausible deniability.

The facts on the ground were that the local people totally supported Castro. Kennedy refused to render U.S. Air support of the invasion in order to comply with Bissell's instructions and later was blamed for not doing so.

Kennedy fired Allen Dulles as Director of CIA and placed Knight of Malta, John McCone in as director.

Kennedy also created the Defense Intelligence Agency (DIA) in an effort to better coordinate Military intelligence. Defense Secretary, Robert S. McNamara and Lieutenant General Joseph Carroll, former FBI special agent and administrative assistant to FBI Director J. Edgar Hoover, took the lead in planning and organizing this new agency. The JCS published Directive 5105.21, "Defense Intelligence Agency" on August 1, and DIA began operations October 1, 1961.

One of Carroll's top subordinates at DIA was an ex-CIA agent who worked closely with Allen Dulles, the man Kennedy had fired. Major General William Quinn worked within an elite group which saw the careers of James Angleton and Richard Helms promoted. He served as Allen Dulles' personal courier on Nazi troop movements during World War II and also pushed forward the overseas spy network aimed at the Soviets - the Gehlen Organization, with its links to Operation Gladio after the war.

One OAS captain who was allegedly involved in a de Gaulle assassination attempt, was Jean Rene Souetre. According to a May 1963 memo from CIA Deputy Director for Plans, Richard Helms, Souetre approached the CIA as the OAS "coordinator of external affairs." OAS had contacts in New Orleans with anti-Castro groups.

In March-April 1963, Souetre met with Howard Hunt in Madrid. Later, Souetre trained that summer with Alpha 66 and the 30th of November (both anti-Castro groups) in the New Orleans Mandeville region. Their headquarters' location in New Orleans was 544 Camp Street. The OAS' Mandeville "cell" worked closely with elements of the Defense Intelligence Agency (DIA).

Centro Mondiale Commerciale (CMC) was, by the US government's own admission, a CIA front. CMC channeled money to the OAS. CMC's parent company founded by the CIA, PERMINDEX, was filled with Nazis and neo-Nazis. President Charles de Gaulle publicly blamed PERMINDEX for attempting to assassinate him.

President Kennedy, after realizing the real situation in Vietnam, was making plans to start withdrawing from that country. Before he was able to carry out this withdrawal, Kennedy himself was assassinated by agents of the CIA, DIA and the Vatican. (11, 12)

Souetre was in Dallas in the afternoon of November 22, 1963. Later, Souetre was flown out of Dallas in the afternoon of November 22, 1963 by a private pilot in a government plane and then expelled from the U.S. 48 hours after the assassination. On the board of directors for CMC was Clay Shaw, indicted for murder of JFK by Jim Garrison. On his death bed, E. Howard Hunt, who had met with Souetre in Madrid, confessed his involvement in the Kennedy assassination.

Later the assassinations of Martin Luther King and Robert Kennedy would follow. In a civil trial against the government by the King family, overwhelming evidence of a Gladio style execution was developed. The 111th Military Intelligence Group was sent to King's location and set up photographers on a roof of a nearby fire station with a clear view of Dr. King's balcony, the usual police protection was pulled away just before the assassination, the 20th Special Forces Group had an 8 man sniper team at the location hiding behind bushes Later, the police cut down the bushes which hid the sniper team. After sanitizing the crime scene, the police failed to use standard procedure to interview witnesses who were in the area of the shooting.

It was obvious that the Military Industrial Complex needed more war to stay in business and the plan was to escalate the Vietnam War – not wind it down. Lynden Baines Johnson, who replaced Kennedy as President, immediately escalated the war with his prefabricated "Gulf of Tonkin Incident", sending thousands of U.S. Troops into Vietnam with U.S. Naval and Air support. The result was a disaster. Sixty five thousand U.S. troops and millions of Vietnamese were killed there. The U.S. ran up so much debt on that war that, in 1968, President Nixon was forced to remove the silver backing of the U.S. Federal Reserve notes, causing the massive inflation of the 1970's.

The CIA also started a secret war in Laos which Congress knew nothing about. No one told them about it or asked them to fund the war. The CIA funded the secret war by trafficking in Opium. The Opium trade had been going on since 1715 when the British East India Company (BEIC) opened up its Far East office in Canton, China and started trading Opium. The Jesuits took over BEIC through the Jesuit Lord Shelburne in 1783. The Jesuit secret agencies like the CIA have been in the Opium trade ever since.

Former OSS and CIA agent, Paul Helliwell had set up two companies for the CIA, Civil Air Transport (CAT) Inc. (Later Air America) and SEA Supply Inc. in Bangkok, Thailand, that became the infrastructure of the CIA's covert operations with drug-trafficking armies in Southeast Asia.

The CIA operatives would trade the Laotian Mao Tribesmen arms for Opium. The Opium would then be flown to Taiwan in CIA company airlines, Civil Air Transport and later, Air America, and converted into Heroin which would then be sold to Mafia leader, Santos Traficante to distribute in the U.S. Theodor Shackly headed the CIA's Laos operation.

Also, the CIA was purchasing Opium from General Khun Sha, head of the Opium Golden Triangle in Cambodia. The CIA's purchaser there was Richard Armitage, who was known to launder the drug money received from Santos Traficante through the Nugan Hand Bank in Austrailia. One Year, Khun Sha said that Richard Armitage brought his entire Golden Triangle Opium crop. (13)

The Opium trade also financed the Secret bombing of Cambodia which was also kept secret from Congress. The bombings primarily on the frontiers between Cambodia and Viet Nam were justified because the Viet Minh were using this region to bring supplies and men into South Viet Nam.

Within Cambodia herself, the strained efforts of Prince Sihanouk to maintain his country's neutrality was causing disenchantment among his people. Many wanted to fight against Vietnamese incursion on Cambodian soil and felt the Prince was shirking his obligation to protect Cambodia's territorial integrity and people. Others had more base motives for being discontent and wanting to oust Sihanouk – greed. Corrupt officials wanted to line their pockets with U.S. largesse and Sihanouk, with his policy of neutrality, hindered their access to such funds.

While Prince Sihanouk was traveling abroad in spring of 1970, several right-wing leaders within his government took the opportunity to overthrow him. It was a bloodless coup that set off over thirty years of bloodshed. Sihanouk was convinced by the Chinese to throw his support behind the Cambodian Communists popularly known as the Khmer Rouge. Full-scale civil war erupted in Cambodia with the Chinese supporting the Khmer Rouge and the Americans supporting an inept and corrupt Khmer Republic regime.

April 17, 1975. The Khmer Rouge finally overcome Khmer Republic forces and enter Cambodia's capital city of Phnom Penh victorious. American bombing during the late 1960s and early 1970s had already caused the estimated death of over a half million people. Under Khmer Rouge rule, people lived in complete misery and despair...if they lived at all. Almost two million people, an estimated 25 percent of the country's total population, died from starvation, disease and execution between 1975 and 1979. The Khmer Rouge leaders were financed by the Vatican's Club of Rome as part of a population reduction program.

Nixon's 1972 visit to the People's Republic of China was an important step in formally normalizing relations between the United States and the People's Republic of China. After President Nixon played the "China Card", U.S. assistance to Communist China increased dramatically.

Public outrage compels Congress to hold hearings on CIA crimes. Senator Frank Church heads the Senate investigation ("The Church Committee"), and Representative Otis Pike heads the House investigation. (Despite a 98 percent incumbency reelection rate, both Church and Pike are defeated in the next elections.) The investigations lead to a number of reforms intended to increase the CIA's accountability to Congress, including the creation of a standing Senate committee on intelligence. However, the reforms prove ineffective, as the Iran/

Contra scandal will show. It turns out the CIA with help from the Illuminati can control, deal with or sidestep Congress with ease.

In an attempt to reduce the damage done by the Church Committee, President Ford creates the "Rockefeller Commission" to whitewash CIA history and propose toothless reforms. The commission's namesake, Vice President Nelson Rockefeller, is himself a major CIA figure. Five of the commission's eight members are also members of the Council on Foreign Relations, the Jesuit/Illuminati organization.

Immediately after gaining independence from Portugal, Angola is up for grabs. Henry Kissinger launches a CIA-backed war in Angola. Contrary to Kissinger's assertions, Angola is a country of little strategic importance and not seriously threatened by communism. The CIA backs the brutal leader of UNITAS, Jonas Savimbi. This polarizes Angolan politics and drives his opponents into the arms of Cuba and the Soviet Union for survival. Congress will cut off funds in 1976, but the CIA is able to run the war off the books until 1984, when funding is legalized again. This entirely pointless war kills over 300,000 Angolans.

In 1966, Miles Copeland, while technically on leave from Booz Allen, made close contact with Adnan Khashoggi, a young Arab who was in the course of becoming both a "principal foreign agent" of the U.S. and also extremely wealthy on the commissions he earned from Lockheed and other military firms on arms sales to Saudi Arabia.

By Copeland's own account in 1989, this encounter with Khashoggi "put the two of us on a 'Miles-and-Adnan' basis that has lasted for more than twenty years of business, parties, and a very special kind of political action."

Copeland adds that "Adnan and I, separately had been called on by our respective friends in Langley [CIA] to… have an official, off-the-record exchange of ideas on the emerging crisis in the Middle East, and come up with suggestions that the tame bureaucrats would like to have made but couldn't."

In November 1962, the CIA, as part of its planning to get rid of Castro, decided to use Edward K. Moss for the Political Action Group of the CIA's Covert Action staff. This was more than a year after the FBI had advised the CIA that Moss's mistress Julia Cellini and her brother Dino Cellini were alleged to be procurers for white slavery rackets in Cuba.

Khashoggi himself was said to have "used sex to win over U.S. executives." The bill for the madam who supplied girls en masse to his Super yacht, *Kingdom 5KR*, in the Mediterranean ran to hundreds of thousands of dollars. Khashoggi made a practice of supplying those he wished to influence with dollars as well as sex. The CIA couldn't legally use these tactics. But, no such prohibition applied to Khashoggi. Apparently the CIA had similar planes for Moss. The power exerted by Khashoggi and Moss was not limited to Khashoggi's access to funds and women. By the 1970s, Moss was chairman of the elite Safari Club in Kenya, where he invited Khashoggi in as majority owner.

Saudi intelligence chief Prince, Turki bin Faisal gave a talk to Georgetown University alumni, in which he said:

"In 1976, after the Watergate matters took place here, your intelligence community was literally tied up by Congress. It could not do anything. It could not send spies, it could not write reports, and it could not pay money. In order to compensate for that, a group of countries got together in the hope of fighting Communism and established what was called the Safari Club.

The Safari Club included France, Egypt, Saudi Arabia, Morocco, and Iran (prerevolutionary Iran)."

When Jimmy Carter became President, he decided to cut back on the CIA's budget and had his appointed Director of CIA, Stansfield Turner, eliminate 600 CIA employees. Also, Panama's Manual Noriega was taken off the CIA payroll which former CIA director; George H.W. Bush had set up for Noriega.

Unless Theadore Shackley took direct action to complete the privatization of intelligence operations soon, the Safari Club would not have a conduit to CIA resources. The solution: create a totally private intelligence network using CIA assets until President Carter could be replaced. The BCCI bank would become the funding sources for many CIA off the books projects, including the Safari Club. So basically, the CIA intelligence and covert operations were being outsourced to private enterprise.

The Jesuit Archbishop of San Salvador, El Salvador, Oscar Romero, pleads with President Carter "Christian to Christian" to stop aiding the military government slaughtering his people. Carter refuses. Shortly afterwards, right-wing leader, Roberto D'Aubuisson has Romero shot through the heart while saying Mass. The country soon dissolves into civil war, with the peasants in the hills fighting against the military government.

About the same time, The Iranian Revolution occurred. Iran had been ruled by the hated Shaw who had been installed by the CIA in the 1953 Coup, which overthrew the then elected leader of Iran for nationalizing Iran's Oil. Since most U.S. Embassies are also CIA centers, the Iranian Revolutionaries captured all the U.S. Embassy employees.

The CIA countered by feeding false intelligence to their secret ally, Saddam Hussein, in Iraq, to the effect that Iran's army was in a state of disarray and now would be a good time to invade Iran. Soon, the Iran Iraq War was underway.

While officially distancing itself from Saddam Hussein, secretly the U.S. was helping Iraq. General Rumsfeld was supplying weapons, including chemical and biological weapons, to Iraq, while the CIA was providing intelligence, including real time satellite imagery over Iran to Iraq's military.

In actuality, not only was the U.S. secretly financing Saddam Hussein in his war against Iran, but also were most of the Persian Gulf Emirates, including Saudi Arabia. The reason was that Iran was a Shia country calling for a fundamentalist Islamic uprising. These countries, that were financing Iraq, were predominantly Shia countries ruled by Sunni leaders. Their leaders decided that Iran could influence a Shia uprising in their countries and possibly throw them out of power. The Iran - Iraq war would keep Iran too busy to cause problems in their countries. Since Saddam had the army and they had the money, they simply hired Saddam's army to do the job.

Since Iran's army had been supplied by the U.S. under the Shaw, all the parts for Iran's military hardware, ammunition and so forth had to come from the U.S. Soon, the Iranian revolutionary council proposed to President Carter to do a U.S. Embassy hostage exchange for arms. Carter refused and started secret consultations with the Joint Chiefs of Staff and CIA to launch a rescue mission.

Also, the U.S. Presidential elections were approaching. In a CIA conducted national opinion poll, the question was asked by pollster Richard Worthland:

"Which Presidential candidate would win the upcoming election if Carter were to launch a hypothetical military rescue mission which was successful in recovering of the hostages – Carter or Reagan?"

The results of the poll indicated that Carter would most likely win the election. The CIA disliked Carter because of his cutbacks at CIA and because Ronald Reagan was a Knight of Malta, they perferred Reagan. But with CIA ineptness (or perhaps on purpose), the poll also tipped off the Iranians of a possible rescue operation.

While all this was going on, Knight of Malta and head of the committee to elect Ronald Regan, William Casey, was secretly negotiating with the Iranian Revolutionary government of Iran. He informed Iranian Ayatollah Khomeini that Reagan - not Carter - would be the next U.S. President and that he should do business with him as Regan's representative.

William Casey already possessed quite a reputation. As president of the U.S. Export-Import Bank, he had negotiated the financing of the Kama River truck plant in the Soviet Union, the largest plant in the world. The Ayatollah knew that Casey was not to be underestimated. In the third week of October, 1980, George Bush and Richard Allen, acting as representatives for William Casey, had a secret meeting with representatives of Iran's Revolutionary Guard at the Hotel Raphael in Paris.

The agreement reached was that the U.S. would supply the requested arms through Israel, acting as a third party, and unfreeze Iran's assets held in international banks. In return, the Iranians would release the hostages as soon as Reagan was inaugurated president, but not before. The first arms shipment would be sent two months after that, in March 1981. (14)

Carters rescue mission "Dessert One" seemed jinxed from the start. Three helicopters, laden with sensitive intelligence, were abandoned in the Iranian dessert. Eight military personnel were killed and the mission was aborted. Richard Secord, Oliver North and Albert Hakim were part of the CIA's sabotage team, Secord was in charge of planning, North would coordinate sabotage of the helicopters on the Carrier Nimitz and Hakim, the man on the ground, would simply go AWOL.

These acts were actually acts of treason against the U.S. government. Their probable reasoning justifying their treasonous deeds could have been like this: "Why should we unnecessarily risk many lives in this dangerous rescue mission when we already know that the hostages will be released?"

Before the election, Knight of Malta, Reagan also had been in secret negotiations with the Vatican. A deal was made that if the Vatican would sway the U.S. Catholic votes to Reagan, and he got elected, he would reopen U.S. diplomatic relations with the Vatican. Ronald Regan, after becoming President, did reinstate diplomatic relations with the Vatican. General Vernon Walters, second in command at CIA under Nixon, was made U.S. envoy to the Vatican. President Lincoln had Vatican diplomatic relations severed during the Civil War, because of the Vatican's efforts to destroy the Union.

Immediately after Reagan was elected, Iran released the hostages. In March, the weapons started flowing to Iran via Israel. Swiss arms dealer, Andreas Jenni teamed up with Miami based arms merchant, Stuart Allen Mc Cafferty , to transport 360 tons of M-48 tank parts worth $27.9 million, in a C-144 turboprop air freighter in flights from Israel to Iran. On July 24-27, 1981, Israeli arms merchant, Yaacov Nimrodi signed a $135 million contract with Iran for 50 U.S. surface to surface Lance missiles,

50 mobile missile launchers and 68 Hawk anti-aircraft missiles. At this time, it was against U.S. Law to arm Iran. Much of this information is well documented in former Reagan/Bush campaign and White House staffer Barbara Honegger' book *October Surprise*.

Once again, the controlled news media's version of events was quite different. Just the tip of the secretive iceberg was publically revealed later, during the Iran Contra hearings.

As president, Ronald Reagan described the Soviet Union as "the evil empire." His hypocritical statement overlooked the U.S. Foreign policy of backing military dictators around the world, particularly in Latin America. At the time, The CIA and U.S. Armed Forces supplied the government of El Salvador with overwhelming military and intelligence superiority. CIA-trained death squads roamed the countryside, committing atrocities like that of El Mazote in 1982, where they massacre between 700 and 1000 men, women and children. By 1992, some 63,000 Salvadorans were killed by the death squads.

Before the Russian Invasion of Afghanistan, a communistic form of government already existed there. In April 1978 Afghanistan's centrist government, headed by Pres. Mohammad Daud Khan, was overthrown by left wing military officers led by Nur Mohammad Taraki. Power was thereafter shared by two Marxist-Leninist political groups, the People's (Khalq) Party and the Banner (Parcham) Party. The new government, which had little popular support, forged close ties with the Soviet Union, launched ruthless purges of all domestic opposition, and began extensive land and social reforms that were bitterly resented by the devoutly Muslim and largely anti-Communist population.

CFR strategist, Brzezinski had this to say: "... According to the official version of history, CIA aid to the Mujahedeen began during 1980, that is to say, after the Soviet army invaded Afghanistan, 24 Dec 1979. But the reality, secretly guarded until now, is completely otherwise Indeed, it was July 3, 1979 that President Carter signed the first directive for secret aid to the opponents of the pro-Soviet regime in Kabul. And that very day, I wrote a note to the president in which I explained to him that in my opinion this aid was going to induce a Soviet military intervention. "

The CIA organized the Muslim Brotherhood fighters in Saudi Arabia into a terrorist band under the leadership of Osama Bin Ladin and had them sent to Afghanistan to launch terror attacks against the government there. The CIA kept a database on all of the Muslim Brotherhood fighters. In Arabic Al Qaeda means "the base" which referred to this database which all their members were in.

These Al Qaeda attacks , along with internal fighting and coups within the government between the People's and Banner factions, prompted the leader of the Banner party to ask the Soviets for help in regaining stability. In response, on Dec. 24, 1979, the Soviets sent in some 30,000 to prop up their new but faltering client state. This was much decried in the controlled U.S. news media as the "Russian Invasion of Afghanistan." There followed a long, protracted war that was basically a stalemate, The Soviet forces controlled the cities and the Mujahidin controlled the countryside.

The Soviet war in Afghanistan of the 1980s saw the enhancement of the covert action capabilities of the Pakistani Inter-Services Intelligence ISI by the Central Intelligence Agency (CIA). A special Afghan Section, the SS Directorate, was created under the command of Brigadier Mohammed Yousaf to oversee the coordination of the war. A number of officers from the ISI's Covert Action Division (Special Activities Division) received training in the United States and many covert action experts of the CIA were attached to the ISI to guide it in its operations against the Soviet troops by using the Afghan Mujahedeen and Al Qaeda forces.

ISI, with CIA funding, also created madrasas which were religious schools which taught among other things that atheistic Russians had no place in an Islamic country like Afghanistan. Later, the ISI with CIA assistance also trained and funded the Chechnya Rebels against Russia.

Finally, the mujahidin were able to neutralize Soviet air power through the use of shoulder-fired Stinger antiaircraft missiles supplied by the U.S. and drove the Soviet military out of Afghanistan.

After that, the Taliban governed Afghanistan with all the extreme fundamentalism of the Wahhabis imported by the Muslim Brotherhood fighters from Saudi Arabia. William Casey at CIA got his "quagmire" which cost the Soviets dearly. At the same time, Casey was conducting a financial war on the Soviets through agent Leo Wanta.

Leo Wanta, a former U.S. Treasury official, was appointed trustee of $150 billion by President Ronald Reagan. He was made US Financial Warfare officer engaged in operations to "collapse" the Soviet Empire through financial maneuvers to prevent the Soviet military devoting larger resources to military expenditure.

The means to carry out this plan was to use the large amount of money trusted to Wanta to set up various corporations around the world, The New Republic Financial Group in Vienna being the primary one. These Corporations would do financial trading between U.S. dollars and Russian rubles. On the "black market" rubles could be brought cheaply and then they could be sold higher at the official Russian rate.

Wanta's traders would take the profits from this disparity in value and recycle the trades for ever higher profits. This was done on such a large scale that it collapsed the Russian economy in what was known in Russia as the "Great Ruble Scam."

The original $150 billion was paid back within 6 months. The profits from these and other financial trades came to $27.5 trillion which was placed in a trust controlled by Leo Wanta on orders from President Reagan, who wanted the money to be used for the benefit of the American people.

When George H. W. Bush became president, he decided that he wanted the money in the Wanta trust. However Leo Wanta had the money hidden in many corporate accounts and banks worldwide and he wouldn't reveal the secret of where the money was hidden. Later, when Bill Clinton became president, he sent Leo Wanta to Switzerland. Wanta was supposed to arrest Mark Rich, indicted in the United States on federal charges of tax evasion and illegally making oil deals with Iran during the Iran hostage crisis. Here is what Wanta said about his mission there:

"I was named Ambassador from Somalia to Switzerland and Canada as a cover to arrest Rich. When I go there, I found myself in a Swiss dungeon and Rich was set free. Foster was also there on behalf of the Clinton's, asking for $250 million to be used for The Children's Fund, which Hillary was the chairman. I thought it was to be used for a good cause so we gave him the money. Later, Vince attempted to help me out of my situation, but I was later notified he was found dead and I never found out what happened to the $250 million." (16)

Wanta was then extradited to the U.S. and sentenced to 22 years in prison on bogus tax evasion charges. Mark Rich was later granted a pardon by President Bill Clinton. It turned out that Rich had ties to Israel's Mossad and was part of the secret Iran deal to trade arms for hostages. Hillary and Bill Clinton were both deep cover CIA agents, recruited when they were in college. The Children's Fund was actually a CIA "cut out" company that Hillary often used as her private slush fund. Vince Foster's so called "suicide", interestingly, occurred just after he returned from his visit to Wanta in Switzerland.

The Reagan administration also increased aid to Communist China, the Bechtel Corporation, with many links to the Reagan Administration, started building nuclear power plants and a space launching facility in China. Secretary of Defense, Casper Weinburger was sending military technology and jet fighter planes to China. The financing of Chinese factories also increased.

The Bush family also has many investments in China. Perhaps that is why President Bush voted the Most Favored Nation trade status for China within months of the Tienamin Square massacre of Chinese students. Now the U.S. is flooded with cheap goods made in China, while U.S. jobs are eliminated.

COSCO Container Lines Americas, Inc. is the national flag carrier of the People's Republic of China, is one of the world's premier full service intermodal carriers. The company utilizes a vast network of ocean vessels, barges, railroad and motor carriers to link the international shipper with the consignee.

COSCO Container Lines is headquartered in Shanghai. COSCO now subtly controls the ports of Vancouver, Seattle, Portland, Oakland, Long Beach as well as East Coast ports of the U.S. and the Panama Canal. This control has been gradually granted by various U.S. Administrations since the Regan Administration. Knight of Malta, Alexander M. Haig, Jr. is a Senior Honorary Advisor to COSCO. Whose interests do these leaders serve? Certainly - not those of the U.S.

In Nicaragua, the Sandinista National Liberation Front (in Spanish, *Frente Sandinista de Liberación Nacional*, or FSLN), was organized by the Jesuits. In 1979 the FSLN threw the Military Dictator Anastasio Somoza out of power. Fearing that Nicaragua was another Cuba, a militia, known as the Contras (contra means against) was formed by the CIA in 1981 to overthrow the Sandinista government. The Contras, funded and trained by the US Central Intelligence Agency, committed many atrocities in Nicaragua. So, we have one branch of the Vatican, the CIA Warring against another branch of the Vatican - the Liberation Theology program promoted by the Jesuits in typical Hegelian style.

The CIA violated international law when they mined the harbor of Corinto, Nicaragua. As a result, Congress passed the Boland Amendment which cut off all funding for the CIA's Contra project. So, the CIA revamped the drug smuggling network used during the Vietnam War. But this time, it would be cocaine not heroin.

One of the "good old boys" networks that flew opium in Laos, Robert Plumlee, joined the Contra resupply network. Plumlee later stated, "I believed in the Contra war at first... But along about 1982, gun running and drug running blurred together and the Contra War eventually became a business. I ended up running drugs for the U.S. Federal government period."

Plumlee stated that he delivered cocaine to Homestead AFB on, at least, 4 occasions and to other air strips in the South West. Another informant stated that he saw Jeb Bush unload the 1000 kilo loads of cocaine flown into Homestead AFB. Jeb Bush would later become Governor of Florida.

One staging area was just south of San Filipe, Mexico - the Delgado Ranch owned by Rafael Quintero.

Plumlee states that he made 4 or 5 stops at this ranch, which was always heavily protected by Mexican police. Quintero was so wealthy that he offered to pay off the Mexican foreign debt, about $104 billion at the time, if allowed to operate freely in Mexico. Quintero eventually ended up spending 40 years in a Mexican prison.

Another staging area was Santa Elena ranch in Northern Costa Rica, formerly owned by Anastasio Somoza. Plumlee states that this ranch was used as narcotics transshipment point long before the Contra War.

This didn't change after Oliver North and Richard Seacord ordered the Ranch's air strip lengthened and improved.

Plumlee's unit was stationed at Fort Huachuca, Arizona. Plumlee's military operations logistic officer was Colonial James Steel who also was chief of the U.S. advisors in El Salvador and in close contact with Vice President George H.W. Bush.

Another "good old boy" that flew Opium in Laos and Contra Resupply Pilot was Barry Seal. Seal joined the Special Forces Reserve in late 1962 and about a month later was photographed in a Mexico City nightclub sitting with CIA operative Porter Goss and the rest of The CIA's Operation Forty group, the special operation charged with assassinating Fidel Castro. On 1 May 1963, Seal was transferred to Company D of the 20th Special Forces Group, composed of a large number of veterans of CIA assassination operations in Southeast Asia. The 20th was also said to have a domestic intelligence network run for them by the KKK.

Fellow Operation Forty pilot, Robert Plumlee maintains that Seal moonlighted as a CIA pilot working for Theodore Shackley in Laos and Vietnam, flying Special Operations missions. On December 1979 he was arrested in Guatemala with $25M worth of cocaine and imprisoned. He bribed the Guatemalan government to release him, but before he could be released, elections were held, forcing him to bribe an entirely new set of Guatemalan officials. In September 1980, he was released without being charged.

While in prison, Barry Seal met William Roger Reeves, a fellow drug smuggler who worked for the Ochoa family of Medellin. In 1981, Reeves, Ochoa's business manager in New Orleans, introduced Seal to Felix Bates. As a result Seal began a close relationship with the Colombians and became part of what became known as the Medellin Cartel. Established in 1980, the Medellin Cartel began when Jorge Ochoa convinced the major cocaine families to contribute $7 million each for the formation of a 2,000-man army in order to destroy the Marxist revolutionary group M-19, that was causing the drug barons problems in Colombia.

Drug barons such as Jorge Ochoa and Pablo Escobar now began working together. It has been estimated that the cartel made up to $60 million per month and its leaders joined the list of the world's richest men. The CIA decided that the Medellin Cartel could be used to help defeat communism throughout Latin America. According to Leslie Cockburn, CIA agent, Felix I. Rodriguez, persuaded the Medellin Cartel to make a $10 million contribution to the Contras.

By 1982, Barry Seal was bringing in drugs to the United States for the Medellin Cartel. Seal moved his base of operations from Louisiana to Mena airport in western Arkansas. Seal told friends that he once made $1.5 million on a single cocaine flight. Seal worked directly for Sonia Atala, the CIA protected drug baron, according to Michael Levine in his book *The Big White Lie: The CIA and the Cocaine/Crack Epidemic.*

By the time Seal was arrested in Ft. Lauderdale in March 1984, he had flown over 100 flights for the Medellin cartel, bringing between $3 Billion and $5 Billion worth of cocaine into the United States -- perhaps more than anyone in history. He tried to cop a deal with the Florida DEA, but they declined. Rebuffed, Seal managed to contact Vice President George H.W. Bush, with whom he struck a deal to testify, before the Task Force on Drugs, that the Sandinistas were complicit in the Columbian cocaine trade. In order to exchange a ten-year sentence for six months probation, he also agreed to participate in a drug sting aimed at Pablo Escobar and other top-ranking members of the Medellin cartel.

Seal agreed to testify against his former employers and associates in the drug trade, putting several of them in jail. Among those Seal testified against were Chief Minister of the Turks and Caicos Islands, Norman Saunders and members of the Medellin Cartel. No CIA employees were mentioned in Seal's testimony. Seal also testified before the President's Commission on Organized Crime in October 1985.

Seal now returned to drug-smuggling with official sanction (if indeed he hadn't had it before) in return for smuggling arms to Contras in Honduras. Seal managed to obtain several photographs of Escobar directing Nicaraguan soldiers loading 1200 kilos of cocaine onto a plane. Ronald Reagan later displayed one of the photographs on national television, denouncing the Sandinistas as "drug smugglers corrupting American youth".

Before 1984 was over, Seal would be again arrested for smuggling drugs, this time marijuana. He posted bail and once again returned to smuggling drugs. In December 1985, Seal was finally sentenced to six months supervised probation. From 6 p.m. till 6 a.m. every day, Seal was required by the terms of his probation to report to the Salvation Army halfway house in Baton Rouge, Louisiana. He complained of the regular schedule and spoke of being made a "clay pigeon".

On February 19, 1986, Barry Seal was shot to death in Baton Rouge, Louisiana in front of the Salvation Army halfway house. Over the next few days the police received information that enabled them to arrest several men for the killing of Barry Seal. This included Miguel Velez, Bernardo Vasquez, Luis Quintero-Cruz, John Cardona, Eliberto Sanchez and Jose Renteria. A seventh, Rafa Cardona, managed to escape back to Colombia. He was murdered later that year.

Eliberto Sanchez and John Cardona were deported and never appeared in court for the crime. Nor did Jose Coutin who supplied the weapons for the killing of Seal. However, he was not charged with any crime and instead testified in court against Miguel Velez, Luis Quintero-Cruz and Bernardo Vasquez. According to Leslie Cockburn in her book *Out of Control*, Coutin was a CIA asset.

Further evidence comes from Dee Ferdinand. She told Daniel Hopsicker that her father, Al Carone, a CIA paymaster and a Colonel in Army Intelligence, had been sent to Dallas to pay off Jack Ruby before the assassination of John F. Kennedy. She also claimed that 33 years later Carone performed the same function for the killing of Barry Seal. According to FAA investigator, Rodney Stich, Carone was Oliver North's bagman.

Al Carone had been a detective in the New York Police Department, but this didn't stop him from becoming a "made" man in the Genovese crime family. He knew all the leading Mafiosi of his day, including Vito Genovese, Sam Giancana, Santos Trafficante, Joe Colombo and Pauley Castellano amongst others. To Carone's daughter, Dee, they were all known as "Uncle". When she got married, her father arranged two different reception rooms to separate the Mob guests from the NYPD guests.

Meanwhile, another "Uncle" was Bill Casey, Director of the Central Intelligence Agency during the Reagan Administration. During his tenure in that role, Casey used Carone as a "cut out" to pass sensitive insider information to Mob capo Pauley Castellano. Carone was also a Knight of Malta which historically has been the military arm of the Vatican. One of Carone's principal functions in the NYPD was to act as the "bagman" in protecting shipments of CIA drugs to the various Mafia families.

Richard Sharpstein, defense attorney for one of Seal's assassins, Miguel Velez, says: "All three Colombians who went on trial always said they were being directed, after they got into this country, on what to do and where to go by an 'anonymous gringo,' a US military officer, who they very quickly figured out was Oliver North," (17)

There was apparently another reason why George Bush wanted Seal dead. According to friends, Seal had a copy of a videotape of a 1985 DEA cocaine sting which showed George Bush's two sons, George and Jeb, picking up kilos of cocaine at Florida Homestead AFB.

Barry Seal's wife, while looking through Barry Seal's papers after his death, discovered a phone number often called by her husband. When she called the number, she discovered she had contacted the Defense Intelligence Agency. She was told to "never call it again". Later that day, the DIA phoned her back. "Debbie, you're young, you have a whole life ahead of you, and you have your kids to think about... Don't call anyone in Washington again."

Another "good old boy" that flew flew opium on Air America in Laos and was a Contra Resupply pilot was Eugene Hasenfus. On October 5, 1986, his C-123K cargo plane was shot down by a Sandinista Patrol in Nicaragua. Hasenfus survived the crash and told his captors that he thought the CIA was behind the operation. He also provided information that several Cuban-Americans were running the operation in El Salvador. This resulted in journalists being able to identify Rafael Quintero, Luis Posada and Felix Rodriguez as the Cuban-Americans mentioned by Hasenfus. Also, it turned that his C-123K cargo plane was previously owned by Barry Seal!

In September 1998, a US $63 million lawsuit (Case No. 98-CV-11829-JLT) was filed by Massachusetts attorney Ray Kohlman on behalf of former Green Beret, William M. Tyree. In the course of the trial Ray Kohlman, Tyree's attorney, received a document titled "Declaration of William Casey". In Kohlman's own affidavit, dated August 27, 1999, he states that "most the contents of this affidavit can be proven" and that he "will testify to the contents of this affidavit in court" The declaration gives revealing insight of the Director of Central Intelligence's rational for his crimes.

Declaration:

I, William J. Casey, declare: I have found that freedom is a priceless commodity that demands constant vigilance to guarantee its longevity.

I was assigned to the Office of Strategic Services (OSS) in London, England, during World War II. During that time I befriended a young German soldier named Gunther Russbacer. I used Gunther and several other anti-Nazi German prisoners of war in OSS operations within Nazi Germany.

I knew this violated Geneva (War) Convention. I did not care. The Geneva Convention was but a set of rules governing man's atrocities committed in the name of political ideology. To wage war with rules is to prolong human suffering. Open warfare is the last resort of a civilized nation and must be used sparingly. Wars must be fought savagely utilizing all tools and tricks at hand. Gunther was a tool. Ignoring the Geneva Convention was the trick.

After I became Director of Central Intelligence (DCI) on January 28, 1981, I was approached and briefed by William Colby, former DCI. My history with Bill Colby is known. Colby notified me off the record of two operations he was still running in Latin America. Both operations were without the knowledge and consent of the United States Congress, President Ronald Reagan or even the United States intelligence apparatus. Colby identified the operations as "A-6" (RED MIST) and "A-7" (PROJECT SANDMAN). A-7 entailed smaller operations

I was told that A-6 identified individuals and the build-up of the communist threat in Latin America. Some intelligence collected in A-6 was used in TASK FORCE-157.

I was told that A-7 was "the Phoenix Program" of Latin America. It involved the assassination of the communist infrastructure throughout Latin America.

I was told that Colby authorized assets involved in A-6 and A-7 to engage in narcotic's trafficking to finance both operations. Colby engaged in similar operations that I know of in Vietnam for the same reason.

Colby candidly informed me that he had prepositioned more than one million pounds of cocaine in Panama between December 1, 1975 and April 1, 1976. This was done with the aid of our gallant ally, General Manuel Noriega. The cocaine was transported into El Salvador, Costa Rica and Honduras between 1976 and 1981. Colby now sat in front of me with hat in hand and requested my help in the delivery of the cocaine to the American market.

I was told that Colby was using a mutual friend of ours, Colonel Albert Vincent Carone, United States Army, Military Intelligence, to field A-6 and A-7. Al Carone is a charismatic patriot that General Joseph W. Stilwell introduced us to in late 1945. Besides the usual qualifications, Al Carone brought to the anti-communist effort a direct connection to his longtime friend, Vito Genovese. Genovese was the head of the gambling and narcotics for the controlling mafia family in New York to which Al Carone was made a member. Carone is a friend of international fugitive Robert Vesco. Carone has several anti-communist intelligence sources that include Maurita Lorenz, a friend of Fidel Castro. Al Carone is the younger brother of Dr. Pasquale

Carone. Dr. Carone worked for Central Intelligence on other matters.

Colby told me that profits from the prepositioned cocaine would be laundered through Al Carone, the New York mafia and Robert Vesco, then redirected to the anti-communist effort through Colby.

After discussion with Al Carone, I made the decision to bring the prepositioned cocaine into Mena airport, Mena, Arkansas. Central Intelligence has used Mena Airport on prior occasions. This time the cocaine is the tool. The trick was to ignore the law and avoid public scrutiny. We were helped in our efforts by William J. Clinton and William F. Weld.

By 1984 all prepositioned cocaine had arrived at Mena airport and additional cocaine sources were secured. Cocaine was being transshipped through Hangar Four and Five at Ilopango Airbase, El Salvador. My point man at Mena was Adler Berriman Seal (Berry Seal).

Bill Clinton has proved invaluable so far by containing the local law enforcement investigations into the intelligence activity at Mena. Bill Weld, as Assistant United States Attorney, was placed in charge of the Criminal Division of the Department of Justice. This was done so that Bill Weld could control investigations into Mena by federal law enforcement agencies. The placement of Weld has proved invaluable.

I ordered John Poindexter, Robert McFarlane and Oliver North to go outside normal channels and use available assets, including the mafia, to ensure the arrival of the cocaine into Mena Airport. The arrivals occurred in no small part through the efforts of personnel assigned to the National Security Agency (NSA) and

Army Security Agency (ASA). The men and women of the NSA and ASA blinded early warning defense satellites and radar grid to enable the aircraft to land undetected at Mena Airport. The NSA and ASA operations were SEA SPRAY and JADE BRIDGE.

I have learned that the course of the democratic struggle for Nicaragua and Latin America is beginning to swing in our direction. I attribute this success to A-6 and A-7 which Bill Colby had the insight, precision and spine to carry out.

I take notice of the heroic efforts of Al Carone, Bill Clinton, Bill Weld, John Poindexter, Bud McFarlane and Ollie North. Without these men, A-6 and A-7 would not have appeared.

Freedom is a priceless commodity. The amount of freedom you enjoy is a result of the amount of vigilance you invest.

My actions may be recorded as criminal, condemning countless American's to drug dependency. I don't care. All wars produce casualties. Generally the more violent the war, the shorter the length. My choice was either to stare down a protracted cold war guerilla insurgency in Latin America or use the means' available to finance and wage a violent war of short duration for democracy. I stand by my decisions. The tool is cocaine. The trick is to understand that the drug user had the freedom to make a choice. They chose the drug. I chose to use their habit to finance the democracy that all Americans enjoy. To keep those American's safe from the communist threat knocking on our back door in Latin America. For a change the drug user will contribute to society.

I declare under penalty of perjury that the above facts are true and correct to the best of my knowledge and belief.

It is interesting that "Maurita Lorenz, a friend of Fidel Castro", mentioned here by Casey, had testified before the House Select Commission on Assassinations, implicating some Anti-Castro Cubans as the gun men and Frank Sturgis and Jack Ruby as their paymasters in the Kennedy Assassination.

Another source of CIA funding for the Contras came from raiding the Savings and Loan companies. A typical example of how this was done, usually with the knowing cooperation of the S&L managers, is as follows: A loan would be taken out by a CIA "cut out" corporation using land as collateral. Typically, the loan would be to build a shopping center. The land was appraised, by a CIA agent, much higher than its actual value. The S&L could lend 80% of the appraised value. After the loan was made the CIA cut out company would default on the loan and the S&L would be stuck with land worth only a fraction of the loan value.

Neil Bush, manager of Silverado S&L authorized so many of these types of loans that Silverado finally collapsed. Charles H. Keating, Jr., Chairman of the Lincoln Savings and Loan Association was running a similar operation. Lincoln Savings and Loan collapsed in 1989, at a cost of over $3 billion to the federal government. Some 23,000 Lincoln bondholders were defrauded and many investors lost their life savings.

Five senators – Alan Cranston (Democrat of California), Dennis De Concini (Democrat of Arizona), John Glenn (Democrat of Ohio), John McCain (Republican of Arizona), and Donald W. Riegle, Jr. (Democrat of Michigan) – were accused of improperly intervening in 1987 on behalf of Charles H. Keating, Jr., Chairman of the Lincoln Savings and Loan Association, which was the target of a regulatory investigation by the Federal Home Loan Bank Board (FHLBB). The FHLBB subsequently backed off taking action against Lincoln. The substantial political contributions Keating had made to each of the senators, totaling $1.3 million, attracted considerable public and media attention.

This was an example going on with many S&Ls around the country in which 747 institutions failed and had to be rescued with $160 billion in taxpayer dollars. Many Savings and Loans were operating more or less as banks, thus requiring the Federal Deposit Insurance Corporation to cover their debts and losses with tax payer money.

The money from drug trafficking, S&L fraud and the money from arming Iran was combined together to fund the CIA's Contra operation. All the sources of money were illegal and hidden from Congress and the U.S. Public. Vice President, George H.W. Bush oversaw the operation. While, his sons Jeb and George W. Bush were unloading pallets of Cocaine at Homestead AFB, another son, Neil Bush was running the Silverado S&L operation.

About the same time that Congress was investigating Iran-Contra, the government of Costa Rica was launching their own investigation of cocaine smuggling in their country.

The result of Costa Rica's investigation was that Oliver North, Richard Seacord, the CIA station Chief in Costa Rica, Joe Fernandez, and US. Ambassador to Costa Rica, Lewis Tambs were all implicated in illegal narcotics trafficking. All four men were expelled and banned from returning to Costa Rica. This made headline news in Costa Rica but not a whisper was heard in the controlled U.S. news media.

The Iran Contra hearings in the U.S. drug on. Part of the problem was the large number of witnesses that died before they could testify. Paper shredding became the strategy of choice at Oliver

North's and Richard Seacord's offices. Director of CIA, William Casey, suddenly came down with cancer of the throat and was unable to testify. President Reagan got Alzheimer's and forgot everything. Only eleven convictions resulted, some of which were vacated on appeal. The rest of those indicted or convicted were all pardoned in the final days of the presidency of George H. W. Bush, who had been vice-president and coordinator of "the enterprise" at the time.

Most of the Iran Contra money was laundered through banks in Panama. At the time , Manual Noriega was president of Panama. On September 15, 1985 Panamanian opposition leader, Hugo Spadafora was kidnapped, tortured and beheaded by F-8, a Panamanian military counter terrorist force.

This caused quite uproar in Panama and the U.S. Manual Noriega was summoned to CIA headquarters at Langley, Virginia where he was warned by William Casey and Deputy CIA Director Robert M. Gates to "find better ways of controlling his special troops." Noriega replied that it wouldn't be so easy because the men in F-8 were trained to be impulsive killers by ex Mossad director, Mike Harrari and they looked towards him as their leader.

In 1988, Israel's primary export was arms and one third of these arms exports were to Columbia. Mike Harrai seemed to have oversight of this operation also. According to Columbia's internal security, Mike Harrari helped to train the paramilitary armies of the Columbian drug cartels. (15)

Evidently the CIA, the Mossad and the Columbian drug cartels had a three way business agreement in the Contra resupply network. Cocaine was delivered from Columbia to primary dealers in the U.S. who would send the money to Panama where money could be laundered through Panamanian Banks and then used to purchase arms for the Contras and the drug cartels. Israel sold the weapons and trained these armies.

When the Contra War ended and Noriega was no longer needed by the CIA, illegal drug charges were brought against him. Two covert CIA attempts to arrest Noriega failed. So, the "Just Cause" invasion of Panama followed. Mike Harrari was tipped off before the attack and escaped to Israel. Noriega hid in the sanctuary of a Catholic Church. Church officials later turned him over to the U.S.

James Steel, the man who probably knew more about the illegal Contra cocaine operations than anyone, was placed in charge of sensitive documents seized from Noriega. He may have shredded more documents than Oliver North! The links between George H. W. Bush, Noriega and ex Mossad director Mike Harrari were all too obvious. So, the Justice Department had to cover up evidence at the Noriega trial and Judge William Hoevelar refused to allow any testimony implicating President George H.W. Bush. This was a telling indictment of the U.S. justice system.

The "Just Cause" invasion of Panama had another purpose. Carter's Panama Canal Treaty was supposed to turn over the Canal to Panama, which would use the Panama Defense force to defend the Canal. In the Invasion, all the members of the Panama Defense Force were killed, many with their hands tied behind their backs, by U.S. Special Forces. Their bodies were buried in mass graves which were later uncovered. Since Panama had no way to defend the Canal, U.S. Military forces continued to be used after the turnover of the Canal.

After "Just Cause", President Bush hand-picked the candidates for the future government of Panama.

For President, Guillermo Endura, director of a Panama bank used exclusively by the Medellin drug cartel to launder their money. For Vice-President, Guillermo Ford, part owner of Dadeland Bank of Florida, a primary drug money laundry. For Attorney General of Panama, Rogello Cruz a boss of the Cali drug cartel in Columbia. With plenty of financial help for their campaigns, all the candidates won.

Journalist, Joseph Caselero had discovered a link between the Pan American Flight 103 explosion over Lockerby, Scotland and CIA drug smuggling and was preparing a news story.

Six CIA agents including the CIA station chief in Beirut were among the many that died in that explosion. They were part of a team headed by Charles McKee bringing back evidence of another CIA group involved in illegal drug smuggling known as the "The Black Rose." The Black Rose was involved with Syrian Drug smuggling rings and trading arms and drugs for hostage deals with terrorist groups. Syrian national Manzar al-Kassar was the head of the smuggling operation.

The CIA agents on the plane had been working to free the five CIA hostages held by William Buckley's Hezbollah murderers, they discovered that al-Kassar was allowed to continue smuggling heroin despite high-level CIA knowledge of his activities. The Beirut hostage team had written and called CIA headquarters in Langley to file complaints about the al-Kassar ring. They got no response. So they decided to fly back to the US and inform their CIA bosses in person. All six agents were on Pan Am 103 when it blew up.

The Black Rose included Richard Seacord, Oliver North,

Rear Adm. John M. Poindexter, William Casey and Iranian Businessman, Albert A. Hakim. The Chairman of The Black Rose was George H.W. Bush. Even though the FAA warned the CIA that a terrorist bomb (perhaps provided for by the CIA) was taken aboard Pan American Flight 103, they gave an order to disregard the report and allow the flight to continue. Whoever gave that order knew that all incriminating evidence against The Black Rose would disappear with the CIA team that died in the explosion.

Within an hour of the bombing CIA operatives arrived at the crash site wearing Pan Am uniforms. The agents removed a suitcase that belonged to one of the CIA agents who died along with 269 others. The suitcase most likely contained incriminating evidence regarding the involvement of both al-Kassar and the CIA's Black Rose unit in the Syrian heroin smuggling ring. It may also have contained a videotape of CIA Beirut Station Chief William Buckley's confessions to his Hezbollah torturers, which could have further revealed CIA involvement in the Middle East drug trade.

A PBS *Frontline* investigation found evidence that the bomb was actually planted while Flight 103 stopped over at London's Heathrow Airport. A suitcase belonging to CIA agent Matthew Gannon, one of the five others on Colonel McKee's team, was switched with bag at Heathrow. Gannon's suitcase probably contained incriminating evidence and the other bag probably had the bomb.

According to the German newsweekly *Stern*, a Pan Am security official in Frankfurt was caught back-dating the critical warning which the FAA issued as soon as he received it. Pan Am was fined $600,000 by the FAA after the bombing. The agency cited lax security in Pan Am's baggage handling operations.

According to the Interfor investigation for Pan Am's insurance company, these baggage operations were more than inept. They had been taken over by al-Kassar. In June 2007 Spanish police arrested al-Kassar for arms trafficking.

When President Bush was sworn into office a month later, he blamed the terrorist act on two Libyans- Abdel Basset Ali al-Megrahi and Lamen Khalifa Fhimah. As chairman of the Black Rose, Bush was probably the one who actually gave the order to bomb flight 103. The Pan American flight 103 bombing was then conveniently blamed on terrorists from Libya by the controlled news media and used as an excuse to bomb that nation .

This was basically the story, along with some others, that Joseph Casolero was researching. The Joseph Casolero murder was made to look like a suicide. All his papers in his room were missing. Wackenhut and NSA officials informed the Martinsburg police that they would secretly take over the investigation of the Casolero death and that the police would maintain the cover. Within three hours of Casolero's body being discovered and before next of kin could be informed, it was taken to a local mortuary and embalmed. His death was officially labeled a suicide.

Muammar Gaddafi, the leader of Libya had nationalized Libya's oil fields and had raised that country standard of living to the highest level on the African continent. Because of Libya's independence from international financial control, it represented a challenge to the New World Order. Also, Gaddafi opposed the U.S. European plan to create a Mediterranean Forum. This sort of Arab NATO would have Egypt and Saudi Arabia act as front men for the U.S., England, Italy and France to impose colonialism on Arab nations. Kaddafi was also organizing an African Union similar to the E.U.

Muammar Gaddafi's 6 year old daughter and many others were killed in the bombing. Also, the Chinese Embassy was hit, causing diplomatic problems between the U.S. and China.

After the Iran Iraq war, Saddam Hussein became upset with Kuwait for several reasons. Kuwait was slant drilling under Iraq's oil field, effectively stealing their oil. Kuwait also owed Iraq about $1 billion in payments for hiring Iraq's war service against Iran that it refused to pay. Also, Saddam Hussein considered Kuwait to actually be a part of Iraq since it was arbitrarily split off from Iraq after World War I by the European powers. For these reasons he was considering an invasion of Kuwait.

But first, he had to make sure it was O.K. with his powerful ally, the U.S. He sent his representative to meet with April Glaspie, U.S. ambassador to Iraq. April Glaspie had been carefully instructed by President Bush's State Department on what to say to the Iraq representative, because with the end of the Iraq Iran war, the U.S. no longer needed Saddam Hussein and was preparing to betray him, as they had done with Noriega.

The Iraq representative explained Saddam Hussein's position and plans to invade Kuwait to April Glaspie and wanted to know how the U.S. would feel about his plans. Her reply to him was "that the U.S. had no interest in Arab - Arab disputes", effectively giving the green light for Saddam Hussein's planned Invasion. If she had said that the U.S. absolutely wouldn't allow it, the invasion Kuwait would have never happened and thousands of lives would have been spared in the wars that followed. This clearly demonstrates just how evil and treacherous the Skull and Bones man, George H. W. Bush was.

Kuwait was invaded and then President Bush raised holy hell, raising a coalition of countries to push Saddam Hussein's army out of Kuwait. An array of nations joined the Coalition, the biggest coalition since World War II. The great majority of the Coalition's military forces were from the U.S., with Saudi Arabia, the United Kingdom and Egypt as leading contributors, in that order.

Much of Saddam Hussein's army was destroyed and the U.S. forces pushed Saddam Hussein's army all the way to Bagdad. United Nations Security Council Resolution 687, passed in April 1991 established formal cease-fire terms, officially ending the Persian Gulf War. But actually, the war continued, with sub fired Tomahawk missiles targeting radar sites and U.S. aircraft enforcing no fly zones. Finally, George Bush's Son would become President of the U.S. and finish off Saddam Hussein with the 2003 U.S. invasion of Iraq.

Cardinal Spellman of New York introduced Bishop of Chicago, Paul Marcinkus to the Pope. By 1971, Marcinkus had become an Archbishop and head of the Vatican Bank. Marcinkus also developed close ties to Masonic Propaganda Due (or P-2) lodge members like Michele Sindona, Roberto Calvi and grand master of P-2, Licio Gelli. P-2 had many links to the Vatican, Opus Dei, and the CIA.

Roberto Calvi, head of the Vatican's Ambrosiano Bank and called God's banker by the media, helped the Vatican transfer $100 million of Vatican funds to finance the Solidarity movement in Poland. Also he was laundering Mafia money through Vatican accounts. He was later involved in the Ambrosiano Bank scandal.

In 1982, Calvi's dead body was found hanging under Blackfriars Bridge in London. The day before his murder, his secretary, Grazella Corrrcher, died after falling from Ambrosiano's fifth floor. Apparently both had crossed the P-2 Masonic Lodge by stealing at least $1.3 billion from P-2. His death was a warning to other Masons - Calvi had taken his Masonic blood oath at Frati Neri (Black Friars) lodge in Italy.

During the years that P-2 was headed by Licio Gelli, P2 was implicated in numerous Italian crimes and mysteries, including the collapse of the Vatican's Banco Ambrosiano, the murders of journalist Mino Pecorelli and banker Roberto Calvi, and corruption cases within the nationwide bribe scandal, Tangentopoli. P2 came to light through the investigations into the collapse of Michele Sindona's financial empire.

P-2 was sometimes referred to as a "state within a state" or a "shadow government". The lodge had among its members prominent journalists, members of parliament, industrialists, and military leaders—including Silvio Berlusconi, who later became Prime Minister of Italy; the Savoy pretender to the Italian throne Victor Emmanuel; and the heads of all three Italian intelligence services (at the time SISDE, SISMI and CESIS).

When searching Licio Gelli's villa, the police found a document called the "Plan for Democratic Rebirth", which called for a consolidation of the media, suppression of trade unions, and the rewriting of the Italian Constitution - a perfect formula for fascism in Italy. Such a scandal arose about P-2 that it was eventually outlawed and a list of its members published.

Occasionally at the Vatican, there would be disputes between the Pope and the Jesuit General. Vatican II, was Proposed by Jesuit General Jean Baptiste Janssens because The Catholic Church needed to change its image to be more acceptable to the modern world. Vatican II included planes to soften the Church's stance on heretics by calling them separated brethren and starting an ecumenical movement to merge the Protestant and other Churches with Catholism. Vatican II also was going to soften the Church's anti communistic stance to appeal more to the Communist Catholics and more easily evangelize communist countries with Catholicism.

Pope Pious XII, described as "Hitler's Pope" by Historian John Cornwell, in his book of the same name, was a conservative and virulent anti-communist and was very much opposed to Vatican II. Apparently, Pious XII had forgotten who was really in charge at the Vatican. On October 9, 1958 Pope Pious XII, died of poisoning, although the controlled press would claim otherwise, and Vatican II stayed on track.

The official swing of the Catholic Church towards Marxism began with election of Angelo Roncalli, Pope John XXIII on October 28, 1958, and would continue with the reigns of Giovianni Montini, Pope Paul VI, and Albino Luciani, Pope Jhon Paul I. Roncalli and Luciani had been raised in poverty and understood from first-hand experience the basic unfairness of the capitalistic system. Montini's father was an atheist and a socialist and by the age of 13 Montini lost faith in the Catholic Church. However he also realized that it could only be changed from the inside. All three Popes wanted to change the Catholic Church into something that would actually follow Christ's teachings and Marxism, rather than capitalism, seemed to provide a closer model to follow.

The Jesuit General, Pedro Arrupe, was working through his subject Jesuits to put the tenants of Liberation Theology into action. This resulted in a period of Marxist revolutions and agitations in Latin America and other parts of the world.

According to Avro Manhattan, one of the best researchers on

the Vatican, in his book, *Vietnam why did we go?*, it was at this time that the Catholic Church started negotiating with Ho Chi Minh to reunify Vietnam under his rule and basically left the U.S. to pursue its own course of action. So, the Catholic Church, under Pious XII got the U. S. started in the Vietnam War and under Pope John XXIII threw its support behind Ho Chi Minh. I have talked with a number of Vietnam veterans that can testify that U.S. conduct of the war, its strategies and so on guaranteed the U.S. would not win the war, most likely because of the Vatican's influence over military commanders.

Pope John Paul I was one of the good Popes and loved by the people. He proposed melting down much of the Vatican's gold and selling it to finance a war against poverty in the poor nations of the world. He was known for creating orphanages in Italy. A statement by him stated: "It is the inalienable right of no man to accumulate wealth beyond his needs while other men starve to death because they have nothing."

He was going to reform the Vatican. One of his first planned acts was to reform the Vatican bank and fire the Superior General of the Society of Jesus, Pedro Arrupe. He also died of poisoning the night before the planned firing of the Jesuit General. His time as Pope was only 33 days! All of the pro-Marxist Popes were killed.

After that, Polish Cardinal Karol Wojtyla, became Pope John Paul II with considerable help from Opus Dei, a secret fascist Masonic Order. A younger Wojtyla had worked in a supervisory position at the Solvay Chemical plant which produced the Zyklon B gas used gas prisoners in the Polish prison camps during World War II. When it became obvious that Germany would lose the War and Germany started drafting Poles, Wojtyla joined a Catholic seminary to avoid being drafted into the German army. After his election as Pope John Paul II, the Catholic Church swung back towards the fascist capitalist camp.

Pope John Paul II also had a conflict with Jesuit General, Pedro Arrupe who was advancing the cause of Liberation Theology and the Marxist guerillas in Latin America. President Reagan prevailed on Pope John Paul II to get the Jesuits under control. In late April 1981, Pope John Paul II ordered Aruppe to resign.

Two weeks later, on May13, 1981, there was an assassination attempt on John Paul II life by Mehmet Ali Agca. Later from his prison cell, Mehmet Ali Agca stated that he was assisted in his attempted assassination by Catholic Cardinals!

However, soon after the attempt on Pope John Paul II, Arrupe himself suffered a massive heart attack which left him partially paralyzed. Many suspect that the CIA played a role in Arrupe's heart attack since the NSA had developed weapons that can stimulate heart attacks electronically from a distance.

Clearly, working at the Vatican can be quite dangerous. Between 1958 and 1978, 4 Popes had been poisoned. Many Cardinals had also been killed. Cardinal Benelli was in the midst of lining up opposition to ratifying the Opus Dei Prelature when he met sudden death. Cardinal Delargey, friend of John Paul I, died mysteriously after John Paul II was elected. Cardinal Felici was investigating Opus Dei's involvement with the Vatican Bank scandal when he dropped dead after drinking wine at a consecration mass. Cardinal Filipiak, arch enemy of John Paul II, died the day before John Paul II's election. Cardinal Suenens, a liberal, was killed. Cardinal Vagnozzi was found dead in his apartment while doing an audit of the Vatican Bank. Cardinal Villot died just after John Paul I did. He would not have allowed the Vatican Bank scandal to happen. Cardinal Violardo was Pope Paul VI's voice in the Italian Parliament and friend of the communist Aldo Morro. He was found dead in a stairway near the Vatican Bank. Cardinal Yu Pin, Archbishop of Taiwan, controlled the eastern votes needed to get Luciani elected, died before the election.

Others with links to the Vatican also died. Metropolitan Nikodim, Archbishop of Leningrad fell dead at John Paul I's feet after sipping a cup of coffee. Paul Marcinkus, President of the Vatican bank was caught up in the Vatican bank scandal Under John Paul II and died while Italy was trying to extradite him from the U.S. Aldo Moro, leader of the Christian Democratic party was kidnapped and murdered on the day he was going to move communist members into control of the Italian Parliament. His assassins were part of Operation Gladio run by the CIA and NATO.

In any case, all these murders at the Vatican got researcher Avro Manhattan writing another book titled *Murder by the Grace of God* which presented compelling evidence linking prominent American and Italian statesmen to the murder of many of these men. However before he could finish his book, he himself was found dead, hanging from a rafter by his wife who had returned from shopping. His book was finished by Lucien Gregoire and is available. Because of the left leaning nature of those murdered many suspect Opus Dei, P2 and the CIA had a role in these killings.

These suspicions were not without merit. In 1958 The CIA and MI6 through NATO established *Operation Gladio*. In the 1970's *Operation Gladio* was involved with right-wing terrorist attacks perpetrated in Italy and attempted to blame these attacks on the Red Brigade. Other Italian fascist organizations were Ordine Nuovo (New Order), Avanguardia Nazional (National

Vanguard), *Operation Condor* which operations were extended to Italy from South America by CIA Director George H.W. Bush in 1976, P2, which was founded by former Nazi Licio Gelli, and Opus Dei originated by Jose Maria Escriva in Franco's fascist Spain. *Operation Gladio* worked together with Ordine Nuovo and Avanguardia Nazional and P-2. Opus Dei's agenda was to gain control of the Papacy and Judicial, branches of nations. Gelli had been in close association with George H.W. Bush and a major campaign contributor to Bush's presidential, bid.

Italian courts established that P-2 was the number 2 killer agency in the 1970's Italian crime wave. The connection between Opus Dei and P-2 came before World War II when Licio Gelli and Jose Maria Escriva were partners in Franco's Cabinet in Spain. Jose Mateos was treasurer for both P-2 and Opus Dei using Ambrosiano Bank. Researchers suspect that much of Ambrosiano's missing money was directed to finance the Contras in Central America.

In 1998 Gelli and Mateos were brought to trial in connection with the Vatican Bank Scandal. Gelli disappeared before serving a 12 year prison sentence. Some officers of Opus Dei escaped trial because Pope John Paul II authorized the Prelature of Opus Dei retroactive to the day before Banco Ambrosiano collapsed. Under the Treaty of Verona, the Vatican is out of Italy's jurisdiction.

In the U.S., Bill Clinton said two influential moments in his life contributed to his decision to become a public figure. One was his visit as a Boys Nation senator to the White House to meet President John F. Kennedy. The other was listening to Martin Luther King, Jr.'s *I Have a Dream* speech, which impressed him enough that he later memorized it.

With the aid of scholarships, Bill Clinton attended the Edmund A. Walsh School of Foreign Service at Georgetown University in Washington, D.C., receiving a Bachelor of Science in Foreign Service degree in 1968. He spent the summer of 1967, interning for Arkansas Senator J. William Fulbright. While in college, he Joined Alpha Phi Omega and was elected to Phi Beta Kappa. Clinton was also a member of the Order of DeMolay and a member of Kappa Kappa Psi honorary band fraternity. At Georgetown, he was also recruited into the CIA.

Upon graduation, he won a Rhodes scholarship to Oxford College. The CIA had him join anti War groups at Oxford to spy on them. He left Oxford without graduating and later attended Yale Law School. At Yale, Bill Clinton met another student recruited by the CIA, Hillary Rodman and fell in love with her. Bill Clinton left Yale Law School in 1973 with a Juris Doctor (J.D.) degree.

Early in Bill Clinton's career at CIA, the agency realized that Bill had a problem with sex which would create potential problems. Although, Bill loved Hillary, with whom he was living, he still couldn't keep away from, other women. The CIA placed Hillary as Bill's "handler". Her job was to keep an eye on Bill and "clean up" after his sexual misbehavior.

After graduating from Yale Law School, Clinton returned to Arkansas and became a law professor at the University of Arkansas. The CIA decided that the best cover was for Bill and Hillary to be married. Since Hillary had lesbian tendencies, she would not be that troubled by Bill's antics with other women. They married on October 11, 1975, and their only child, Chelsea, was later born on February 27, 1980.

Clinton was elected Arkansas Attorney General in 1976. Later,

Bill Clinton was elected Governor of Arkansas in 1978 with considerable help from Dan Lasater, Stephens Inc. and Don Tyson. He served one term and wasn't reelected in 1980 because he didn't "play ball" with those who helped him into power. Having learned his lesson, he went back to his backers and promised to do whatever they wanted if placed back into the Governor's position. In 1982, Bill Clinton won back the Governor's office.

While Governor of Arkansas, Bill Clinton's CIA covert job was to kill any investigations into the CIA cocaine trafficking at Mena air Port in Arkansas. Clinton was on a first name basis with a number of Arkansas state police officers that would often drive him over to visit with his girlfriends. L.D. Brown was one of these officers, who was assigned to the governor's mansion. Clinton offered to reward Brown by getting him a job at CIA, using his contacts there.

After Bill Clinton called Langley, a CIA contact man, Donald Gregg, was sent to Dallas to meet with Officer Brown. Gregg was the Intelligence Directorate at NSC, worked with Panama's Noriega and was George Bush's right hand man. After, meeting with Donald Gregg, who used the alias Dan Magruder, Officer Brown got a phone call from Barry Seal. What surprised Brown was how familiar Barry Seal was with Governor Clinton.

After venturing out with Seal on a drug operation at Mena Airport, Brown, a seasoned narcotics officer, became quite disillusioned and approached Clinton at the governor's office. "Do you know what they are bringing back on those planes?" he asked Clinton. "They are bringing in coke", he added. "Don't worry, that is Lasater's deal and your hero, Bush knows all about it," Bill Clinton replied.

Dan Lasater was Bill Clinton's biggest campaign donor and a well-known Arkansas businessman and less well known cocaine distributer. Lasatar brought a horse ranch, the Carver Ranch and had an airstrip built on it. Carver Ranch was used by the Medellin cartel and Barry Seal to bring narcotics in and refuel. Lasater also was a friend of Bill Clinton's mother and gave Bill Clinton's brother, Roger a job as his driver.

Roger Clinton had a cocaine addiction problem that was well known. Often when Hillary was gone, there would be huge parties at the governor's mansion with plenty of cocaine and women to go around. Roger got seriously in debt to some cocaine dealers that started to threaten him if not repaid. Lasater loaned Roger Clinton the money to pay off his cocaine debt.

Sometimes, even murder was used to hide the Mena illegal narcotics smuggling operation. Near Mena Airport there was a Drop Zone called "A-12" by CIA operatives. Sometimes, the illegal narcotics would be air dropped at A-12 and picked up by narcotics traffickers, including Roger Clinton and Skeeter Ward, who were given protection by Sheriff, Jim Steed. At other times the drops would be picked up by police who were in on the drug operation. Sometimes the drops would be money. Someone, not part of the network, had picked up a previous money drop. The police and Dan Harmon, a corrupt prosecuting attorney for Arkansas's 7th judicial district, were hiding at the site hoping to catch the culprit.

Two boys, Don Henry and Kevin Ives, were Deer hunting near A-12. They were spotted by the police and made to lay on the ground with their hands tied behind their backs. They were interrogated and then brutally murdered. Then, their bodies were placed across some rail road tracks and covered with a tarp. Later, a train ran over the bodies. According to Sharlene

Wilson, Dan Harmon was scared and had blood stains all over his clothes when he rejoined her in the car after the murder.

These murders were covered up with the help of the notorious Arkansas State Medical Examiner, Fahmy Malak, whose autopsy findings, making murders looking like suicides, were so outrageous that many in the State were calling for his replacement.

However, Governor Bill Clinton merely gave Malak a pay raise, making his salary the second highest in the state government. Neither would the head of the State Medical Examiner Commission, Dr. Jocelyn Elders, take action against Malak. Later on January 1993, Bill Clinton appointed Dr. Jocelyn Elders to be United States Surgeon General. Thus, demonstrating how Clinton rewarded those who served his covert purposes.

The cocaine trafficking in Arkansas was prolific. High political figures were involved and many of them were paranoid of getting caught. Hillary Clinton asked Vince Foster to get Jerry Parks, a private security firm owner , to spy on Bill Clinton, as any normal red blooded wife would do if they had a philandering husband like Bill.

Jerry Parks was also a friend of Barry Seal.

In addition to spying on Bill and keeping files and photographs on his infidelities, Parks also became a money runner for the Mena operation, delivering the money to Vince Foster himself.

Parks would leave his Lincoln at the airport after a drug shipment came in and go for a Coke. By the time he would return, the trunk of his Lincoln was filled with bundled $100 bills by other operatives. He would drive home and remove the money, a suitcase load at a time. The money was then delivered to

Vince Foster in a switching suitcase routine in the K-Mart parking lot on Rodney Parham Boulevard in Little Rock.

Later during Clinton's 1992 presidential campaign, Larry Parks was hired as the head of campaign security. When the campaign was strapped for cash, Vince Foster would provide an infusion with Mena drug money.

Bill Clinton did his job so well at hiding the CIA Mena operation that he was invited to join the Bilderberg Group. A year after that, Clinton became President of the U.S. This was partly because the people of the U.S. were getting sick of the corruption of President H.W. Bush, but mainly due to the support of the CIA, Bilderbergers and major corporations.

After becoming President, the Bill Clinton and his wife, had to continually worry about being caught for their nefarious deeds. Vincent Foster and Larry Parks knew too much and had to go. Vincent Foster's "suicide" was clearly not a suicide. There was little blood found by his body at Fort Mercy Park, no witness there had heard a gunshot, and his cloths were covered with carpet fibers. In a typical mob hit, the body is rolled up in a carpet, which soaks up the blood, thrown in the trunk of a car and dumped somewhere else. Obviously, someone had taken out a "contract" on Vince Foster. Eleven days before the murder of Larry Parks, his apartment was broken into and all the files he had on Bill Clinton were taken.

Mochtar Riady started his financial empire gun and drug running in the East Indies before World War II. Riady joined with Jackson Stephens in Arkansas's biggest bank – Worthen Bank. Worthern Bank had contributed $600,000 to the DNC to help finance Bill Clinton presidential bid. And Bill Clinton owed the owners of Worthern some favors.

The favors came due when Riady asked Clinton to place John Huang in the Commerce Department. On the pretext that Huang's services were urgently needed by Ron Brown's Commerce Department, Huang was given a Top Secret security clearance. In this position, Haung was given CIA clearance and would pass classified U.S. economic intelligence on to Riady and Chinese Intelligence. So, Basically the Clintons were engaged in treason, in addition to other crimes.

The head of Commerce, Ron Brown knew what was going on because he himself was involved, having accepted bribes from Riady. The Independent council was getting ready to issue a criminal grand jury indictment against Brown. If called to the stand, Brown would have testified against Hillary and Bill Clinton.

So, the Clinton's quickly arranged for Ron Brown and the Assistant Secretary of Commerce to make a fund raising trip to the Balkans. Brown was never subpoenaed by the independent Council because he died in a plane crash on the way to Croatia. Researcher Victor Thorne and others have compiled sufficient evidence that the plane crash was no accident and that Ron Brown and others on the plane were murdered. Many other deaths of people linked to the Clintons also occurred. Researcher, Victor Thorn estimated that 120 deaths were in the "Clinton body count." (20)

6

Nation Destroying for the New World Order

In the 1990s, The Vatican decided to renew its war on the Eastern Orthodox Christians in Yugoslavia. Their chief agencies to carry out this war were the German BND, the U.S. CIA, the controlled Western news media, NATO and Non-Governmental Organizations (NGOs). The CIA had used many front corporations to successfully carry out its agendas. NGO's were privately funded organizations to carry out their founders agendas.

The Jesuits had already been hard at work in the different ethnic regions of Yugoslavia which no longer had the strong man, Tito to hold these regions together. The Jesuits, wishing to Balkanize Yugoslavia, started separation movements in the different regions much like they had in the U.S. preceding the Civil War. These separation movements took advantage of the ethnic and religious differences of the region.

One separation method used were the NGOs, in particular one called Otpor which meant resistance in English. Otpor was funded by other NGOs, the U.S. National Endowment for Democracy (NED), U.S. AID and the International Republican Institute (IRI). In typical Jesuit style, Otpor worked at the University level, recruiting students for the cause. Also, the CIA started importing

Muslim Brotherhood terrorists from many Islamic countries into Bosnia. The head of Otpor was Srdja Popovic, a CIA agent.

Initially the Yugoslav People's Army (JNA) sought to preserve the unity of the whole of Yugoslavia by crushing the secessionist movements in what became known as the "Yugoslav Wars." Slobodan Milosevic controlled the JNA. So, the Vatican put him on their "hit list".

The US government had installed the US diplomat William Walker as head of the Organization for Security and Co-operation in Europe (OSCE) in Kosovo. Before that, Walker had managed the dirty business of the US in Latin America, supporting regimes friendly to the US, especially in El Salvador when the death squads were rampant.

The OSCE is the world's largest security-oriented intergovernmental organization. Its official mandate includes issues such as arms control and the promotion of human rights, freedom of the press and fair elections. But, the OSCE actions in Yugoslavia proved otherwise.

Despite its links to organized crime and Al Qaeda, the Kosovo Liberation Army (KLA) rebel army had been skillfully heralded by the Western media in the months preceding the 1999 NATO bombings as broadly representative of the interests of ethnic Albanians in Kosovo. Its leader Hashim Thaci had been "designated" by US Secretary of State Madeleine Albright as chief negotiator at the Rambouillet peace talks which sought to separate Kosovo from Yugoslavia.

The fact of the matter is that the Atlantic Alliance had been supporting a terrorist organization. The KLA was not supporting the rights of ethnic Albanians. Quite the opposite was true. The

Muslim fighters in the KLA were Al Qaeda forces brought in from Muslim countries by the CIA. Another group trained and financed by the CIA and the German BND were the UCK terrorists. In one incident, the Serbian Police had cornered a UCK terrorist cell and a shootout ensued. The OSCE had been informed beforehand by the Serbian police that they had cornered the UCK terrorists near Racak.

William Walker, head of OSCE in Kosovo, got on T.V. and lied about the circumstances. He converted the dead terrorists into "civilian victims" and that the "cruel massacre" was committed by Serbians. This became the much decried Racak massacre which provided NATO and the US with the pretext to intervene on humanitarian grounds, claiming that the Serb authorities had committed human rights violations against ethnic Albanians. President Bill Clinton pushed NATO to act.

On March 24, 1999, NATO, headed by the Catholic and Rhodes Scholar, Commander Wesley Clark, started the bombings on Yugoslavia as air support for the terrorist KLA army. This was in violation of the NATO charter which was set up to defend Europe from a Soviet invasion - not to be used to attack countries having internal conflicts!

But then, the criminals running the New World Order have no actual concern for laws. As we have seen, many of the people running the U.S. and other nations are criminals, like Bill and Hillary Clinton and the Bush crime family.

This is in accordance with the ninth Protocol which states, "... Our directorate must surround itself with all those forces of civilization among which it will have to work...persons which in case of disobedience to our instructions, must face criminal charges – or disappear. This, in order to make them defend our interests to their last gasp."

On the other hand, Milosevic was made out to be a War Criminal instead of the Patriot that he was, trying to hold his country together. Today, there are a number of lawsuits against the Vatican from Serbia for the damages caused in their country by that criminal organization, the Vatican, disguised as a religion.

The Vatican's war on Yugoslavia was also supported by the nations of Georgia, Uzbekistan, Ukraine, Azerbaijan and Moldova, the GUUAM nations which make up a regional military alliance surrounding the oil rich Caspian Sea region. GUUAM was created in1999 by Bill Clinton as a further attack on Russia by removing the GUUAM nations out of CIS, the Commonwealth of Independent States of the former Soviet Union.

The NGOs were the method of removal. These organizations which are funded by multinational corporations and in some cases by the U.S. State department itself, organize young people to agitate for human rights and regime change in targeted nations. These nations are chosen because; they are part of U.S. anti-Russian foreign policy, they are too independent of the New World Order or they have nationalized their Oil. These actions lead to the so called "color revolutions" and the "Arab spring" in the twenty first century.

Three revolutions – the "rose revolution" in Georgia (November 2003-January 2004), the "orange revolution" in Ukraine (January 2005) and the "tulip revolution" in Kyrgyzstan (April 2005) – each followed a near-identical trajectory; all were spearheaded by the American democratization NGOs working at the behest of the US foreign policy establishment.

The Project for the New American Century (PNAC) was an

Illuminati think tank based in Washington, D.C. established in 1997 as a non-profit educational organization founded by William Kristol and Robert Kagan. The PNAC's stated goal is "to promote American global leadership. Some will say that PNAC is a Zionist – not Illuminati - organization because of their strong support of Israel's policies. To that, I would counter that Israel has always been led by high degree Freemason Jews who are ultimately controlled by the Jesuit's Illuminati.

Section V of PNAC's Rebuilding America's Defenses, entitled "Creating Tomorrow's Dominant Force", includes the sentence: "Further, the process of transformation, even if it brings revolutionary change, is likely to be a long one, absent some catastrophic and catalyzing event—like a new Pearl Harbor"

The goal of regime change in Iraq remained the consistent position of PNAC. Perle and other core members of the PNAC - Paul Wolfowitz, R. James Woolsey, Elliot Abrams, and John Bolton - were among the signatories of a letter to President Clinton calling for the removal of Hussein.

President Clinton did not remove Saddam Hussein from power. That job was left to George W. Bush who replaced Clinton at the White House, in a fraudulent election in which Democrat, Al Gore actually won the popular vote. With Bush in power, it became relatively easy for PNAC's goals to proceed. A large number of PNAC members were placed in positions in the George W, Bush Administration.

A pipe line from Turkmenistan to Pakistan was being planned to connect Oil rich Caspian Sea resources to Western markets. On 21 October 1995, The U.S. company, Unocal, in conjunction with the Saudi oil company Delta, signed a separate agreement with Turkmenistan's president Saparmurat Niyazov. In August

1996, the Central Asia Gas Pipeline, Ltd. (CentGas) consortium for construction of a pipeline, led by Unocal, was formed. On 27 October 1997, CentGas was incorporated in formal signing ceremonies in Ashgabat, Turkmenistan, by several international oil companies along with the Government of Turkmenistan.

Since the pipeline was to pass through Afghanistan, it was necessary to work with the Taliban. The U.S. ambassador to Pakistan, Robert Oakley, moved into CentGas in 1997. In January 1998, the Taliban, selecting CentGas over Argentinian competitor, Bridas Corporation, signed an agreement that allowed the proposed project to proceed. Enron had spent $400 million on a "feasibility study" for the pipeline, most of which was used as bribes to the Taliban. This is probably why The Taliban chose Cent Gas over Bridas.

On August 7, 1998, American embassies in Nairobi and Dar es Salaam were bombed, allegedly under the direction of Osama bin Laden, and all pipeline negotiations halted, as the Taliban's leader, Mullah Mohammad Omar, announced that Osama bin Laden had the Taliban's support. Unocal withdrew from the consortium on 8 December 1998, and soon after closed its offices in Afghanistan and Pakistan.

It wasn't until oilmen, George Bush and Richard Cheney gained the White house that pipeline negotiations with the Taliban resumed. Between April 19 and August 17, 2001, Francesc Vendrell, the UN Secretary-General's Personal Representative for Afghanistan, made 5 trips to Kabul and Kandahar to talk with the Taliban. If the Taliban would form a peace with the Northern Alliance, to form a stable government in Afghanistan and turn over Osama Bin Ladin – a pipeline could be built in their country with very profitable royalties for the Taliban.

It was known beforehand that the negotiations might fail and a military invasion of Afghanistan was being planned if the talks failed. Niaz Naik, a former Pakistani Foreign Secretary, was told by senior American officials in mid-July that military action against Afghanistan would go ahead by the middle of October.

Mr. Naik said US officials told him of the plan at an UN-sponsored international contact group on Afghanistan which took place in Berlin. Mr. Naik told the BBC that at the meeting the US representatives told him that unless Bin Laden was handed over swiftly, America would take military action to kill or capture both Bin Laden and the Taliban leader, Mullah Omar. The wider objective, according to Mr. Naik, would be to topple the Taliban regime and install a transitional government of moderate Afghans in its place - possibly under the leadership of the former Afghan King Zahir Shah. Mr. Naik was told that Washington would launch its operation from bases in Tajikistan, where American advisers were already in place.

A larger plan was to launch a "war on terror", which could continue indefinitely and give the U.S.an excuse to act militarily anywhere on the globe anytime it would further the Illuminati's plan for economic gain and world rule.

This war on terror could also be used to nullify parts of the U.S. Constitution that the Jesuits wanted eliminated. So, it could also quite correctly also be called a "war on freedom."

The "Patriot Act" was already being written up by Knight of Malta, Michael Chertoff and the Jesuit Viet D. Dinh, a Professor of Law at Georgetown University Law Center. Dinh was also involved in the selection and confirmation of 100 district and 23 appellate judges in his role representing the U.S. Department of Justice. After 9/11, Dinh conducted a comprehensive review of

DOJ priorities, policies and practices, and revising the Attorney General's Guidelines, which govern federal law enforcement activities and national security investigations. Chertoff would become the head of the Department of Homeland Security.

All PNAC needed was their new "Pearl Harbor" to kick off the "War on Terror", attack Afghanistan and remove Saddam from power.

Countless books have been written on the 9/11 attacks. So, I won't write down all the evidence that the November 11, 2001 attacks on the Trade center towers and the Pentagon were an inside job, done by traitors in the U.S. military and intelligence agencies, acting in unison with the intelligence agencies of other countries primarily Israel, Saudi Arabia, Pakistan, Germany and Briton. However, I might cover some of the more important aspects.

Most of the alleged hijackers originated from Saudi Arabia – not Afghanistan. The alleged hijackers, most of who were originally barred by U.S. Immigration from entering the U.S., had the CIA intervene on their behalf. They were taking flight lessons at CIA company airports and the Pensacola Naval Air Station. None were good enough to fly commercial air liners. No records of Muslim named passengers were on the passenger list of the two planes that hit the Trade Center towers. Nine of these alleged hijackers, including the alleged leader, Mohammed Atta, were found to be alive after the 9/11 attacks.

The type of planes that hit the Trade Center Towers were equipped to be flown by remote control. So, there was no need for alleged hijackers to be on the planes to cause the collision with the Twin Towers. Private non-governmental investigations have proven beyond any doubt that the Pentagon was hit by a guided missile – not a passenger aircraft!

There had been a reported $2.3 Trillion missing at the pentagon. The section of the Pentagon that was hit by the missile was the accounting division – destroying any accounting records there.

The rules of engagement of hijacked aircraft were changed by Dick Cheny 6 months prior to the 9/11 attacks.

24 stimulated hijacking war games were taking place on the very day of the attacks - the only time in history this many was ever done at once. Air Force General Meyers, who was in charge of Air Security for the North East U.S. should have been court marshalled for the abject lack of air security during the 9/11 attacks. Instead, he was promoted to the Joint Chiefs of staff.

The Head of Pakistan's ISI, Mahmoud Ahmad, sent Mohammed Atta, the alleged leader of the hijackers, a money wire for $100,000 prior to the attacks – yet was never charged as an accomplice the 9/11 attacks! After Indian Intelligence showed absolute proof of Mahmoud Ahmad guilt in sending the money wire, Mahmoud Ahmad was merely asked to resign from his post.

At this time, the CIA and ISI worked closely together. Ahmad came to the U.S. on September 4, 2001 and met with CIA director George Tenent until September 9. On September 12 & 13 Ahmad met with Deputy Secretary of State, Richard Armitage, former primary illegal narcotics purchaser for the CIA. Agreements on Pakistan's collaboration with the U.S. were discussed. And finally, Ahmad met with Senator Joseph Biden, Chairman of the Senate Foreign Relations Committee before returning to Pakistan.

It must be remembered that the ISI was a launch pad for CIA covert operations against Russia and that ISI was responsible for training Al Qaeda fighters and the Taliban. Without the ISI aid to the Taliban, the Taliban government wouldn't have even existed in Afghanistan! Mahmoud Ahmad was a U.S. approved appointee for ISI head and since 1999, was in liaison with his counterparts at CIA, DIA and the Pentagon.

Larry Silverstein, who some say was involved in heroin trafficking, illegal money laundering and other illicit activities, purchased a 99 year lease on the Trade Center Complex from the new York Port Authority less than 3 months before the 9/11 attacks. The Trade Towers were built of concrete reinforced with steel, but had problems with the rivets that meant the towers would only have a useful life of about 7 more years and then would have to be demolished. Some businessmen were wondering why Silverstein would make such a terrible business decision, where he would lose more money that he had invested. Before the 9/11 attacks, Silverstein had the Trade Center insured against terrorist attacks and profited considerably from the insurance damages after the attacks.

Silverstein also was a personal friend of Ariel Sharon and Benjamin Netanyahu, both high level Freemasons and Prime Ministers of Israel. Before the 9/11 attacks, Silverstein and Netanyahu would be on the telephone every Sunday afternoon. Also, before the attacks, Silverstein was on the phone with the insurance company to see if he could get double damages if there were two terrorist attacks.

As any competent architect would tell you, steel reinforced buildings don't collapse from fires, even from airplane collisions. The Twin Towers and Tower 7 were brought down with some kind of controlled demolitions. What kind remains to be determined. Some independent researchers say that nano-thermate was used and others suspect a secret directed energy weapon was used because close examination of videos by researcher, Judy Woods, show steel beams turning into dust in a process she labeled "dustification"!

The Comptroller of the Pentagon at the time of the attack was Dov Zakheim, who was appointed in May of 2001. Before becoming the Pentagon's money-manager, he was an executive at System Planning Corporation, a defense contractor specializing in electronic warfare technologies including remote-controlled aircraft systems. Zakheim is a member of the Project for a New American Century and participated in the creation of its 2000 position paper *Rebuilding America's Defenses* which called for "a New Pearl Harbor."

After Zakheim became comptroller, the Pentagon could not account for $2.3 Trillion in missing money according to Donald Rumsfield. Could the missing money have gone into paying off all the traitorous operatives in the 9/11 attacks?

The CIA was monitoring the alleged hijackers and two of them lived near CIA headquarters. It was George Tenet, who exhibited extremely suspicious behavior when he apparently knew after the first attack that it was an attack, that Bin Laden was involved, and that Moussaoui was involved. Tenet was Jesuit-trained at Georgetown University and a Knight of Malta.

The other 'spook' agency is the NSA. Five of the alleged hijackers lived near NSA headquarters and the NSA monitored some of them. They received intercepts the night before the attacks that they claim they weren't able to translate until Sept.12. The director of the NSA on 9/11 was Michael Hayden. He is Roman Catholic and was trained at a Roman Catholic school and University.

George H.W Bush, certainly a mover and shaker in world events, is alleged by numerous sources to be a Knight of Malta. There are photos of him side by side with the Pope. He was the man behind Iraq War I. He was also a big name in the Carlyle Group and was in a meeting with Carlyle on 9/11. He met with Bin Laden's brother, Shafig, on the morning of 9/11.

As was the case of the Bolshevik Revolution, the Jesuit General used its Masonic Labor Zionist "Court Jews" to play leading roles in the 9/11 debacle. Those traitors to their own race have willingly served the Jesuits in this crime and subsequent cover-up so as to enable Jesuit-controlled operatives to blame the Jews for 9/11 if the Muslim scapegoats didn't work out.

Many private investigators of 9/11 who didn't look deep enough into the conspiracy have taken the bait. Although there were some foolish and greedy Muslims and Jews involved, very few investigators realize the Jesuit General, Adolf Nicolas and his man in New York, Cardinal, Edward Egan were the masterminds of the whole affair.

In any case, the greatest crime in the 21 Century, the 9/11 attacks, has yet to be officially solved. And, that is primarily because the government refuses to investigate it. The 9/11 Commission was a total cover up, as most independent experts will agree. One wonders if the true perpetrators of this crime will ever be brought to justice.

The 9/11 attacks gave PNAC their "new Pearl Harbor" and dramatic changes soon followed. Officials of the Bush Administration claimed Osama Bin Ladin was behind the 9/11 attacks and again demanded the Taliban turn him over. They replied "show us the proof that Bin Ladin was behind the 9/11 attacks and then we will turn him over". Since the U.S. had no such proof to show, the Taliban refused to turn over Bin Ladin.

Then, the U.S. started military operations against Afghanistan On October 7, 2001 as predicted earlier by Pakistani Foreign Secretary, Niaz Naik, as a "War on Terror" was declared. So, the main promoter of terrorism, the U.S. , through its secret agencies, was proclaiming a "War on Terror." How hypocritical can you get?

The CIA and the President ran much of the Afghanistan War, working with the Northern Alliance, the enemies of the Taliban. By November 2001, the Northern alliance had the Taliban surrounded at Kunduz. Since the CIA had also created the Taliban through the Pakistani ISI which actually ran Pakistan using Musharraf as their front man, President George W. Bush, ordered the rescue of much of the Taliban at Kunduz. It is estimated that 8,000 Taliban and Al Qaeda forces were airlifted from Kunduz by the U.S military into the Kashmir province of Pakistan.

Three weeks later, a Terrorist attack on India's Parliament almost triggered a nuclear war between Pakistan and India. Indian Intelligence determined that the Terrorists originated in the Kashmir region of Pakistan and that they were funded by the ISI.

The Patriot Act was fast tracked before Congress which wasn't even allowed to read the bill. Because of the uproar over the 9/11 attacks, it would have been considered unpatriotic not to pass the act. Vice President, Dick Cheney stated that anyone who didn't vote for the bill would be responsible for the next terror attack. Had congress been allowed to read the bill, they might have realized that some provisions of the act were totally unconstitutional.

The Patriot Act gives the Attorney General and the Secretary of State the power to designate domestic groups including political and religious organizations as "terrorist organization" under the "enemy combatant" designation. These "enemy combatants" can be held indefinably, without charge, without legal representation and can be tried and executed in secret military tribunals. These are similar to the legal tactics used by the fascist Pinochet government in Chili in their "Dirty War" when thousands of political activists simply disappeared.

Section 213 of the Patriot Act allows any Federal or State agency to break into your home or office to remove (or place) any items they wish without a warrant. It also enforces silence on the victims of this unconstitutional procedure. It is not hard to see that this allows planting of incriminating evidence and violates the forth Amendment of the Constitution.

Section 215 allows law enforcement access to library and book store records and prohibits librarians and store workers from informing patrons of this spying.

TSA now searches people at air ports and NSA taps and records their phone conversations, in violation of their fourth amendment rights.

As the Afghanistan war drug on, a war against Iraq was also being planned by PNAC and Illuminati controlled intelligence agencies in the U.S and England. There were multiple agendas involved in attacking Iraq. Iraq was a military threat against Israel, the oil companies wanted Iraq's nationalized oil and Iraq would be a good base of military operations against Iran and Syria. And of course, Vice President, Cheney would make sure his company Halliburton got lucrative no-bid, contracts to service the military operation, while the defense contractors would make huge profits at tax payer expense.

The 9/11 attacks and "weapons of mass destruction" were used as an excuse to attack Iraq even though Iraq had nothing to do with 9/11 and had no weapons of mass destruction. The controlled press and the Bush Administration, as so often occurs, used lies and propaganda to promote the Iraq War.

In George W. Bush's second administration, Richard Armitage, who was the leak in the Valery Plame affair, was replaced as United States Deputy Secretary of State at the State Department and sent to Afghanistan, which at the time had the world's largest supply of opium. One can only wonder if he was once again purchasing opium for the CIA.

Since January 1, 2010, Armitage has been a Member of the Board of Directors and Chairman of the American-Turkish Council (ATC), a Washington-based, corporate membership NGO dedicated to the promotion of a strong and peaceful business, military and foreign policy relationship between Turkey and the United States.

FBI investigations of the ATC also show it to be complicit in illegal narcotics trafficking, money laundering and selling U.S. military secrets and nuclear hardware to the highest bidder. This is written about in *Classified Woman* by Sibel Edmonds.

Her book documents just how broken the Constitutional government of the U.S. actually is, with a Justice Department that protects high level criminals, a FBI that incompetently allows itself to be infiltrated by the same groups that they are investigating, a Congress that is so brought and blackmailed that they are ineffective in investigating high level crime and National Security secrecy that is used to cover up high level crime.

Classified Woman also shows that the 9/11 commission should have been called the 9/11 Omission because of all the important information that was omitted from the report. The book also shows why the actual criminals behind the 9/11 attacks will never be prosecuted under our present government system.

NGOs were used in the Color Revolutions in Eastern Europe to pull nations away from Russia's influence and integrate them into EU and NATO. And NGOs were used to create the Arab Spring. Many of the young activists received training and financing from NGO groups like the International Republican Institute, the National Democratic Institute, The National Endowment for Democracy and Freedom House, a nonprofit human rights organization based in Washington D.C. Most of these NGOs are organized and controlled by the Jesuits and, the war mongering, Neo Cons that were pulling a Neo "Con job" on the U.S. public.

After its success, Serbia's Otpor would continue receiving funds from the West and become a "CIA-coup college" of sorts, under the name change to CANVAS, or "Center for Applied Non-Violent Action and Strategies." Amongst CANVAS's current partners are the Albert Einstein Institution, Freedom House, and the International Republican Institute (IRI). The IRI includes amongst its board of directors John McCain, Lindsey Graham, and Brent Scowcroft. The then director of CANVAS was Srdja Popovic, a CIA agent and the former head of Otpor.

Egyptian activists from the now infamous April 6 movement were in New York City for the inaugural Alliance of Youth Movements (AYM) summit, also known as Movements.org. There, they received training, networking opportunities, and support from AYM's various corporate and US governmental sponsors, including the US State Department itself. UN IAEA

Chief, Mohammed ElBaradei assembled his "National Front for Change" and began preparing for the coming "Arab Spring" in Tunisia, Egypt, Syria and Lebanon.

During Egypt's Hosni Mubarak's government, the Muslim Brotherhood was attempting a comeback in Egypt with limited success. They put on an outward face of good works and charity to get public approval in Egypt. But they were sporadic clashes with the Egyptian Government and often there would massive arrests of Muslim Brotherhood members. During the upheaval of the Arab Spring of 2011, the Muslim Brotherhood gained enough support for their candidate, Mohamed Morsi, to have him elected President of Egypt. Then, he would fully legalize the Muslim Brotherhood in that country.

Muslim Brotherhood fighters (Al Qaeda) moved across the border into Libya for PNAC's planned overthrow of the Libyan government. While the CIA was coordinating the Al Qaeda fighters from Benghazi, NATO Bombers provided air support. And finally, the country with the highest standard of living in Africa, Libya, was destroyed.

Like the destruction of Iraq as an independent country, the destruction of Libya had a lot to do with privatizing the nationalized oil fields of Libya. Chaos and terrorism has plagued both countries since their destruction by the U.S.

And again the controlled news media was spewing propaganda to justify the criminal actions against Libya.

As part of the war on terror, on December 2011, President Obama signed the 2012 NDAA, codifying indefinite military detention without charge or trial into law for the first time in American history. The NDAA's dangerous detention provisions would authorize the president — and all future presidents — to order the military to pick up and indefinitely imprison people captured anywhere in the world, far from any battlefield. This is a violation of international law. A U.S. Citizen could be labeled a terrorist under this provision and be detained by the military indefinitely.

The Patriot act is the enabling legislation that allows international law to supersede national law through the Department of Homeland Security which is the Military Industrial Complex's fascist enforcing agency. It seems the planned coup of U. S. Constitutional government, planned for so long by the Jesuits, has finally taken place.

A big problem with all the PNAC un-necessary wars is the tremendous debt that they add to the national debt. The Iraq War cost about $2 trillion and the Afghanistan War, a similar amount. It will be interesting to see what the Libya War cost.

An additional problem is the tremendous amount of graft and corruption at the Department of Defense. On Sept 10, 2001, Donald Rumsfeld admitted, 'There is a $2 trillion hole in the Pentagon's accounting". In May 2012 Secretary of Defense, Leon Panetta acknowledged that the DOD "is the only major federal agency that cannot pass an audit today." The Pentagon will not be ready for an audit for another five years, according to Panetta. Reuters quantifies these numbers today:

The Pentagon is the only federal agency that has not complied with a law that requires annual audits of all government departments. That means that the $8.5 trillion in taxpayer money doled out by Congress to the Pentagon since 1996, the first year it was supposed to be audited, has never been accounted for. That sum exceeds the value of China's total economic output last year. According to a report by the Inspector General, the Pentagon cannot account for 25 percent of what it spends

The disclosure by Rumsfield of the missing $2.3 Trillion normally might have sparked a huge scandal. However, the commencement of the attack on New York City and Washington the next morning would assure that the story remained buried. To the trillions already missing from the coffers, an obedient Congress terrorized by anthrax attacks would then add billions more in appropriations to fight the "War on Terror."

Since the presidency of Jimmy Carter, all presidents of the U.S. have been members of secret societies or agencies. Barak Obama's life is also shrouded in secrecy. His maternal grandfather, Stanly Armour Dunham, worked for the OSS with his wife Madelyn in Lebanon. Later, Madelyn Dunham would become the first female vice president at the Bank of Hawaii, handling secret escrow accounts for CIA clients.

Barak Obama's parents were both CIA employees as well as his stepfather. Barack Obama, Sr. worked on the CIA-sponsored operations in Kenya to counter rising Soviet and Chinese influence there. CIA espionage activities were conducted by his mother, Ann Dunham, and stepfather, Lolo Soetoro, in 1960s Indonesia on behalf of a number of CIA front operations working to overthrow Sukarno, including the East-West Center at the University of Hawaii, the U.S. Agency for International Development (USAID), and the Ford Foundation.

Barack Obama, Sr., who met Ann Dunham in 1959 in a Russian language class at the East West Center at the University of Hawaii, had been part of an air lift of 280 East African students to the United States to attend various colleges. The airlift was a CIA operation to train and indoctrinate future agents of influence in, the newly independent, Kenya, which was becoming a battle-ground for influence between the United States, China and the Soviet Union.

Obama, Sr., who was already married with an infant son and pregnant wife in Kenya, married Ann Dunham in Maui on February 2, 1961 and was also the university's first African student. In 1964, Obama Sr. would get divorced from Ann Dunham. Later, Ann Dunham would meet Lolo Soetoro at the University of Hawaii and married him in 1965. Shortly after the marriage, Lolo Soetoro returned to Indonesia to assist in the CIA/ Suharto coup that overthrew Sukarno.

On September 30, 1965, six of the military's most senior officers were killed in an action (generally labeled an "attempted coup") by the so-called 30 September Movement, a group from within the armed forces. Within a few hours, Major General Suharto mobilized forces under his command and took control of Jakarta.

Ann Dunham and her son, Barak Obama, moved to Jakarta, Indonesia to join Lolo Soetoro in 1966. They first lived in a house owned by Lolo Soetoro near the St. Fransiskus School, where Barak was enrolled from grade 1 to grade 3. Later, they moved to the expensive diplomatic quarter of Menteng, Jakarta where Barak attended Menteng Elementary School. The interesting thing is that only Indonesian citizens were allowed in either school. Since at the time, dual citizenship was not allowed in Indonesia, Lolo Soetoro and Ann Dunham would have both have had to renounce their U.S. Citizenship and become Indonesian Citizens to enroll Barak in either school.

In 1968, Ann Dunham worked at the Indonesian-American Friendship Institute in Jakarta and in 1970 at the Institute of

Management Education and Development (IMED) in Jakarta. Both organizations are CIA fronts. During this period the CIA was using anthropologists to gain information on tribal groups to discover their ways of thinking and political loyalties. Target lists were being compiled to determine which groups were sympathetic to the communist PKI.

Anti-communists, initially following the army's lead, went on a violent purge of communists throughout the country, killing an estimated half million people and destroying the PKI, which was officially blamed for the crisis which was a typical CIA "false flag" operation. After Suharto came into power, Indonesia's natural resources were brought up by multinational corporations. Typically, Indonesian "CIA assets" would be given jobs in these corporations. Eventually, Lolo Soetoro went to work at Exxon.

In 1972, Ann Dunham moved back to Hawaii to obtain her MA in Anthropology at University of Hawaii with a grant from the CIA funded Asia Foundation while still being paid by IMED. Ann Dunham would return to Indonesia in 1975 to do more anthropological field work before the CIA/Suharto Indonesian invasion of East Timor. She also worked there with USAID, another CIA front.

Obama (born in 1961) enrolled at the, very pricey, Occidental College in Los Angeles, California in 1979 where the CIA recruited him in 1980. In 1981, Obama allegedly transferred from Occidental to Columbia University to major in Political Science with a specialization in international relations. A search of Columbia's records yield no evidence that Barak Obama or Barry Soetoro was ever there. No students at Columbia at that time remember Barak Obama. In fact, his records at Columbia are sealed.

The CIA needed Muslims or others who could easily blend into the Muslim environment in the Middle East. The CIA persuaded Columbia University to extend their foreign student program to Obama, now a Columbia student, so that he might travel to Pakistan and enroll in the universities around Karachi in addition to the Patrice Lumumba School in Moscow. The 20-year-old Obama, who then was known as "Barry Soetoro," traveled to Pakistan in 1981 and was hosted by the family of Muhammadmian Soomro, a Pakistani Sindhi who became acting President of Pakistan after the resignation of General Pervez Musharraf on August 18, 2008.

Officials have publicly acknowledged that Obama went to Pakistan in 1981. There is no way of knowing how often Obama traveled between Pakistan and Russia. According to Dr. Manning, Obama was an interpreter for the CIA during the war in Afghanistan. When Obama completed his CIA operations in the mid-1980s he returned to the United States. Apparently, the State Department then maneuvered his entrance into Harvard Law School. The CIA has always functioned as the president's personal agency for black operations throughout the world. Most likely, the CIA created the false story of Obama attending Columbia University while he was actually in Pakistan and Russia.

President Obama has maintained a personal correspondence with private military company (PMC) whose senior personnel includes numerous Afghan Mujahedeen-Soviet war veterans who fought with the late Northern Alliance commander Ahmad Shah Massoud and who became Afghanistan's Defense Minister in 1992. The PMC is also involved in counter-insurgency operations in Colombia, where Obama is building seven new military bases. In 2009, Obama signed an agreement to station U.S. personnel at these seven military bases in Columbia, ostensibly to combat terrorism and narco-traffickers.

President Obama's own work in 1983 for Business International Corporation, a CIA front that conducted seminars with the world's most powerful leaders and used journalists as agents abroad, dovetails nicely with CIA espionage activities conducted by his mother and father. Then, Obama moved to Chicago where he became a "community organizer" for the CIA to spy on the Black Panthers, The Nation of Islam and the El Runkns gang. These radical organizations had links to foreign leftist governments, hence the CIA's interest.

In late 1988, Obama enrolled in Harvard Law School, and eventually moved back to Chicago to enter politics.

He served as an Illinois State Senator from Chicago's South Side. In 2004 he ran for the U.S. Senate. In the primary election he was running against Blair Hull. The CIA released sealed divorce records of Blair Hull to *The Chicago Tribune*. After that, Hull went from first place in the polls to third place and Obama won the primary race. At the general election, Obama ran against Jack Ryan. Ryan's sealed divorce records were leaked by the CIA to The *Chicago Tribune*, sinking Ryan's chances and Obama became the U.S. Senator from Illinois. Both opponents had such scandalous divorces that Judges had ordered the divorce proceedings sealed. The CIA had their ways of opening up sealed cases.

The CIA recruited John O. Brennan, who speaks fluent Arabic, after his college graduation. Brennan became deputy executive director of the CIA in March 2001. In about 2005, about the time that the international bankers like George Soros were interviewing Obama as presidential material, Brennan left government service and became the Chairman of the Intelligence and National Security Alliance (INSA) and the CEO of The Analysis Corporation (TAC) now known as Sotera Defense Solutions, quite conceivably a CIA front. At the same time, Brennan began working with the Obama 2008 presidential campaign as Obama's top intelligence adviser.

Obama promised change in his campaign. Many people, including myself, were quite upset with the criminal activities of the George W. Bush Administration. We did not know who this mysterious Obama, who seemed to come out of nowhere was, but we knew that we wanted a change. At the time, I joined the Democrats and placed my energies to get Obama elected because of my strong opposition to Bush. After he became president, I wanted to know more, as did others, and started investigations of the man. To my dismay, I discovered his CIA links. We ended up getting more of the same kind of criminal government, with little change.

The Obama Administration not only maintained the Bush Administration's policies which sought confrontation with the progressive block of Latin American nations but seems to be trying to repeat the fascists policies of President Nixon which caused the bloody overthrow of the Allende government in Chile and the "Dirty War", which followed, where thousands of people were "disappeared" by the government of Pinochet. President Obama not only authorized CIA planned Coups in Honduras and Ecuador, but also has launched a new generation of the Contras called Neo-Contras to harass the government of President Daniel Ortega in Nicaragua.

This Anti-Ortega policy is overseen by U.S. Ambassador Robert Callahan, an old CIA hand who assisted former Ambassador to El Salvador, Negroponte, run the death squads there. U.S. Ambassador to Honduras, Hugo Llorens, provides support to the Neo-Contras. These Neo-Contras are nothing more than an illegal terrorist band. But then, what else could you expect from a President put into office with considerable help from the CIA?

After the destruction of Libya, Syria was next on PNAC's agenda. NGOs in Syria started agitating against President Assad. The Muslim brotherhood fighters were moved from Libya into Turkey where they were supplied with arms and smuggled across the border into Syria. One can only wonder to what degree Richard Armitage as Chairman of the American-Turkish Council, was coordinating these efforts. Other Al Qaeda fighters were smuggled in from Anbar province, Iraq.

After the death of Osama Bin Ladin, Abdelhakim Belhadji was to become Al Qaeda's new leader. Not all of the Muslim Brotherhood leaders in Turkey supported a war on Syria to overthrow Assad. Abdelhakim Belhadji persuaded nine of the most vigorous opponents of the war policy to go on a rescue mission to Gaza on the freedom flotilla vessel, Mavi Marmara to deliver vital medical aid and other supplies to that blockaded area.

When the Israel Defense Force illegally boarded the Mavi Marmara in international waters, nine Turkish citizens were killed in the conflict. They were the only ones killed and - you guessed it - they were the ones opposed to the war to overthrow Assad! This goes to show you the behind the scenes intrigue in CIA -Mossad relations between Turkey and Israel.

At first, the CANVAS trained young people would stage massive anti-Assad demonstrations in Damascus. Then, some Muslim Brotherhood fighters smuggled in from Turkey would take up sniper positions on the roof tops and fire on the demonstrators and the Syrian police and security forces alike. This tactic would anger both demonstrators and security forces, each who thought that the other side was doing the shooting and cause the violence to escalate. Then, the news media would run stories about how cruel Assad was for cracking down on and shooting the demonstrators.

Many of the weapons captured from Muammar Gaddafi's armies were being collected and sent to Benghazi to be shipped on to the Syrian rebels. The U.S. Embassy there was used as a trans-shipment base, with the U.S. Ambassador Stevens working with the CIA, in charge of the operation. About 35 CIA personnel were working at the Embassy annex in Benghazi.

Iran intelligence got wind of the Benghazi operation and sent a hit squad there to sabotage the operation. The attack was well planned and supplied with weapons and highly trained fighters. It was not a spontaneous anti-American demonstration as some have claimed. The demonstration was only a cover. The television network said that a CIA team was working in an annex near the consulate on a project to supply missiles from Libyan armories to Syrian rebels.

Sources said that more Americans were hurt in the assault spearheaded by suspected Islamic radicals than had been previously reported. CIA chiefs were actively working to ensure the real nature of its operations in the city did not get out. So only the losses suffered by the State Department in the city had been reported to Congress.

The reason for the secrecy behind what happened at Benghazi was the U.S. trying to hide its role in causing the Syrian upheaval.

According to the Examiner, fighters were recruited from the various Libyan militias that fought against the Gaddafi regime. About 4,000 fighters volunteered to fight with anti-Assad forces, accepting the offer of a $1,000 signing bonus in addition to a $450 monthly wage. These fighters were then flown to Turkey in

---

unmarked aircraft, where they were then loaded on trucks and taken to join the Free Syrian Army bases on the Turkish border with northwestern Syria.

Prince Bandar had been appointed ambassador to the United States by King Fahd on October 24, 1983. During his tenure as ambassador, he dealt with five U.S. presidents, ten secretaries of state, eleven national security advisers, sixteen sessions of Congress, and the media. He had extensive influence in the United States. He had arranged $32 million in Saudi financing for the Nicaraguan Contras. Bandar has formed close relationships with several American presidents, notably George H.W. Bush and George W. Bush and has funded many U.S. covert operations. Prince Bandar is now doing the same for President Obama.

Much of the supplies and pay to the Al Qaeda fighters in Syria came from Prince Bandar in Saudi Arabia. When the Chemical weapons attack occurred, one rebel band complained that they hadn't been given sufficient training in how to use them and over a dozen of their own men were killed as a consequence. Their leader was so angry that he talked and said that the chemical weapons and their pay was provided by Prince Bandar.

The Mint Press News report adds an important dimension to the story, totally contradicting the claims of the US government that Assad was responsible for the chemical attacks. It quotes a female insurgent fighter who says "the supplier didn't tell them what these arms were or how to use them and that they didn't know they were chemical weapons. When Saudi Prince Bandar gives such weapons to people, he must give them to those who know how to handle and use them," she is quoted.

The atrocities committed by the Syrian rebels included

kidnapping, rape, mass murder of whole villages and chemical attacks. The general destruction caused by them was reminiscent of Hitler's incursion into Yugoslavia in 1938. However the Western news media placed the blame for these atrocities on the Assad government. There can be little doubt of the fascist nature of the governments backing the rebel forces, including the E.U. Saudi Arabia, Qatar and the U.S.

In any case, President Obama said that Assad had crossed a "red line" with his alleged chemical attack and that the U.S. was prepared to take military action. Many in the U.S. Military became nervous. Syria had a powerful ally in Russia and China. Russia's only naval base in the Mediterranean Sea is at Tartus, Syria. Russia wasn't going to allow another Libya to happen in that country. Russia moved a number of navy cruisers into the area around Syria which were later joined by Chinese ships. A military conflict in Syria would not be a "cake walk", like Libya had been. And there was a very real danger that a U.S. attack on Syria could escalate into World War III.

At a U.N. conference U.S. Secretary of State, John Kerry was asked by the Russian representative what it would take to stop the planned U.S. air strikes on Syria. "The only way the air strikes could be prevented was if Assad would completely eliminate his chemical weapons stockpiles," Kerry replied. "O.K. we will see that it gets done." the Russian representative basically said. Soon after, diplomacy rather than war was the preferred course of the Obama Administration. And, Assad started eliminating Syrian chemical weapons.

While all this was going on the European Union as well as the United States was facing economic problems brought on by the tremendous debt their nations were running up. In the meantime Russia, under Putin's governance, was brought from financial collapse to prosperity. According to Time Magazine, Moscow had more millionaires than any other city in the world.

Ukraine declared independence from the old Soviet Union in 1990. In 2004-2005 Western NGOs worked with CIA/Mossad/MI6/BND assets to stage the phony Orange Revolution. Victor Yuschenko became Prime Minister but was poisoned. Western media blamed it on the Russians, but it was likely CIA/Mossad hit, since he was succeeded by Yulia Tymoshenko, a good looking blond lady favored by the western financiers and oil companies.

In 2007, Yulia Tymoshenko traveled to the US to meet with Vice-President Dick Cheney and National Security Advisor Condoleezza Rice to talk energy. Tymoshenko became rich as an executive at a natural gas company. Ukraine was working with Cheney's crooked Energy Policy Task Force, which opened the planet to unregulated oil & gas exploration, including fracking. Tymoshenko privatized over 300 state industries during her reign,

In 2010 they voted in Prime Minister Viktor Yanukovych with 48% of the vote because many Ukrainians were upset with all the privatization. Later, Tymoshenko was convicted of embezzlement of state funds and abuse of power. She was given a seven year prison sentence and fined $188 million.

In October 2013 the International Monetary Fund (IMF) met with Ukrainian officials to discuss the country's alleged "budget crisis". The IMF demanded that Ukraine double consumer prices for natural gas and electricity, devalue its currency, slash state funding for schools and the elderly, and lift a ban on the sale of its rich farmland to foreigners. In return for this Ukraine was promised a measly $4 billion in further loans.

On the other hand, Russia was making President of the Ukraine, Viktor Yanukovych and his country an offer they could not refuse. It appears to involve an emergency loan of $15 billion (actually the purchase $15 Billion in Ukrainian Bonds) for Ukraine's stricken economy without the tough conditions required in any deal with Western lenders such as the IMF. These considerations led the President of the Ukraine, Viktor Yanukovych, to change his mind about joining the European Union.

In the middle of February 2014 Tymoshenko was released from prison, as part of a deal hatched at a secret meeting between Yanukovych, EU, NATO and Russian officials, while NGO organized demonstrations were again agitating in Maidan Square in Kiev. The U.S. State Department clearly did not like the turn of events in the Ukraine as the golden goose for the multinational corporations was threating to go toward Russia.

Demonstrators once again filled Kiev's Independence Square, demanding that their country move closer to the EU and further away from Russia. And once again, NGOs, particularly CANVAS, was behind the demonstrations, using the same insignia used by Utpor in Serbia and the April 6 movement in Egypt - the clenched fist.

In the Ukraine, fascist political parties were being formed after the first color revolution. One notable party was the National Socialist Party of the Ukraine which later changed its name to the Svoboda (Ukrainian for freedom) party. Another was the Ukrainian National Assembly-Ukrainian National Self Defense (UNA-UNSO). The hero of Svoboda and UNA-UNSO is the Nazi collaborator Stepan Bandera, leader of the Ukrainian Insurgent Army (OUN), which aided the Nazis in horrific massacres of the Jewish population.

In 2010, Svoboda's official forum posted a statement reading: "To create a truly Ukrainian Ukraine in the cities of the East and South...we will need to cancel parliamentarism, ban all political parties, nationalize the entire industry, all media, prohibit the importation of any literature to Ukraine from Russia...completely replace the leaders of the civil service, education management, military (especially in the East), physically liquidate all Russian-speaking intellectuals and all Ukrainophobes (fast, without a trial shot. Registering Ukrainophobes can be done here by any member of Svoboda), execute all members of the anti-Ukrainian political parties...."

Svoboda was the major political force in the Maidan protests that overthrew Ukrainian president Viktor Yanukovych. In return for providing the shock troops for the coup, it has been given control of vital ministries.

Svoboda co-founder Andriy Parubiy acted as "security commandant" in the protests, directing attacks and providing the snipers which shot at riot police and demonstrators alike, by the Right Sector—an alliance of fascists and extreme right-wing nationalists, including the paramilitary UNA-UNSO.

Dressed in uniforms modelled on Hitler's Waffen SS, its members boast of fighting Russia in Chechnya, Georgia and Afghanistan. The UNA –UNSO is led by Andriy Shkil, and is part of the CIA/ NATO operation Gladio, responsible for many terrorist operations against communists and non-communist alike in Europe.

An interview with Russia's Rossiya-1 TV channel on Thursday (3/13/14), former head of the Security Service of Ukraine Aleksandr Yakimenko said shots that killed both policemen and protesters in February were fired from the building which was under the full control of the opposition and particularly

Maidan Commandant Andrey Parubiy. "Shots came from the Philharmonic Hall. Maidan Commandant Parubiy was responsible for this building. Snipers and people with automatic weapons were 'working' from this building on February 20," Yakimenko said.

According to Yakimenko, during the massacre the opposition leaders contacted him and asked him to deploy a special force unit to scoop out the snipers from buildings in central Kiev, but Parubiy made sure that didn't happen.

"The Right Sector and Freedom Party have requested that I use the Alpha group to cleanse these buildings, stripping them of snipers," Yakimenko said. According to him Ukrainian troops were ready to move in and eliminate the shooters. "I was ready to do it, but in order to go inside Maidan I had to get the sanction from Parubiy. Otherwise the 'self-defense' would attack me from behind. Parubiy did not give such consent," Yakimenko said noting that the Maidan leader had full authority over access to weapons on Maidan, and not a single gun, including a sniper rifle, could get in or out of the square.

The Estonian Foreign Minister, Urmas Paet said that the medical and on the ground people all confirm that the riot police and the protestors were shot by the same group. Paet also stated that the new interim government at Kiev had no interest in finding out who was responsible for the shootings.

Ukrainian Rabbi Moshe Reuven Azman, called on Kiev's Jews to leave the city and even the country if possible, fearing that the city's Jews will be victimized in the chaos, Israeli daily Maariv reported Friday. "I told my congregation to leave the city center or the city all together and if possible the country too," Rabbi Azman told Maariv. "I don't want to tempt fate," he added, "but there are constant warnings concerning intentions to attack Jewish institutions."

According to the paper's report Azman closed the Jewish community's schools but still holds three daily prayers. He said the Israeli embassy told members of the Jewish community to avoid leaving their homes. Edward Dolinsky, head of the umbrella organization of Ukraine's Jews described the situation in Kiev as dire, telling Maariv "We contacted Foreign Minister Avigdor Lieberman requesting he assist us with securing the community.

Shkil also has direct ties to Yulia Tymoshenko, as does newly installed Prime Minster Oleksandr Turchynov, former Tymoshenko advisor who took over after Yanukovych fled under threat to his life. In 2006 state prosecutors had opened a criminal case against Turchynov, who was accused of destroying files which showed Tymoshenko's ties to organized crime boss Semion Mogilevich. With Turchynov as Prime Minister, Ukraine is now under the thumb of fascist organized criminals known collectively as the "Right Sector."

These people organized the burning of government buildings and murdering demonstrators and police alike. Then they, against the Ukraine constitution and all legal procedure, had parliament declare them-selves national leaders without the required elections. Then, they issued arrest warrants for the former, duly elected leaders. Parubiy is now secretary of the National Security and Defense Council, overseeing the Defense Ministry and the armed forces. Dmytro Yarosh, leader of the Right Sector, is his deputy. Deputy Prime Minister Oleksandr Sych is another leading Svoboda figure, as is Oleh Makhnitsky (prosecutor-general), Serhiy Kvit (Education Ministry), Andriy Makhnyk (Ecology Ministry) and Ihor Shvaiko (Agriculture Ministry).

So, it is not hard to understand why Russia, and any right minded person for that matter, would question the legitimacy of the new provisional government of Ukraine. What is truly sickening is that the leaders of the U.S. and E.U. actually recognize these criminals as the legitimate government of the Ukraine.

While U.S. leaders were hypocritically speaking of respecting national sovereignty and international law, after their dismal record of doing just the opposite in Afghanistan, Iraq, and Libya, U.S. Ambassador to Ukraine, Victoria Nuland bragged that the "U.S. had spent $5 billion to build democratic skills and institutions in the Ukraine." The fact remains that if the wrong people get elected "regime change" will soon follow. The "right people" mean ones that open up their country to rape and pillage by the multinational corporations as Yulia Tymoshenko had previously done in the Ukraine.

In an interview with Press TV on March 9, Scott Rickard, a former American intelligence official said the United States started to boost its military presence in the Baltic region in January this year, showing that Washington knew then what was in store for Ukraine.

"Regarding the Americans' sending more fighters to and also more military presence into the Baltic areas, unfortunately, this is actually another show of force that the Americans have done. They actually did a preemptive move in January," said Rickard, "So they had some anticipation of what they were doing because there were some moves in January whereby the Americans and NATO made the decision where the United States assumed control of all the air-policing that is over these Baltic countries, including Estonia, Latvia, and Lithuania in January this year," he added.

Again Russia was not about to lose a primary naval base in Crimea. When the criminal government in Kiev took power, Putin with the approval of the Russian Parliament sent additional Russian military forces into Crimea. Since Crimea has a majority of Russians living there, these military forces were welcomed with open arms. Also contrary to western propaganda, Russia was within the law in sending these forces there.

The Russian/Ukrainian 1997 Partition Treaty provisions let Moscow maintain up to 25,000 troops in Crimea. They permit 24 smaller than 100 mm artillery systems, 132 armored vehicles, and 22 military aircraft. Russian naval and air force units are legally based in Sevastopol. They include: (1) the 30th Surface Ship Division 11th Antisubmarine Ship Brigade, six warships, and the 197th Landing Ship Brigade. (2) The 41st Missile Boat Brigade. (3) The 247th Separate Submarine Division. (4) The 68th Harbor Defense Ship Brigade. (5) The 422nd Separate Hydrographic Ship Division. (6) Two air bases in Kacha and Gvardeysky. (7) The 1096th Separate Anti-Aircraft Missile Regiment. (8) The 810th Marine Brigade, as well as several other units. Leasing arrangements run through 2042. If exercised, an additional option is binding until 2047. The Russians have less than 25,000 troops in the Crimea.

So the "Russian invasion" of the Ukraine is just more controlled news media propaganda. The equivalent would be the U.S. sending more ships and men to their base at Guantanamo, Cuba being construed as a U.S. invasion of Cuba. I haven't heard many of these propaganda outlets stating that Russia was within its legal rights sending some more military forces to Crimea have you?

Next, the Crimean Parliament voted to have Crimea break away from the Ukraine and join Russia. All areas East of the Dnieper river in the Ukraine have a large portion of Russian and Russian speaking people. It is not inconceivable that these areas of the Ukraine may also vote to join Russia. So, at this time (March 6, 2014), the Balkanization of the Ukraine is already underway.

President Obama started talk about economic sanctions against Russia. The suggestion of the EU to impose sanctions could hurt the EU economy even further and possibly bring it to a halt. This is according to experts, both from the economic and security industry. According to the European Centre for Information Policy and Security the imposing of sanctions would bring about more tension and could have catastrophic results in the EU due to the Oil & gas relation with Russia. About 42% of Europe's oil comes from Russia.

Russia could easily retaliate by dumping U.S. T bills, not paying U.S. loans, and using non-dollar currency for its foreign trade. China stands with Russia on this issue and if China and Russia both dumped their U.S. T bill holdings at the same time it would ruin the weak U.S. economy and send us into a real depression. So, trade sanctions are a bad idea. In fact, most of U.S. foreign policy is a bad idea and that is because it is secretly directed by agents of the Vatican who don't really care about what is good for the American people.

As I have said, the Vatican has always coveted Jerusalem. As we have seen, the Jesuits are in back of the secret societies and their agents which created the U.N. and are still in control of that governing body. So realistically speaking, U.N. control means Vatican control. And it is the New World Order's plan to eventually make Jerusalem their world capital.

Israel could be entering the final stages of negotiations to turn over control of Mount Zion to the Vatican, according to a report by Israel National News (February 22, 2014.) According to the online news source, a secretive meeting took place this week between the Jerusalem Municipality, Prime Minister's Office, Ministry of Tourism and senior Catholic officials. During the meeting, the Catholic delegation reportedly pressed Israel to follow through on a years-old proposal to give the Church control over the compound that houses the traditional "Hall of the Last Supper."

The problem is that the same compound also houses the traditional "Tomb of David," a holy site revered and frequented by religious Jews. Not to mention that Mount Zion is symbolic of Jerusalem as a whole, and surrendering it to the Vatican would be seen by many Israelis as a repudiation of Judaism's claim to the city. In response to reports regarding the negotiations, the Jerusalem Municipality released a statement insisting that it would remain "the central sovereign power on Mount Zion." Others are not so sure, and believe Prime Minister Benjamin Netanyahu intends to turn over control of Mount Zion prior to Pope Francis' visit to the Holy Land in May.

The entire City of Jerusalem could eventually come under U.N. control. When the U.N. was first considering partitioning the State of Israel, it passed U.N. Resolution Number 181 which would place the city of Jerusalem under U.N. Control. The General Assembly revisited the question of Jerusalem at its fifty-fifth session. In a resolution adopted on December 1, 2000, the Assembly determined that the decision of Israel to impose its laws, jurisdiction and administration on the Holy City of Jerusalem was illegal and, therefore, null and void.

The Assembly also deplored the transfer by some States of their diplomatic missions to Jerusalem in violation of Security Council resolution 478 (1980). These statements and resolutions, as well as many others adopted by United Nations bodies, international organizations, non-governmental organizations and religious groups, demonstrate the continuing determination of the international community to remain involved in the future of Jerusalem.

7

Propaganda and Mind Control

One means of controlling the populations of nations is a process called social conditioning. In 1922, the RIIA instructed John Rawlings Reese, a British Army technician, to establish the Tavistock Institute for Human Relations at the University of Sussex in England.

This Institute developed into the core of Briton's Psychological Warfare Department. Its methods were used, under the direction of Dr. Kurt Lewin in the United States, using the press, radio and the movie "news reels" to gradually condition the U.S. public into supporting the U.S. entry into World War II prior to Pearl Harbor.

During the War, Silent weapon technology evolved from *Operations Research* (O.R.), a strategic and tactical methodology developed under the Military Management in England during World War II. The original purpose of Operations Research was to study the strategic and tactical problems of air and land defense with the objective of effective use of limited military resources against foreign enemies. Part of the results of O.R. was a secret document called *Silent Weapons for Quiet Wars, An Introduction Programming Manual.*

This manual was uncovered quite by accident on July 7, 1986 when an employee of Boeing Aircraft Co. purchased a surplus IBM copier for scrap parts at a sale, and discovered inside details of a plan, hatched in the embryonic days of the "Cold War" which called for control of the masses through manipulation of industry, peoples' pastimes, education and political leanings. It called for a quiet revolution, putting brother against brother, and diverting the public's attention from what is really going on.

The document can be found online. So, I won't write all of it here. But I will point out some of the more interesting parts:

Immediately, the Rockefeller Foundation got in on the ground floor by making a four-year grant to Harvard College, funding the *Harvard Economic Research Project* for the study of the structure of the American Economy. One year later, in 1949, The United States Air Force joined in. In 1952, the grant period terminated, and a high-level meeting of the elite was held to determine the next phase of social operations research. The Harvard project had been very fruitful, as is borne out by the publication of some of its results in 1953 suggesting the feasibility of economic (social) engineering. (*Studies in the Structure of the American Economy* - copyright 1953 by Wassily Leontief, International Science Press Inc., White Plains, New York).

Theoretical Introduction

Give me control over a nation's currency, and I care not who makes its laws. -- Mayer Amschel Rothschild, 1743 - 1812)

Today's silent weapons technology is an outgrowth of a simple idea discovered, succinctly expressed, and effectively applied by the quoted *Mr. Mayer Amschel Rothschild*. Mr. Rothschild discovered the missing passive component of economic theory known as economic inductance. He, of course, did not think of his discovery in these 20th-century terms, and, to be sure, mathematical analysis had to wait for the Second Industrial Revolution, the rise of the theory of mechanics and electronics, and finally, the invention of the electronic computer before it could be effectively applied in the control of the world economy.

What Mr. Rothschild had discovered was the basic principle of power, influence, and control over people as applied to economics. That principle is "when you assume the appearance of power, people soon give it to you."

The basics of mechanical theory also apply to electrical theory and economic theory and can be modeled with mathematical equations. Operation Research clarifies all the variables and place them into a predictable program.

Social programming or engineering can likewise be modeled once the basic human functions are understood.

The following gives an idea of what the elite think of the masses and how the masses will react to a given stimulus:

1. The Artificial Womb

   From the time a person leaves its mother's womb, its every effort is directed towards building, maintaining, and withdrawing into artificial wombs, various sorts of substitute protective devices or shells.

   The objective of these artificial wombs is to provide a stable environment for both stable and unstable activity; to provide a shelter for the evolutionary processes of growth and maturity - i.e., survival; to provide security for freedom and to provide defensive protection for offensive activity.

This is equally true of both the general public and the elite. However, there is a definite difference in the way each of these classes go about the solution of problems.

The Political Structure of a Nation – Dependency

The primary reason why the individual citizens of a country create a political structure is a subconscious desire to perpetuate their own dependency relationship of childhood. Simply put, they want a human god to eliminate all risk from their life, pat them on the head, kiss their bruises, put a chicken on every dinner table, clothe their bodies, tuck them into bed at night, and tell them that everything will be alright when they wake up in the morning.

This public demand is incredible, so the human god, the politician, meets incredibility with incredibility by promising the world and delivering nothing. So who is the bigger liar? The public? Or the "godfather"? This public behavior is surrender born of fear, laziness, and expediency. It is the basis of the welfare state as a strategic weapon, useful against a disgusting public.

1. The Draft (As military service)

Few efforts of human behavior modification are more remarkable or more effective than that of the socio-military institution known as the draft. A primary purpose of a draft or other such institution is to instill, by intimidation, in the young males of a society the uncritical conviction that the government is omnipotent. He is soon taught that a prayer is slow to reverse what a bullet can do in an instant. Thus, a man trained in a religious environment for eighteen years of his life can, by this instrument of the government, be broken down, be purged of his fantasies and delusions in a matter of mere months. Once that conviction is instilled, all else becomes easy to instill.

Even more interesting is the process by which a young man's parents, who purportedly love him, can be induced to send him off to war to his death. Although the scope of this work will not allow this matter to be expanded in full detail, nevertheless, a coarse overview will be possible and can serve to reveal those factors which must be included in some numerical form in a computer analysis of social and war systems.

We begin with a tentative definition of the draft.

2. The draft (selective service, etc.) is an institution of compulsory collective sacrifice and slavery, devised by the middle-aged and elderly for the purpose of pressing the young into doing the public dirty work. It further serves to make the youth as guilty as the elders, thus making criticism of the elders by the youth less likely (Generational Stabilizer). It is marketed and sold to the public under the label of "patriotic = national" service.

Once a candid economic definition of the draft is achieved, that definition is used to outline the boundaries of a structure called a Human Value System, which in turn is translated into the terms of game theory. The value of such a slave laborer is given in a Table of Human

Values, a table broken down into categories by intellect, experience, post-service job demand, etc.

Some of these categories are ordinary and can be tentatively evaluated in terms of the value of certain jobs for which a known fee exists. Some jobs are harder to value because they are unique to the demands of social subversion, for an extreme example: the value of a mother's instruction to her daughter, causing that daughter to put certain behavioral demands upon a future husband ten or fifteen years hence; thus, by suppressing his resistance to a perversion of a government, making it easier for a banking cartel to buy the State of New York in, say, twenty years.

Such a problem leans heavily upon the observations and data of wartime espionage and many types of psychological testing. But crude mathematical models (algorithms, etc.) can be devised, if not to predict, at least to predeterminate these events with maximum certainty. What does not exist by natural cooperation is thus enhanced by calculated compulsion. Human beings are machines, levers which may be grasped and turned, and there is little real difference between automating a society and automating a shoe factory.

These derived values are variable. (It is necessary to use a current Table of Human Values for computer analysis.) These values are given in true measure rather than U.S. dollars, since the latter is unstable, being presently inflated beyond the production of national goods and services so as to give the economy a false kinetic energy ("paper" inductance).

The silver value is stable, it being possible to buy the same amount with a gram of silver today as it could be bought in 1920. Human value measured in silver units changes slightly due to changes in production technology.

1. Enforcement

Factor I

As in every social system approach, stability is achieved only by understanding and accounting for human nature (action/reaction patterns). A failure to do so can be, and usually is, disastrous.

As in other human social schemes, one form or another of intimidation (or incentive) is essential to the success of the draft. Physical principles of action and reaction must be applied to both internal and external subsystems.

To secure the draft, individual brainwashing/programming and both the family unit and the peer group must be engaged and brought under control.

Factor II - Father

The man of the household must be housebroken to ensure that junior will grow up with the right social training and attitudes. The advertising media, etc., are engaged to see to it that father-to-be is pussy-whipped before or by the time he is married. He is taught that he either conforms to the social notch cut out for him or his sex life will be hobbled and his tender companionship will be zero. He is made to see that women demand security more than logical, principled, or honorable behavior.

By the time his son must go to war, father (with jelly for a backbone) will slam a gun into junior's hand before father will risk the censure of his peers, or make a hypocrite of himself by crossing the investment he has in his own personal opinion or self-esteem. Junior will go to war or father will be embarrassed. So junior will go to war, the true purpose notwithstanding.

Factor III - Mother

The female element of human society is ruled by emotion first and logic second. In the battle between logic and imagination, imagination always wins, fantasy prevails, maternal instinct dominates so that the child comes first and the future comes second. A woman with a newborn baby is too starry-eyed to see a wealthy man's cannon fodder or a cheap source of slave labor. A woman must, however, be conditioned to accept the transition to "reality" when it comes, or sooner.

As the transition becomes more difficult to manage, the family unit must be carefully disintegrated, and state-controlled public education and state-operated child-care centers must be become more common and legally enforced so as to begin the detachment of the child from the mother and father at an earlier age. Inoculation of behavioral drugs [Ritalin] can speed the transition for the child (mandatory). Caution: A woman's impulsive anger can override her fear. An irate woman's power must never be underestimated, and her power over a pussy-whipped husband must likewise never be underestimated. It got women the vote in 1920.

Factor IV - Junior

The emotional pressure for self-preservation during the time of war and the self-serving attitude of the common herd that have an option to avoid the battlefield - if junior can be persuaded to go - is all of the pressure finally necessary to propel Johnny off to war. Their quiet blackmailing of him are the threats: "No sacrifice, no friends; no glory, no girlfriends."

Factor V - Sister

And what about junior's sister? She is given all the good things of life by her father, and taught to expect the same from her future husband regardless of the price.

Since World War II, the methods of social conditioning have been improved considerably. The advent of television has provided an excellent medium for social conditioning. Subliminal messages can be flashed over the TV screen so rapidly that the conscious mind is not aware of them. However the subconscious mind is aware of them. The subconscious mind can then affect the person to act in irrational ways. The subliminal message technique was used for a while by advertisers, until public awareness and outrage caused them to be made illegal.

However the subliminal method can still be used for non-advertising means, like social conditioning. As already stated, the control of the media sources has been consolidated into basically 6 major global corporations. Social conditioning is now a global situation operated by a near monopoly.

The CIA became very interested in mind control for several reasons. One reason was to find ways to interrogate persons of interest in such a way that the subject would not be able to hide anything. Another reason was more sinister, to develop a means of creating assassins that would kill on command and then forget what had happened.

Headed by Sidney Gottlieb, the MK Ultra project was started on the order of CIA director Allen Dulles on April 13, 1953. Its remit was to develop mind-controlling drugs for use against the Soviet bloc, largely in response to alleged Soviet, Chinese, and North Korean use of mind control techniques on U.S. prisoners of war in Korea. The CIA wanted to use similar methods on their own captives.

The CIA was also interested in being able to manipulate foreign leaders with such techniques. Experiments were often conducted without the subjects' knowledge or consent. In some cases, academic researchers being funded through grants from CIA front organizations were unaware that their work was being used for these purposes.

Once Project MK Ultra officially got underway in April, 1953, experiments included administering LSD to mental patients, prisoners, drug addicts and prostitutes, "people who could not fight back", as one agency officer put it. In one case LSD was administered to a mental patient in Kentucky for 174 days. LSD was also administered to CIA employees, military personnel, doctors, other government agents, and members of the general public in order to study their reactions. LSD and other drugs were usually administered without the subject's knowledge or informed consent, a violation of the Nuremberg Code that the U.S. agreed to follow after World War II. The aim of this was to find drugs which would irresistibly bring out deep confessions or wipe a subject's mind clean and program him or her as "a robot agent."

MK-ULTRA used hypnosis, psychotropic drugs, and trauma to create multiple personalities, known as "alters" in a subject. One alter could be the persons normal personality which presented itself to the normal world. Another alter could be triggered using a key phrase, this alter would kill a target person that the alter was programmed to kill. Another key phrase would then snap the alter back to the normal alter. One alter had no idea that the other alter even existed within that person.

This process was not only used to create assassins but also spies. One alter if captured by the enemy could pass lie detector tests, torture and other techniques to uncover deception if the other alter was actually doing the spying. However, as usually happens in war, the enemy quickly catches on and develops countermeasures. Soon the CIA had to develop alters three layers deep to have sufficient security in their multiple personality agents.

Dr. Estabrooks was a Rhodes Scholar and worked with Military intelligence. He took his Doctorate at Harvard in 1926 and has authored many articles and books on clinical hypnosis and human behavior. This is what he had to say:

"....One of the most fascinating but dangerous applications of hypnosis is its use in military intelligence. This is a field with which I am familiar though formulating guide lines for the techniques used by the United States in two world wars. Communication in war is always a headache. Codes can be broken. A professional spy may or may not stay bought. Your own man may have unquestionable loyalty, but his judgment is always open to question. The "hypnotic courier," on the other hand, provides a unique solution. I was involved in preparing many subjects for this work during World War II..."

Research continued into early 70's by CIA's own admission during the Church hearings. John Marks, author of the best study of CIA mind control experiments, makes the subtle differentiation that the CIA congressional witnesses might truthfully say that all research done by the TSS Directorate had ended, since the programs were moved into other areas like the DIA, ONI and other agencies, once operational techniques had been developed.

Electronic methods of mind control were also developed. Patrick Flannigan had developed a device called a Neurophone which allowed deaf people to hear. A high frequency RF signal that would act directly on the brain was amplitude modulated by an audio signal and the deaf person would "hear" the audio signal inside his head -bypassing the ears entirely. The military became interested in his device and modified it so that a microwave signal could be directed at a person and that person would hear "voices" inside their head. This would work on anyone whether deaf or not.

Patrick Flannigan was not the only one to discover this effect. In 1975, researcher A. W. Guy stated that "one of the most widely observed and accepted biologic effects of low average power electromagnetic energy is the auditory sensation evoked in man when exposed to pulsed microwaves."

He concluded that at frequencies where the auditory effect can be easily detected, microwaves penetrate deep into the tissues of the head, causing rapid thermal expansion (at the microscopic level only) that produces strains in the brain tissue. An acoustic stress wave is then conducted through the skull to the cochlea, and from there, it proceeds in the same manner as in conventional hearing. It is obvious that receiver-less radio has not been adequately publicized or explained because of national security concerns.

Today, the ability to remotely transmit microwave voices inside a target's head is known inside the Pentagon as "Synthetic Telepathy." According to Dr. Robert Becker, "Synthetic Telepathy has applications in covert operations designed to drive a target crazy with voices or deliver undetected instructions to a programmed assassin."

In 1975, a primitive mind reading machine was tested at Stanford Research Institute. The machine was invented by Psychologist, Lawrence Pinneo and Computer experts, Daniel Wold and David Hall. Their stated goal was to put a computer programmer in direct contact with a computer. The military quickly saw the applications for military use.

Eventually this technology evolved into Radio Hypnotic Intra Cerebral Control – Electronic Dissolution of Memory or RHIC-EDOM technology. With this technology people could be programmed to carry out assigned tasks and then totally forget what they had done. Many theorize that Sirhan Sirhan, a 24-year-old Palestinian/Jordanian immigrant, who was convicted of Robert Kennedy's murder and is serving a life sentence for the crime was a victim of RHIC-EDOM programming.

Another scientist involved in mind control Was Jose Delgado, who performed experiments using permanent brain implants in bulls, primates, and humans beginning in the 1950s, with extremely successful results. The bulk of Delgado's research took place at Yale University in the 1950s and 1960s. Delgado manually positioned electrode assembles within the brain, assemblies that stimulate a desired area of the brain when a particular FM frequency is present. He called his units stimoceivers.

In 1963, Delgado became a matador to demonstrate the abilities of stimoceiver manipulation. He stepped into a closed bull ring with an implanted bull armed only with a radio frequency controller. When the bull charged at him, Delgado stimulated the bull's motor cortex with the remote control, causing the bull to come to a full stop only feet away. After this stunt, he was interviewed by a *New York Times* reporter. Delgado made this statement:

"The individual may think that the most important reality is his own existence, but this is only his personal point of view. This lacks historical perspective. Man does not have the right to develop his own mind. This kind of liberal orientation has great appeal. We must electronically control the brain. Someday armies and generals will be controlled by electric stimulation of the brain."

Delgado illustrated some of his hopes for mind control in 1969's *Physical Control of the Mind: Toward a Psychocivilized Society.* The book makes for a phenomenal read, with Delgado going into the intimate details of his research with images, along with a treatise on ethical implications of the technology.

These implants have been improved and miniaturized over the years so that they are smaller than the size of a grain of rice and can actually be implanted via a hypodermic needle. There have been times when these implants were placed in in persons without their knowledge. They were used at the Pelican Bay California State Prison, explicitly designed to keep California's alleged "worst of the worst" prisoners. These implants have been placed in violent prisoners during medical checkups, where the prisoner is sedated unconscious and implanted. The implants are used to calm prisoners down during violent confrontations among inmates. Also, some military personnel, like Special Forces have been implanted to give them superior combat abilities.

In the 1980s, Fort Hero, an abandoned Air force base on Long Island, was taken over by a secret group, not officially connected with the U.S. government to conduct mind control experiments using the huge Sage Radar antenna located there. It had been discovered that the 425 to 450 megahertz band could access the human brain.

According to electronics expert, Preston Nichols, in his book *The Montauk Project,* considerable mind control experimenting was done using this radar antenna on people in towns within range of the antenna. The book also gives detailed information on other physical effects of the Montauk Project including teleportation and time travel. But, I won't cover that aspect here as it will be covered in a planned future book.

Alan Yu, a former lieutenant colonel in the Taiwan National Defense Department, says that the United States has not only developed an operational mind control machine, but has also distributed models for use by allied countries. Yu states that such machines pose a great threat to human rights and the American way of life. He calls the device the "Mind Reading Machine" (Mind Machine).

Yu writes that there are two sources of information detailing the existence of the Mind Reading Machine. In the 1970s, The South China Morning Post reported that the University of Maryland had invented a Thought Reading Machine.

In the spring of 1984, Yu was a lieutenant colonel serving in the National Defense Department of Taiwan. At that time, Yu read a classified document from the department that he served under. The document said the Military Police Department of Taiwan had purchased several of the Mind Reading Machines from the United States (In Taiwan, it was called Psychological Language Machine).

The document was a request to the United States for parts to repair several malfunctioning machines. The machine allegedly uses microwaves to deliver spoken messages directly to the human brain, as well as using radio waves to hypnotize people or change their thoughts. Yu reports that before he left, this machine had become the most effective weapon for the security departments of Taiwan.

In 1993, Defense News announced that the Russian government was discussing with American counterparts the transfer of technical information and equipment known as "Acoustic Psycho- correction." The Russians claimed that this device involves the transmission of specific commands via static or white noise bands into the human subconscious without upsetting other intellectual functions.

Demonstrations of this equipment have shown encouraging results after exposure of less than one minute and have produced the ability to alter behavior on unwilling subjects. A US Department of Defense medical engineer claimed in 1989 that the U.S. and Israel had regularly used microwaves to condition and control the minds of Palestinians.

The mind-altering mechanism is based on a subliminal carrier technology: the Silent Sound Spread Spectrum (SSSS) sometimes called "S-quad" or "Squad". It was developed by Dr. Oliver Lowery of Norcross, Georgia, and is described in US Patent #5,159,703, "Silent Subliminal Presentation System", dated October 27, 1992.

The ability to read the mind has been perfected via the use of supercomputers. Different brain wave patterns are recorded by extra sensitive sensors and fed into these computers. Not only are thoughts recorded but also emotions.

A vast library of thoughts and emotions and their equivalent brain waves are stored in these computers.

From this data any set of thoughts and emotions can be transmitted into human beings with the proper electromagnetic gear using SSSS technology. The most insidious aspect of SSSS is that it is completely undetectable by those being targeted. Because it delivers its subliminal programming directly to the human brain via the auditory sense at frequencies that humans are incapable of perceiving as sound, there is no defense against it. Everyone on the planet is equally susceptible to mind control via SSSS and there isn't any escape from it, as the UHF waves can be transmitted over very long distances from remotely located sources and will pass through walls and other objects as if they are not there. UHF is the frequency (100 mega Hz) that has been used for television and radio broadcasting for as long as these media have existed. SSSS is designed to utilize UHF as a carrier wave.

This type of technology was used successfully in Operation Desert Storm to cause thousands of Iraq soldiers to leave their battle hardened bunkers and surrender to U.S. forces.

Thomas Beardon, has written numerous books on scalar wave technology. A standard electromagnetic wave is a vector wave having transverse directions of magnetic field, electric field and propagation. A scalar wave is like a sound wave or pressure wave. Pressure is equal in all directions and is non directional or non-vectorial. If you have two equal and opposite electric vectors, they cancel, but there is still a stress in the vacuum. This is a scalar stress which can have interesting effects.

In the early 1970's Hundreds of inmates at the Gunniston Facility of the Utah State Prison were subjected to scalar wave mind control. This was brought out in the Utah U.S. District Court, because inmates who had been subjected to this Tesla-wave mind-control in prison had tried unsuccessfully to fight back in court The University of Utah researched at that time how scalar waves could induce the mind into hearing voices, overriding and implanting thoughts into the mind, as well as reading the thoughts.

The process was also tested at Draper Prison in Utah. A prisoner, called David Fratus, in Draper Prison, in 1988 wrote:

"I began to receive, or hear, high-frequency tones in my ears. When I plug my ears, the tones are still inside and become amplified. It's as if they had become electrified echo chambers with the sounds coming from the inside out. I began to hear voices into my inner ears as vivid as though I were listening to a set of stereo head phones with the end result being that I am now having my brain monitored by an omnipotent computerized mind reading or scanning machine of some sort."

There are companies creating products out there that can counter these electronic mind control tactics. One Company is Quwave: http://www.quwave.com/

In 1904, Nikola Tesla had developed transmitters to harness scalar energy from one transmitter to another, undetectably by-passing time and space. Tesla himself stated that he was using non-Hertezian waves that were like sound waves in the Aether.

Fourier transforms change waves from the time domain to the frequency domain. An ideal square wave has all the frequencies under a Fourier transformation. A continuous wave of one frequency shows up as a spike in the frequency domain. Whittaker was able to show that D.C. potentials could be represented by conjugate waves of many frequencies combined. Thomas Townsend Brown was able to demonstrate that high D.C. potentials produced gravitational effects. Tesla also experimentally discovered time effects from high voltage fields. So, high voltage potentials have the ability to warp gravity, space and time.

Finer scalar wave-forms also have been discovered periodically by other mathematicians, who have been able to calculate new equations especially in harmonics (used in hyper dimensional physics) connecting the wavelengths of matter, gravity and light to each other and how all these lock in and create our expression of time (as it manifests in space) - which has been now discovered to be untapped 'potential' energy flowing in hyperspace. Time flows like a wave-form river in hyperspace in a grid pattern. According to Thomas Beardon in his book *Energy from the Vacuum*, time itself can be a source of energy.

Both Russia and the U.S. have weaponized scalar wave technology in highly classified programs. Some applications of this technology involve weather modification and triggering earth quakes, using the HAARP microwave antenna systems in Alaska to generate scalar waves which can be steered to any place on the planet. But, I am straying from the subject of mind control here.

The use of mind controlled computer interfaces are now commercially on the market. So, a sceptic could purchase one and test it out. For example, the Cyberlink Mind Mouse is a revolutionary hands-free computer controller which allows you to move and click a mouse cursor, play video games, create music, and control external devices, all without using your hands. A headband with three sensors detects electrical signals on the forehead resulting from subtle facial muscle, eye, and brain activity. This headband connects to an interface box that amplifies and digitizes the forehead signals and sends them to your computer.

Even though science says there is no evidence of soul or spirit, science may be wrong. Robert Allan Monroe, was a radio broadcasting executive who became known for his research into altered consciousness and founding the Monroe Institute. His 1971 book *Journeys Out of the Body* is credited with popularizing the term "out-of-body experience".

In *Journeys Out of the Body*, Monroe describes experimenting with his "astral body", which after leaving his physical body, normally could travel through walls and go anywhere desired. In one experiment, he placed a bed inside a faraday cage, a complete enclosure of copper screen, which could be charged to 20 thousand volts.

With no voltage, he could lie in the bed and go into his astral body and easily pass through the copper wire faraday cage. However with the high voltage turned on, which wouldn't affect his physical body inside the faraday cage, his astral body could not pass through the faraday cage. This interesting experiment proved that electric fields can affect the astral body.

Monroe achieved world-wide recognition as an explorer of human consciousness. His research, beginning in the 1950s, produced evidence that specific sound patterns have identifiable, beneficial effects on our capabilities. For example, certain combinations of frequencies appeared to enhance alertness; others to induce sleep; and still others to evoke expanded states of consciousness. Assisted by specialists in psychology, medicine, biochemistry, psychiatry, electrical engineering, physics, and education, Robert Monroe developed Hemi-Sync, a patented audio technology that is claimed to facilitate enhanced performance.

A NeuroMap system was purchased by the Institute. This was a computerized system that was fed inputs from noninvasive electrodes on the head that would display a color map of changes within the brain. NeuroMap would be used with Hemi-Sync to view changes caused within the brain by variations in the audio signal input.

Monroe would write two more books about his out of body experiments and experiences, *Far Journeys* and *Ultimate Journey*. In some of his out of body travels he would meet acquaintances of his that had already died. This seemed to demonstrate the survival of the soul after physical death. He also visited his own past lives and concluded that his present personality was a composite of all of his previous personalities. This seemed to prove reincarnation.

The way in which Monroe was able to leave his physical body at will and travel far beyond the time space continuum, was absolutely fascinating. Moreover, his ability to traverse time, moving both back in time as well as into the future, is one of the most interesting aspects of his out of body experiences. It was these astral travels that would also attract the attention of the U.S. Military Intelligence complex.

Both the U.S. Central Intelligence Agency and the National Security Agency would eventually utilize Monroe and his Hemi-Sync process to train agents in the arcane sciences of remote viewing. Two of these agents were Captain Frederic Atwater and Chief Warrant Officer Joseph McMoneagle.

Frederic Atwater, after leaving the military, ended up living within a mile of Monroe Institute. He also wrote the book, *Captain of My Ship - Master of My Soul*.

Joseph McMoneagle was the best remote viewer at NSA's Ft. Mead in Maryland. He worked in operation *Star Gate* with Ingo Swann. After leaving the military, he also ended up living within a mile of Monroe Institute. He started a business called Intuitive Intelligence Applications, Inc. His website is at: http://www.mceagle.com.

Also, the Russians, working on paraphysics and physic phenomena had developed spies that could travel in their astral bodies and gather information from remote locations. The U.S. military intelligence developed a classified program of astral guards and spies to counter the Russian program.

Mind control technology provides the New World Order an excellent tool for control of the people of the world. To what extent it is being used is yet to be determined.

8

Deep Underground
Military Bases

World War II involved massive aerial bombardments of enemy cities, factories, ports, roads and rail transport systems. Germany was particularly badly hit with air raids, in an Allied effort to destroy Germany's ability to make war.

Germany countered by placing some of their factories underground and inside of mountains. Nordhausen was such an underground factory, located in the Hartz Mountains, built and operated with slave labor from the prison camps, which built the German V-2 Rockets. Nordhausen was an impressive engineering feat, well camouflaged at its entrance and not easily seen from the air. Even if it were to be seen, it was impervious to bombing attacks.

After the war, the U.S. forces captured the Nazi engineers that designed Nordhausen and bought them, along with a number of V-2 rockets back to the United States in "Operation Paperclip." The engineers were put to work designing underground levels for Wright Patterson air base. The rockets and Nazi rocket scientists were sent on to White Sands, New Mexico for the start of America's space program.

By January 1946, 160 Nazi Scientists had been secreted into the U.S. The largest group consisted of 115 Rocket scientists under Wernher Von Braun at Fort bliss, Texas, eighty miles from White Sands proving grounds.

At Wright Field, there were 30 Nazi scientists pouring over 1,500 tons of German documents captured by Allied intelligence agencies after the war and transported to Air material Command. The subject matter had to be translated into English and committed to microfilm. So abundant was the information that more than one hundred thousand new words had to be added to the Air material Command's English dictionary. The German scientists at Wright Patterson however were getting restless. They were used to be innovators - not librarians. Also, they were confined to the base and not allowed to go to town and were segregated from personnel at the base who were not essential for their job.

By the summer of 1946, things started to change. Gehelen's Intelligence on Eastern Europe and Russia was starting to alarm military and political figures in Washington. Russia, a former ally was starting to look like a potential new enemy. Loathing for the Nazis started to transform into fear of the Russians. Operation Paperclip got under way and thousands more Nazi scientist would be brought into the U.S. These scientists were allowed to bring their families to live with them and were given greater freedom and eventually U.S. citizenship.

Wright Patterson had an alien property division which evaluated and back engineered alien (non-American) weapons. During the war, this division was used to examine advanced German and Japanese captured weapons.

After the war, it was used to examine recovered extra-terrestrial "flying Saucers" and their crew. The underground levels at Wright Patterson were quite useful in hiding classified projects from personnel without high enough security clearances.

The event of the atom bomb and later the hydrogen bomb made the creation of underground facilities impervious to nuclear attack a high priority program. This was the start of the Deep Underground Military Bases (DUMB) program.

Some of these underground bases like NORAD's facility at Cheyanne Mountain in Colorado are well known. It is purported to be able to take a direct hit by a hydrogen bomb and still keep in operation. Most of the DUMB bases are not known about. A vast tunnel system connecting these DUMB bases has also been built.

There is also a Continuation of Government (COG) program in the event of a nuclear war, an underground facility for members of the U.S. government and their families to live and work has been built at the Greenbrier Facility, in White Sulfur Springs, West Virginia under the Greenbrier Resort. The Continuity of Government facility intended to house the United States Congress is located on the grounds of the prestigious Greenbrier resort.

The bunker is beneath the West Virginia wing, which includes a complete medical clinic. Construction of the facility, which began in 1959, required 2.5 years and 50,000 tons of concrete. The steel-reinforced concrete walls of the bunker, which is 20 feet below ground, are 2 feet thick. The facility includes separate chambers for the House of Representatives and the Senate, as well as a larger room for joint sessions. These are located in the "Exhibit Hall" of the West Virginia Wing, which includes vehicular and pedestrian entrances which can be quickly sealed by blast doors. They don't hide this one, and it's even a tourist attraction.

In the United States alone, there are over 132 Deep Underground Military Bases situated under most major cities, US AFBs, US Navy Bases and US Army Bases, as well as underneath FEMA Military Training Camps and DHS control centers.

However, the military has been quite secretive about most of these bases and the subject is classified. Richard Souder, a Ph.D. architect, risked his life by talking about this. He is the author of the book, *Underground Bases and Tunnels: What is the Government Trying to Hide*. Later Sauder wrote *Underwater & Underground Bases: Surprising Facts the Government Does Not Want You to Know*. Here, he reveals that there are also under-sea naval bases with submarine pens. Most of Sauder's information comes from government contractor documents which he had been researching.

The United States has a history of government agencies existing in secret. The National Security Agency (NSA) was founded in 1952, its existence was hidden until the mid1960's. Even more secretive is the National Reconnaissance Office, which was founded in 1960 but remained completely concealed for 30 years.

Recent leaks from Edward Snowden, a former intelligence contractor, have shed light on the black budget world. This is a world full of Special Access Programs (SAP) that garnishes trillions of dollars every year to conduct operations the general public knows nothing about. These programs do not exist publicly, but they do indeed exist. They are better known as 'deep black programs.' A 1997 US Senate report described them as "so sensitive that they are exempt from standard reporting requirements to the Congress". One aspect of these 'deep black programs' is the development of deep underground military bases, and they can go up to several miles underneath the surface.

There are also known underground facilities in existence. Take for example, the Swedish underground military facility at Musko. It's a large naval base built underneath a mountain. The hospital alone within this facility holds over 1,000 beds. Musko engineers blasted out 1,500, 000 cubic meters of stone in order to build it

One major contractor is Bechtel Corporation. They have a nuclear powered laser drilling machines that can drill a tunnel seven miles long in one day. The September, 1983 issue of Omni (Pg. 80) has a color drawing of 'The Subterrene,' the Los Alamos nuclear-powered tunnel machine that burrows through the rock, deep underground, by heating whatever stone it encounters into molten rock. This machine is used to create the inter-connecting tunnels to the different DUMBs. These tunnels use a tube system with mag lev trains that can move up to Mach 2 in the vacuum inside the tubes. Travel across the entire U.S. would take about 2 hours in this system.

Many of these tunnels are made with Nuclear Subterrenes, which work by melting their way through the rock and soil, actually vitrifying it as they go, and leaving a neat, solidly glass-lined tunnel behind them.

The heat is supplied by a compact nuclear reactor that circulates liquid lithium from the reactor core to the tunnel face, where it melts the rock. In the process of melting the rock the lithium loses some of its heat. It is then circulated back along the exterior of the tunneling machine to help cool the vitrified rock as the tunneling machine forces its way forward. The cooled lithium then circulates back to the reactor where the whole cycle starts over. In this way the nuclear subterrene slices through the rock like a nuclear powered, 2,000 degree Fahrenheit (1,100 Celsius) earthworm, boring its way deep underground.

The United States Atomic Energy Commission and the United States Energy Research and Development Administration took out Patents in the 1970s for nuclear subterrenes. The first patent, in 1972 went to the U.S. Atomic Energy Commission. A cost analysis and diagrams of this machine by Los Alamos Labs. is at: http://projectcamelot.org/la5354ms.pdf

The Nuclear Subterrene has an advantage over mechanical tunnel boring machines, in that it produces no muck that must be disposed of by conveyors, trains, trucks, etc. This greatly simplifies tunneling. The tunnels they make could be very hard to detect, for the simple reason that there would not be the tell-tale muck piles or tailings dumps that are associated with the conventional tunneling activities.

There is the Deep Underground Military Base underneath Denver International Airport, which is over 22 miles in diameter and goes down over 8 levels. Constructed in 1995, the government and politicians were hell bent on building this airport in spite of it ending up vastly over budget. Charges of corruption, constant construction company changes, and mass firings of teams once they had built a section of their work was reported so that no "one" group had any idea what the whole blueprint of the airport was. Not only did locals not want this airport built nor was it needed, but everything was done to make sure it was built despite that.

There are acres of fenced-in areas which have barbed wire pointing into the area as if to keep things in, and small concrete stacks that resemble mini-cooling towers that rise out of the acres of land around the airport to apparently vent underground levels. The underground facility is 88.3 square miles. Basically this Underground Base is 8 cities on top of each other! The holding capacity of such bases is huge. These city-sized bases can hold millions and millions of people.

Here are the locations of some other Deep Underground Military Bases in the U.S.:

ALASKA 1. Brooks Range, Alaska 2. Delta Junction, Alaska 2a. Fort Greeley, Alaska, in the same Delta Junction area.

ARIZONA 1. Arizona Mountains Function: Genetic work. Multiple levels. Fort Huachuca, Arizona Function: NSA Facility 2. Luke Air Force Base. 3. Page, Arizona Tunnels to: Area 51, Nevada, Dulce base, New Mexico 4. Sedona, Arizona Located under the Enchantment Resort in Boynton Canyon. Also, there is an underground Base in Secret Mountain with tunnels to the Navajo Weapons Depot and the Cement plant near Clarkdale. There have been many reports by people in recent years of "increased military presence and activity" in the area. 5. Wikieup, Arizona Tunnels to: Area 51 6. Yucca Mountain, Arizona.

CALIFORNIA 1: 29 Palms, California Tunnels to: Chocolate Mts., Fort Irwin, California 2: Benicia, California 3. Catalina Island, California Tunnels to Port Hueneme Naval Weapons Division Base in and also to Edwards Air Force Base. 4. China Lake Naval Weapons Testing Center. 5. Chocolate Mountains, California Tunnels to: Fort Irwin, California 6. Death Valley, California. 7. Deep Springs, California Tunnels to: Death Valley, Mercury, NV, and Salt Lake City 8. Edwards AFB, California Function: Aircraft Development - antigravity research and vehicle development Levels: Multiple Tunnels to: Catalina Island

Fort Irwin, California Vandenberg AFB, California Notes: Delta Hanger - North Base, Edwards AFB, Ca. Haystack Butte - Edwards, AFB, Ca. 9. Fort Irwin, California Tunnels to: 29 Palms, California Area 51, Nevada Edwards AFB, Mt. Shasta, California 10. Helendale, California Function: Special Aircraft Facility 11. Lancaster, California Function: New Aircraft design, anti-gravity engineering, Stealth craft and testing Levels: 42 Tunnels To: Edwards A.F.B., Palmdale 12. Lawrence-Livermore International Labs, California The lab has a Human Genome Mapping project on chromosome #19 and a newly built $1.2 billion laser facility 13. Moreno Valley, California Function unknown 14. Mt. Lassen, California Tunnels to: Probably connects to the Mt. Shasta main tunnel. 15. Mt. Shasta. Function: Genetic experiments, magnetic advance, space and beam weaponry. Levels: 5 Tunnels to: Ft. Irwin, California North 16. Napa, California Functions: Direct Satellite Communications, Laser Communications. Continuation of Government site. Levels: Multi-level Tunnels to: Unknown Notes: Located on Oakville Grade, Napa County, Ca. 87 Acres 17. Needles, California Function unknown 18. Palmdale, California Function: New Aircraft Design, anti-gravity research 19. Tehachapi Facility Tejon Ranch Function: Levels: 42 Tunnels to: Edwards, Llona and other local areas Notes: 25 miles NW of Lancaster California, in the Tehachapi Mountains. 20. Ukiah, California Function unknown

COLORADO 1. Near Boulder, Co. in the mountains Function: unknown. 2. Cheyenne Mountain -NORAD -Colorado Springs, Colorado Function: Early Warning systems - missile defense systems - Space tracking Levels: Multiple Tunnels to: Colorado Springs, Function: Early warning systems, military strategy, satellite operations Levels: Multiple NORAD is a massive self-sustaining 'city' built inside the mountain Tunnels to: Creede, Denver, Dulce Base, Kinsley. 3. Creede, Colorado Function unknown Tunnels to: Colorado Springs, Colorado - Delta,

Colorado - Dulce Base, New Mexico 4. Delta, Colorado Function unknown Tunnels to: Creede, Salt Lake, Utah 5. Denver International Airport Function: Military research, construction, detainment camp facilities Levels: 7 reported Tunnels to: Denver proper, Colorado and Rocky Mountain "safe housing", Colorado Springs, Colorado Cheyenne Mtn. 6. Falcon Air Force Base, Falcon, Colorado Function: SDI, Satellite Control Levels: Multiple Tunnels to: Colorado Springs, possibly more. 7. Fort Collins, Colorado Function: Suspect high precision equipment manufacturing for space. 8. Grand Mesa, Colorado Function unknown 9. Gore Range near lake, west of Denver, Co. Function: Library and Central Data Bank 10. San Juan Valley, Colorado hidden beneath and in an operating Buffalo Ranch Function unknown 11. Telluride, Colorado Function unknown 12. University of Denver, Co (Boulder area) Function: Genetics, geology/mining as related to tunneling and underground construction. 13. Warden Valley West of Fort Collins, CO Function Unknown Tunnels to: Montana

GEORGIA Dobbins Air Force Base, Marietta GA Function: test site for plasma and antigravity air craft, experimental crafts and weapons

INDIANA Kokomo, Indiana Function Unknown Notes: for years people in that area have reported a "hum" that has been so constant that some have been forced to move and it has made many others sick. It seems to come from underground, and "research" has turned up nothing although it was suggested by someone that massive underground tunneling and excavating is going on, using naturally occurring caverns, to make an underground containment and storage facility.

KANSAS 1. Hutchinson, Kansas Function unknown Tunnels to: Kinsley, Nebraska. The entrance to the tunnel is underneath

Hutchinson Hospital and is huge 2. Kansas City, Kansas Function unknown Notes: Entrance near Worlds of Fun 3. Kinsley, Kansas Function unknown Tunnels to: Colorado Springs, Colorado; Hutchinson, Kansas; Tulsa Kokoweef Peak, SW California Notes: Gold stored in huge cavern, blasted shut. Known as the "midway city" because it's located halfway between New York and San Francisco.

MARYLAND Edgewood Arsenal, Maryland (from Don) Martins AFB, Aberdeen Proving Ground, Maryland

MASSACHUSETTS Maynard MA, FEMA regional center. Wackenhut is here too.

MONTANA Bozeman, Mont. Function: Genetics

NEVADA Area 51 - Groom Lake - Dreamland - Nellis Air Force Base Area 51 Function: Stealth and cloaking Aircraft research & development. 'Dreamland (Data Repository Establishment and Maintenance Land) Elmint (Electromagnetic Intelligence), Biological weapons research and genetic manipulation/warfare storage, Cold Empire, EVA, Program HIS (Hybrid Intelligence System),BW/CW; IRIS (Infrared Intruder Systems), Security: Above ground cameras, underground pressure sensors, ground and air patrol Area S-4 back engineered ET saucers and antigravity technology. 2. Blue Diamond, Nevada Function unknown 3. Fallon Air Force Base area (the flats, near Reno) "American City" restricted military sites southwest of Fallon 4. Mercury, Nevada Function unknown 5. Tonopah, Nevada Function unknown 69: San Gabriel (mountains) On Western side of Mojave Desert Function unknown Notes: Heavy vibrations coming from under the forest floor which sounds like geared machinery. These vibrations and sounds are the same as heard in Kokomo, Indiana and are suspected underground building/tunneling operations.

NEW MEXICO 1. Albuquerque, New Mexico (AFB) Function unknown Levels: Multiple Tunnels to: Carlsbad, New Mexico Los Alamos, New Mexico Possible connections to Datil, and other points. 2. Carlsbad, New Mexico Functions: Underground Nuclear Testing Tunnels to: Fort Stockton, Texas. Roswell 3. Cordova, New Mexico Function unknown 4. Datil, New Mexico Function unknown Tunnels to: Dulce Base 5: Dulce Base, New Mexico. Tunnels to: Colorado Springs, Colorado Creed, Colorado Datil, N.M. Los Alamos. Page, Arizona Sandia Base Taos, NM. 6. Los Alamos, New Mexico Functions: Psychotronic Research, Psychotronic Weapons Levels: Multiple Tunnels to: ALB AFB, New Mexico Dulce, New Mexico Connections to Datil, Taos 7. Sandia Base, New Mexico Functions: Research in Electrical/magnetic Phenomena Levels: Multiple Tunnels to: Dulce Base Notes: Related Projects are studied at Sandia Base by 'The Jason Group' (of 55 Scientists). They have secretly harnessed the 'Dark Side of Technology' and hidden the beneficial technology from the public. 8. Sunspot, NM Function unknown 9. Taos, New Mexico Function unknown Tunnels to: Dulce, New Mexico; Cog, Colorado Notes: Several other sidelines to area where Uranium is mined or processed. 10. White Sands, NM Function: Missile testing/design Levels: Seven known

NEW YORK New York, New York Function unknown Tunnels to: Capitol Building, D.C.

OHIO Wright-Patterson Air Force Base - Dayton, Ohio Function: Air Force Repository. Rumored to house stealth technology and prototype craft

OREGON 1. Cave Junction, Oregon Function: Suspected Underground UFO Base Levels: At least one Notes: Suspected location is in or near Hope Mountain. Near Applegate Lake, Oregon, just over into California. Multiple shafts, access areas to

---

over 1500 feet depth. Built using abandoned mine with over 36 known miles of tunnels, shafts. 2. Crater Lake, Oregon Tunnels: possible to Cave Junction 3. Klamath Falls, Oregon 4. Wimer, Oregon (Ashland Mt. area) Function: Underground Chemical Storage Levels: At least one

PENNSYLVANIA Raven Rock, Pa (near Ligonier) Function: working back up underground Pentagon - sister site of Mt. Weather Notes: 650' below summit, 4 entrances.

TEXAS 1. Calvert, Texas Function unknown 2. Fort Hood, Texas (also reported detainment camp) Levels: Multiple 3. Fort Stockton, Texas Function: Unknown Tunnels to: Carlsbad, New Mexico UTAH 1. Dugway, Utah Function: Chemical Storage, Radiation storage. 2. Salt Lake City Mormon Caverns Function: Religions archives storage. Levels: Multiple Tunnels to: Delta, Colorado & Riverton, Wyoming

VIRGINIA Mount Poney - Near Culpepper, Virginia Function unknown. Mount Weather known COG base.

WASHINGTON 1. Mt. Rainier, Washington Function unknown. Levels: Multiple Tunnels to: Yakima Indian Reservation. Function: unknown Notes: Southeast of Tacoma Washington, on the Reservation, in an area 40 by 70 miles. Unusual sounds from underground Toppenish Ridge. Low flying Silver Cigar shaped craft seen to disappear into the Middle fork area of Toppenish creek.

Washington DC: The Function: Part of a massive underground relocation system to house select government and military personnel in the event of cataclysmic event. Tunnels to: New York City; Mt. Weather.

This list is only what researchers could uncover and is only for the U.S. many more underground bases are all over the planet. Some bases are under the sea.

The Army Corps of Engineers have tunneled hundreds of miles from shore out to sea. For example, the Treadwell gold mine on Alaska's Douglas Island has tunneled 2,000 feet beneath the sea under the Gastineu Channel. A tunnel has been constructed from San Diego, California called the South Bay Outfall Tunnel.

On Kauai, Hawaii, there is an undersea base at Majors Bay, Barking Sands Naval Base near the Pacific Missile range. There is what could be a huge joint Naval- E.T. undersea base in Puerto Rico that is 40 miles due south of Punta Brea on one end and about 32 miles due south of the western end of St. Croix Island on the other end. The base is about 120 Miles long by about 5 miles wide at an average depth of 2,300 feet below sea level. Thirty miles from the west end of the undersea base, there are two connecting tunnels heading in the direction of the city of Ponce, Puerto Rico.

Local fishermen working south of Vieques Island have witnessed flying saucers and other strange phenomenon in this area. For more Information check out:

http://jorgemartin-enigmasdelmilenio-english.blogspot. com/2012/08/did-we-discover-large-undersea-alien.html

Another reason for constructing these underground bases and cities was that there was fear of global catastrophes from increased solar activity when the sun passed through the galactic disk around 2012. This fear now (2014) seems unfounded. Although the planets in our solar system, including earth are slightly warming and extreme weather is on the increase.

So who is peopling and maintaining all these underground installations? Some researchers theorize that missing persons have been taken to these underground places. The National Crime Information Center's (NCIC) Missing Person File was implemented in 1975. Records in the Missing Person File are retained indefinitely, until the individual is located, or the record is canceled by the entering agency. During 2012, 661,593 missing person records were entered into NCIC, a decrease of 2.5 % from the 678,860 records entered in 2011. Notably, about 4 times as many missing persons are under the age of 18. Younger people are easier to condition if they are indeed being taken to these underground installations.

I personally spoke with the wives of persons working on an underground tunnel between Las Vegas and Area 51. Their husbands were picked up from their homes near Las Vegas and placed in vans with darkened windows. They were blind folded and were driven many miles out into the dessert. The van would stop in the middle of nowhere and there would be a single building there. The blindfolds were taken off and the men would enter the solitary building and take an elevator down a long ways.

Finally, the elevator would stop and they would enter a tube transport device. This device would take them to the end of the tunnel construction. Each man would work fabricating metal with their welding equipment. And, each man had an armed guard watching over them the whole time they were working.

One wife told me that her husband finally could not handle the stress of all the secrecy and having an armed man watching over him while he was working. Even though he was well paid, he finally quit the job and moved to California. Only after he quit the job, did his wife find out what was going on because of his secrecy contract.

The other wife had a similar story.

9

The Extra-Terrestrial Presence

One of the biggest secrets in the U.S. with the highest classification is the extra-terrestrial presence on our planet.

According to Wilber Smith, an upper level person in the Canadian government, the subject was classified higher than the hydrogen bomb project was. Extra-terrestrials have been visiting our planet for thousands of years. But, the event of the atom bomb dramatically increased the rate of their visitation.

Several months after Pearl Harbor, in the early morning hours of February 25, 1942. An unidentified saucer shaped aircraft flew over L.A. County that sparked an air raid alert. Searchlights and Guns were locked onto the aircraft for about an hour as anti-air craft guns fired away at the craft which hovered over the city of Los Angeles. The saucer was unharmed from all the flack shells exploding around it and eventually flew away. The only damage to the city was from falling debris from the anti-aircraft fire. This was reported as the "Battle of Los Angeles" in the Los Angeles Times.

What was not well known was that the Navy had recovered a crashed flying about the same time. A Top Secret memo dated

March 5, 1942, addressed to President Roosevelt explained how the Navy had recovered an "unidentified airplane... of interplanetary origin". Army Chief of Staff, George Marshall ordered the crashed saucer studied and created a highly classified unit called the Interplanetary Phenomenon Unit (IPU), within the Army's G-2 Intelligence Agency, to do the study.

Head of Navy Intelligence, Admiral James Forrestal and General Eisenhower were also informed of the saucer recovery by the Navy. Later, John F. Kennedy, who spent the war in Naval Intelligence, and was a close friend of Forrestal, would accompany him on a 1945 trip to Europe. At this time, Forrestal informed Kennedy of the recovered saucer and told him to keep it secret. (21)

According to the Army's Directorate of Intelligence, The IPU existed until the 1950s when it was disbanded and all of IPU's records were turned over to the U.S. Air Force Office of Special Investigations in conjunction with Operation BLUEBOOK.

The next incident of recorded UFO recovery was the well-known Roswell incident. Actually there were two separate UFO crashes near Rosewell as well as others at Corona, Arizona around the same time. The Army Air Force was not concerned with the crashes around Corona since they were in remote locations and could be secretly recovered and the crash sites cleaned up without danger of the public discovering what had happened.

However, one UFO crash was just north of the city of Roswell and easily accessible to the public. So, the psychological warfare department of G-2 had to do a "bait and switch operation" to direct attention elsewhere.

They leaked a story that the Roswell Army Air Force had

recovered a crashed flying saucer on the Brazel Ranch which was in a more remote location and more difficult to for investigators to reach. The Crashed UFO north of the city was quickly recovered and the site cleaned up by special crashed UFO recovery teams, while public attention was directed elsewhere.

Then, Air Force Major Jesse Marcell posed by some silvery fragments of an alleged ballon while photos were taken. Meanwhile, a second recovery team was cleaning up the Brazel Ranch crash site. The next day the Air Force's Story was changed to recovered balloon fragments – not a flying saucer and the story quickly died out.

All the remains were taken to Wright Paterson Air Force Base (then called Wright Army Air Field) in Daton, Ohio. Wright Paterson was chosen because it already had the facilities and personnel to analyze and back engineer recovered alien technology. (22)

At the time, it was estimated that Nazi technology was about 25 years ahead of the U.S. The brilliant Paperclip Nazis; Siegfried Kneeler, the former head of the German RLM (The Reichsluftfahrtministerium), the Third Reich's Air Ministry for aircraft development for the Luftwaffe, Dr. Hans Amtmann, an expert in vertical takeoff aircraft and Dr. Alexander Lippisch a pioneer in tailless aircraft, who would later develop the US Delta wing fighter, the F-102A Delta Dagger were among the specialists at Wright Patterson and would help back engineer the alien craft.

Some of the Paperclip Nazis at Wright Patterson themselves had developed Nazi flying saucers in Germany, some of which used technology recovered and taught from extraterrestrial beings. Oberth himself was asked how the Nazis had developed such advanced technology. His reply was "We had help from beings not of this world."

All of the Roswell UFO recovery was reported to President Truman who then signed a memo to then Secretary of Defense, James Forrestal, authorizing the creation of "Operation Majestic Twelve" headed by Dr. Vannevar Bush, then director of the Office of Scientific Research and Development.

MJ-12 or Majestic-12 would be a secret group of two leaders from each military service; Air Force, Navy and Army and six leaders in the scientific fields to study the UFO phenomenon. The 12 members of the original MJ-12 can be found by looking at the, well researched, Top Secret / MAJIC preliminary briefing document to President Eisenhower dated November 19, 1952 from MJ-2 Admiral Roscoe Hillenkoetter; Dr. Vannevar Bush, Roscoe Hillenkoter, James Forrestal, Nathan Twining, Hoyt Vandenburg, Detlev Bronk, Jerome Hunsaker, Sidney Souers, Gordon Grey, Donald Mensel, Robert Montague and Lloyd Barkner.

When Eisenhower replaced Truman as President he was briefed on UFOs and the extra-terrestrial situation as described in the "Eisenhower Briefing Document." Further confirmation of MJ-12 is a Top Secret Memo from Wilbert Smith to the Canadian Department of Transportation on November 21, 1951 concerning a small group in the U.S. headed by Vannevar Bush secretly studying flying saucer technology.

At first, Eisenhower was worried about keeping the lid on MJ-12 and IPU secrets. On January 24, 1953, Eisenhower established the Advisory Committee on Government Organizations. He hired Nelson Rockefeller to be chairman of the committee. Rockefeller passed on to Eisenhower his recommendations on reorganizing the National Security Agency to protect the secrecy of MJ-12. MJ-12 should be headed by the Director of Central Intelligence.

Rockefeller was also appointed Special Assistant for Cold War Planning by Eisenhower and therefore also worked directly with the covert operations division at CIA headed by Frank Wisner. Rockefeller ensured that MJ-12 now would have greater autonomy from the office of the president and the uncertainties of the political process.

The problem with MJ-12 working out of Wright Patterson was that it was a military base and therefore under the control of the U.S. President. In 1955, a remote section of the Atomic Energy Commission test site in Nevada was handed over to the CIA and called Area 51. It was an ideal test site for secret spy planes to be used against the Soviets.

Richard Bissell, working under Frank Wisner at CIA's covert operations was placed in charge of the acquisition of Area 51. Groom dry lake was an ideal place to build lengthy airstrips for testing their spy planes. Lockheed Aircraft Corporation was given access to Area 51 by the CIA to test their secret aircraft.

On the other side of Papoose Mountain, approximately 10 miles south-west of Groom Lake was Papoose dry lake. This was where MJ-12 would relocate in an area called S-4. S-4 was hidden inside of Papoose Mountain. There were multi levels of the underground facility. The first level housed the secret planes and flying saucers, which were in hangars that looked like part of the mountain from outside. Hangar doors could be opened and planes or saucers could fly right out of the mountain. The second level was the dining and meeting area. The third level down housed MJ-12 personnel. The fourth level down housed the aliens. The fifth level was a clean room laboratory where aliens and humans worked together on various classified technologies and genetics.

The CIA had total responsibility for the security at Area 51 and total control on who had access to the facilities there. The CIA's Directorate of Plans had the resources and personnel to relocate the extra-terrestrial technologies to S-4 and the CIA's Counter Intelligence Division made sure this was done without any leaks. Now, total secrecy was insured and even the U.S. president had no idea what was going on at Area 51, much less at S-4.

Later, Eisenhower would regret taking the President out of the loop with MJ-12. He wanted to know the progress of the alien program. In 1958, CIA agent Richard Dolan and his boss were called into oval office. Eisenhower was accompanied by the Vice President, Richard Nixon. The president explained:

"We called the people in from MJ-12 from Area51 and S-4, but they told us that the government had no jurisdiction over what they were doing...I want you and your boss to fly out there. I want you to give them a personal message...I want you to tell them, whoever is in charge, I want you to tell them that they have this coming week to get into Washington and report to me. And if they don't, I'm going to get the First Army from Colorado. We are going to go over and take the base over. I don't care what kind of classified material you got. We are going to rip this whole thing apart."

Dolan and his CIA boss went to Area 51 and relayed Eisenhower's message. Then, they were allowed to observe the flying saucers and Grey aliens at S-4. Dolan's boss interviewed the Grey alien. After returning to Washington D.C., Dolan and his boss reported what they had learned to the president, who was this time accompanied by J. Edgar Hoover, director of the FBI. The CIA agent observed that Eisenhower was visibly shaken from what he had learned.

Secretive portions of the Military Industrial Complex were working with the CIA and aliens on programs that the president had little or no control over. Future presidents would have even less ability to discover what was going on than he had. So, effectively MJ-12, and corporations that it worked with, would become beyond the control of the constitutional government of the U.S. In Eisenhower's farewell speech, he warned about the dangers of the Military Industrial Complex.

Lt. Colonel Phillip Corso was head of the U.S. Army's Foreign technology Desk from 1961 to 1963. In his book *The Day After Roswell,* he describes how alien technology was sent to various companies to back engineer into useful devices. He claims that the transistor and the laser were offshoots of this alien technology, which the company scientists at Bell Labs were allowed to patent themselves to better hide the actual source of the alien technology.

Information from S-4 is highly classified and has only become available via whistle blowers who have actually worked there. The first Whistle blower was Robert Lazar who felt that the government had no right to hide something as important as ET contact and technology from the American people.

Robert Lazar is a scientist with two masters degrees, one in physics, the other in electronics. He wrote his thesis on magneto hydrodynamics (MHD). He has worked in Los Alamos as a technician and then as a physicist in the Polarized Proton Section dealing with particle accelerators. In his spare time, he has built a jet powered car _and_ a jet powered motorbike (max. speed 350mph!), as well as a car capable of running off of hydrogen.

In March 1989, Lazar appeared on KLAS-TV in the US claiming to have worked in an above Top Secret installation known as S-4, ten miles south of AREA 51 in the Nevada desert. He was a scientist who was employed between December 1988 and April 1989 to examine a captured flying saucer to try and reverse engineer the saucer's propulsion mechanism.

He claims that there were nine different saucers at S-4, although he was only working on one of them. He was told that the crafts used a propulsion system that uses gravity waves, a theory that mainstream science hasn't discovered yet and the energy needed is supplied by irradiating Element 115, an element not found on Earth and which, at the time, could not be synthesized. He says that he had 500 pounds (227.27kg) of the element to work with, but each craft only needed 223 grams of the element.

When element 115 is bombarded with a proton, it is transmuted to element 116 which is unstable and undergoes a decay which releases large amounts of anti-matter. The matter – anti-matter reaction is efficiently and directly converted into electricity using a back-engineered alien device. Whilst working on one of the craft, he was allowed to actually go inside the craft and he was also present at a test flight in which the craft underwent a few simple maneuvers in the air.

Having knowledge of the testing schedule, on 29/3/89, Lazar took three of his friends, one of them John Lear, to the edge of S-4 to observe any UFO test flights through a telescope. They saw (and filmed) a bright light rise in a step maneuver, that is, it would hover in the air, briefly disappear and reappear a few feet higher, and then the light went down in the same way.

After Lazar went public, his university and work records at Los Alamos were destroyed and attempts were made to discredit him. However, since his claim was made in 1989, Element 115 has actually been artificially created and called Ununpentium.

Dan Burish was a microbiologist who was another whistle blower that worked at S-4. Dan Burish's work on classified "black" programs began in the 1990-1991 time period. Concurrently, he was deployed in Operation Desert Storm as a defense bio-warfare expert in black ops operations. He refuses to discuss much about his role in bio defense unless given immunity from possible prosecution for war crimes. Biological and chemical warfare constitutes a war crime.

By 1994, Dan received and accepted an offer to work on a TOP SECRET program known as Project Aquarius, located at an underground facility known as Papoose Lake facility S-4, located 10 miles south of Area 51 in Nevada.

Security measures at the facility were very oppressive. This included armed guards, optical scans, voice print identification, showering, weighing, shaving, and decontamination. Dan was told he had been commissioned by the department of the Navy, and was given a secret "Q" clearance. At times he was assigned to work under the direction of the prestigious Naval Research Laboratory, and the Defense Intelligence Agency. These assignments were designated on official documents to legitimize his presence while working for a group called Majestic.

It was here at S-4, that Dan learned that the United States Government was working with extraterrestrial "visitors" for decades, and that many technological advancements directly associated with the field of military aerospace, were actually made through a "reverse engineering" program beginning in the 1940's. Dan described the facility as having five working floors. He also claims that he saw some of the flying saucers that Robert Lazar worked on.

Dan was transported from McCarran International Airport in Las Vegas to Area 51 via "Janet" 737-200 airliner. The staging point for pick-up and drop off is the EG&G building across from the main terminal. These aircraft feature a painted white exterior, with a single red stripe running along both sides of the fuselage.

During the flight to Area 51, no talking was allowed between personnel that Dan was allied with. When entering the aircraft, Dan was instructed to sit near the aft end of the cabin, and then, a drape was pulled, thereby separating his section with that of the rest of the cabin. Seating arrangements are carefully chosen so that passengers are "quarantined" from various personnel who may be working on various different programs on the base.

So what was project Aquarius that Dan Burish worked on? Here is the wording of a document recovered by UFO researchers:

TOP SECRET
CLASSIFICATION AND RELEASE INSTRUCTIONS

(TS/ORCON) The information contained in this document is classified TOP SECRET with ORCON. (Only the originator may release the information). Only MJ12 has access to Project Aquarius. No other government agency, to include the military has access to the information contained in this briefing. There are only two copies of Project Aquarius and the location is known only to MJ12. This document will be destroyed after the briefing. No notes, photographs, or audio recordings may be made of this briefing.

PROJECT AQUARIUS

(TS/ORCON) (PROWORD: DANCE) Contains 16 volumes of documented information collected from the beginning of the United States Investigation of Unidentified Flying Objects (UFOs) and Identified Alien Crafts (IAC). The Project was originally established in 1953, by order of President Eisenhower, under control of NSC and MJ12. In 1966, the Project's name was changed from Project Gleem to Project Aquarius. The Project was funded by CIA confidential funds (non-appropriated). The Project was originally classified SECRET but was upgraded to its present classification in Dec. 1969 after Project Blue Book closed. The purpose of Project Aquarius was to collect all scientific, technological, medical, and intelligence information from UFO/IAC sightings, and contacts with Alien life forms. This orderly file of collected information has been used to advanced the United States Space Program.

The proceeding briefing is an historical account of the United States Government's investigation of Aerial Phenomena, Recovered Alien Aircrafts, and Contacts with Extraterrestrial Life Forms.

EXECUTIVE BREIFING (TS/ORCON) In June 1947, a civilian pilot flying over the Cascade Mountains of Washington State observed nine flying discs (later referred to as UFOs). The Commander, Air Force Technical Intelligence Center of the then Army Air Forces became concerned and ordered an inquiry. This was the beginning of the United States involvement with the UFO investigations. In 1947, an aircraft of extraterrestrial origin crashed in the desert of New Mexico. The craft was recovered by the military, four Alien (non-homo-sapiens) bodies were recovered in the wreckage. The Aliens were found to be creatures not related to human beings. Atch. 1.

In late 1949, another Alien aircraft crashed in the United States and was recovered partially intact by the military. One Alien of extraterrestrial origin survived the crash. The surviving Alien was male and called itself "EBE". The Alien was thoroughly interrogated by military intelligence personnel at a base in New Mexico. The Alien's language was translated by means of picture graphs. It was learned the Alien came from a planet in the Zeta [sic] Reticuli star system, approximately 40 light years from Earth. EBE lived until June 18, 1952, when he died [sic] to an unexplained illness. During the time period EBE was alive, he provided valuable information regarding space technology, origins of the Universe, and exobiological matters. Further data is contained in Atch 2.

The recovery of Alien aircrafts led the United States on an extensive investigation program to determine whether these Aliens posed a direct threat to our national security. In 1947, the newly created Air Force initiated a program to investigate incidents involving UFOs. The program was operated under three different code names: Grudge, Sign, and finally Blue Book. The original mission of the Air Force program was to collect and analyze all reported sightings or incidents involving UFOs and determine whether the information could be interpreted as having any bearing on the security of the United States. Some information was evaluated with the idea of using the gained data to advance our own space technology and future space programs. Ninety percent of the estimated 12,000 reports analyzed by the Air Force were considered hoaxes, explained aerial phenomena's, or natural astronomical objects. The other 10 percent were considered legitimate Alien sightings and/or incidents. However, not all UFO sightings or incidents were reported under the Air Force program. In 1953, Project Gleem was initiated by order of President Eisenhower, who believed the UFOs presented a threat to the national security of the United States. Project

Gleem, which became Project Aquarius in 1966, was a parallel reporting system for UFO sightings and incidents. Reports collected under Project Aquarius were considered actual sightings of Alien aircrafts or contacts with Alien life forms. Most reports were made by reliable military and Defense Department civilian personnel.

In 1958, the United States recovered a third Alien aircraft from the desert of Utah. The aircraft was in excellent flying condition. The aircraft was apparently abandoned by the Aliens for some unexplained reason, since no Alien life forms were found in or around the aircraft. The aircraft was considered a technological marvel by United States scientists. However, the operating instrumentations of the aircraft were so complex that our scientists could not interrupt their operation. The aircraft was stored in a top security area and analyzed throughout the years by our best aerospace scientists. The United States gained a large volume of technological data from the recovered Alien aircraft. A detailed description and further information regarding the aircraft is explained in Atch. 3

Several independent scientific investigations, at the request of the Air Force and CIA, were initiated during the era of Project Blue Book. MJ12 decided that officially, the Air Force should end their investigation of UFOs. This decision was arrived at during the [unreadable] meeting in 1966. The reason was twofold. First, the United States had established communication with the Aliens. The United States felt relatively sure the Aliens' exploration of Earth was non-aggressive and non-hostile. It was also established that the Aliens' presence did not directly threaten the security of the United States. Secondly, the public was beginning to believe that UFOs were real. The NSC felt this public feeling could lead to nationwide panic. The United States was involved in several sensitive projects during this time period. It was felt that public awareness of these projects would have jeopardized the future space program of the United States. Therefore, MJ12 decided that an independent scientific study of the UFO phenomena would be needed to satisfy public curiosity. The study concluded that sufficient data did not exist that would indicate UFOs threatened the security of the United States. The final conclusion satisfied the government and allowed the Air Force to officially step out of the UFO investigating business.

When the Air Force officially closed Project Blue Book in Dec. 1969, Project Aquarius continued operation under control of NSC/MJ12. The NSC felt investigations of UFO sightings and incidents had to continue in secrecy without any public knowledge. The reasoning behind the decision was this: If the Air Force continued its investigation of UFOs, eventually some uncleared and un-briefed Air Force or Defense Department civilian officials would obtain the facts behind Project Aquarius. Obviously (for operational security reasons) this could not be allowed. In order to continue the investigation of UFO sightings and incidents in secrecy, investigators from CIA/DCD and MJ12 were assigned to military and other governmental agencies with orders to investigate all legitimate UFO/IAC sightings and incidents. These agents are presently operating at various locations throughout the United States and Canada. All reports are filtered either directly or indirectly to MJ12. These agents are collecting reports of UFO/IAC sightings and incidents occurring on or near sensitive governmental installations.

NOTE: Aliens have been extremely interested in our nuclear weapons and nuclear research. Many reported military sightings and incidents occur over nuclear weapons bases. The Alien's interest in our nuclear weapons can only be attributed to the future threat of a nuclear war on Earth. The Air Force have initiated measures to insure the security of the nuclear weapons from Alien theft or destruction. MJ12 feels confident the Aliens are on an exploration of our solar system for peaceful purposes. However, we must continue to observe and track the Aliens' movements until it is determined that the Aliens' future plans contain no threat to our national security or the civilization of Earth.

Most governmental documents pertaining to UFO sightings, incidents and governmental policies, including Project Blue Book, have been released to the public under FOIA or under various other release programs. MJ12 felt the remaining documents and information (not related to Project Aquarius) relating to technological facts regarding Aliens' medical matters, the fact that an Alien was captured alive and survived for three years, ca not be released to the public for fear the information would be obtained by SHIS There was other information obtained from EBE that was deemed sensitive and not releasable to the public. Notably, Project Aquarius Volume IX, which pertains to tracing the Aliens' first visitation of Earth back some 5,000 years. EBE reported that 2,000 years ago his ancestors planted a human creature on Earth to assist the inhabitants of Earth in developing a civilization. This information was only vague and the exact identity or background information on this homo-sapien was not obtained. Un-doubtfully, if this information was released to the public, it would cause a worldwide religious panic. MJ3 has developed a plan that will allow release of Project Aquarius, Volumes I thru III. The release program calls for a gradual release of information over a period of time in order to condition the public for future disclosures. Atch 5 of this briefing contains certain guidelines for future public releases.

In the 1976 MJ3 report (Atch 6), it was estimated the Aliens' technology was many thousands of years ahead of United States technology. Our scientists speculate that until our technology develops to a level equal to the Aliens, we cannot understand the large volume of scientific information the United States has already gained from the Aliens. This advancement of United States technology may take many hundreds of years.

SUB PROJECTS UNDER PROJECT AQUARIUS
1. (TS/ORCON) PROJECT BANDO: (PROWORD: RISK) originally established in 1949. Its mission was to collect and evaluate medical information from the surviving Alien creature and the recovered Alien bodies. This Project medically examined EBE and provided United States medical researchers with certain answers to the evolution theory. (OPR: CIA) (Terminated in 1974)

2. (TS/ORCON) PROJECT SIGMA: (PROWORD: MIDNIGHT) originally established as part of Project Gleem in 1954, it became a separate project in 1976. Its mission was to establish communication with Aliens. This Project met with positive success, when in 1959, the United States established primitive communications with the Aliens. On April 25, 1964, a USAF intelligence officer met two Aliens at a prearranged location in the desert of New Mexico. The contact lasted for approximately three hours. Based on the Alien's language given to us by EBE, the Air Force officer managed to exchange basic information with the two Aliens (Atch 7). This project is continuing at an Air Force base in New Mexico. (OPR: MJ12/NSA).

3. (TS/ORCON) PROJECT SNOWBIRD: (PROWORD: CETUS) originally established in 1972. Its mission was to test fly a recovered alien aircraft. This project is continuing in Nevada. (OPR: USAF/NSA/CIA/MJ12)

4. (TS/ORCON) PROJECT POUNCE: (PROWORD: DIXIE) originally established in 1968. Its mission was to evaluate all UFO/IAC information pertaining to space technology. PROJECT POUNCE continues. (OPR: NASA/USAF)

End of Document. The attachments were not recovered by researchers.

When Allen Dulles became Director of CIA, he also became MJ-1 and privy to all the information at S-4. As a Knight of Malta Agent of the Vatican, he also relayed this information to the Jesuit Superior General to keep him advised of the current extra-terrestrial situation. The Vatican of course keeps all of this secret, for fear that public knowledge of extra-terrestrials visiting our planet would jeopardize their religious mission.

The military was not the only ones communicating with the extra-terrestrials; there were many individual contactees, men like George Adamski, Billy Mier, Daniel Fry, Truman Berthurum and George Van Tassle who claimed they were communicating with the beings in the flying saucers. Many contactees have written books about their experiences and communications with these alien beings.

George Adamski was one of the first contactees and wrote a number of books on his experiences with the aliens On November 20, 1952, Adamski and six friends were in the Colorado Desert near the town of Desert Center, California, when they purportedly saw a large submarine-shaped object hovering in the sky.

Believing that the ship was looking for him, Adamski is said to have left his friends and to have headed away from the main road. Shortly afterwards, according to Adamski's accounts, a scout ship landed close to him, and its pilot, an ETcalled

Orthon, disembarked and sought him out. Adamski's six friends observed the contact with Orthon through binoculars and have signed documents attesting to the reality of Adamski's contact claims.

Adamski described Orthon as being a medium-height humanoid with long blond hair and tanned skin. Orthon communicated with him via telepathy and through hand signals. During their conversation, Orthon is said to have warned of the dangers of nuclear war and to have arranged for Adamski to be taken on a trip to see the Solar System, including the planet Venus, where Orthon claimed he was from.

Adamski also took some photos of flying saucers and cigar shaped mother ships and included them in some of his books. He also went on many speaking tours and became quite famous.

Billy Meier, a German Citizen has perhaps the best photos of flying saucers and claims to have ridden in them. Lt. Colonel Wendell Stevens, retired Air Force Intelligence officer and a UFO researcher, has the largest collection of UFO photos in private hands and has authored a number of books on the subject, including *Messages from the Pleiades Volume I and II* which have the contact notes and photos of Billy Meier.

Here, we have a conflict of stories. Billy Meier said he took a trip to Venus on Samjase's beam ship. He observed no life on Venus and was told that Venus was still in an early stage of its evolution. Yet, Orthon told Adamski that he was from the Planet Venus. According to NASA, information from their space probes indicates the surface temperature on Venus is hot enough to melt lead. Perhaps Orthon was not being truthful. Just because they are extra-terrestrials does not mean that they, like humans on this planet, cannot sometimes tell an untruth.

MJ-12 with the CIA developed a Physiological Warfare Division to counter public interest in flying saucers and extra-terrestrials. Their job was to debunk and discredit the contactees and observers of UFOs. So, swamp gas, the planet Venus and weather balloons became the "real explanation for UFO sightings. Only the most uninformed and gullible could accept these ridiculous explanations, which makes one wonder just how intelligent people running these intelligence agencies really are.

Most of the aliens seem to be concerned that mankind is on a course of destroying the earth, through pollution, over population, harmful technology and nuclear war. The nuclear weapons have effects our scientists don't understand on the space-time continuum and affect other parts of the universe, which is one of the reasons for their alarm and their increased monitoring of our planet. Their influence on our national leaders probably had a lot to do with the Nuclear Test Ban Treaty.

Many of the contactees have expressed their respect for the extra-terrestrial more advanced spirituality, intellect and wisdom and help to spread the words of their other worldly contacts through their writings and speaking engagements. However, world governments continue to dishonestly cover up the ET presence in our planet.

Conclusions

We see that Christianity was first distorted by the Orthodox Christian Church fathers to gain more followers and gain greater control over them. The Catholic Church of Rome would later make even more changes in order to appeal to Pagan Rome, while violating laws set down by the God of the Jews and the teachings of Jesus Christ. Changing the day of worship from the Sabbath on the seventh day of the week to Sunday on the first day of the week violated the law to keep the Sabbath holy. The worship before statues of the Virgin Mary violated the commandment against Idol worship. Jesus never wished anyone to worship his mother. The Church policy of killing heretics violated the commandment against killing. The cruelty of burning people at the stake went against Jesus' Love thy neighbor concept.

The Church also committed numerous frauds and outright lies violating the commandment to not bear false witness. Some of these frauds were the lie that the Pope was Jesus's representative on Earth and that the Pope held the keys of Heaven and Hell. Other lies were the priest's ability to absolve sins; the fraud of Constantine's Donation, giving all of the Western Roman Empire to the Catholic Church and the Sale of Indulgences, where for the right price, your sins could be absolved.

Using these Pagan rituals, the Church of Rome clothed itself in Christianity and after Rome's defeat evolved into the Holy Roman Empire. This Empire lasted about 1,000 years. The Protestant reformation threatened this empire and lead to the installation of the Society of Jesus by the Catholic Church to counter the Reformation.

Some of the leaders of the Reformation noting that many Church rituals dated back to Babylon and the Church's departure from Biblical scripture called the Catholic Church the "Whore of Babylon" mentioned in Revelations and called the Pope the anti-Christ.

The members of the Society of Jesus became known as the Jesuits. The Jesuit's mission was to make war on all heretics. The Jesuits started a spy network using the confessional to gather information. They would become advisors to princes and kings. Often using the confessional and their assumed ability to absolve sins and sometimes using the intelligence gathered from their spy network to blackmail, they exercised considerable influence these national leaders. This influence led to many wars against Protestant kingdoms and massacres of Protestants.

Bowing to pressure from the kings of Europe who were alarmed by the Jesuits criminal activity, the Jesuits were finally outlawed by the Catholic Church itself. The Jesuits went underground and created secret societies like the Illuminati. They controlled Napoleon who ended the Holy Roman Empire and who had the Pope arrested –not to be released until the Society of Jesus was reinstated. After this, the Jesuits were re-instated and had more actual worldly power than the Pope.

The Illuminati took over Freemason lodges and organized the American, French and Bolshevik Revolutions. Most of the Wars of Europe and the twentieth and twenty first centuries were also instigated by the Jesuits through their secret societies, vast wealth from the corporations they secretly owned through third parties and their influence over world leaders. The ultimate reason for these wars was world control, in a world government with its capitol at Jerusalem. This is the New World Order and their plan.

Before World War II, industrialists in the U.S., which supported fascism, planned a military coup against President Roosevelt. After World War II, the fascists were integrated into a secret stay behind army under the CIA and NATO which allowed the Nazi Ghelen to operate Nazi cells in Europe. This secret army was supposed to counter a Soviet threatened invasion based on false intelligence supplied by Ghelen. This secret army was later used to commit acts of terrorism in Europe and the U.S. and blame the communists; generically these operations were called "Operation Gladio."

Before and after World War II the Nazi government and the U.S. government secretly made contact with extra-terrestrials and developed advanced technology, including antigravity, based on these contacts. While some of this technology like; transistors, printed circuits, charge coupled devices, lasers, Etc. have been developed into computers LED T.V.s, miniature digital cameras, Etc. for public use, much of the technology like free energy and antigravity technology has been kept secret from the public. These secret technologies would upset the money flow for the big energy companies and give too much freedom to the public and therefore have been withheld.

Electronic mind control technology has also been developed

which can transmit thoughts and emotions into the mind and receive thoughts and emotions from the mind. This technology has been used by the U.S. military on Iraq military forces, causing them to surrender in mass.

Massive underground constructions called Deep Underground Military Bases were created to have a continuation of government in the event of a nuclear war. Some also feared a giant world cataclysm around 2012 when the solar system passed through the galactic disk. Some researchers posit that these underground base/cities are peopled by many of the missing persons, which run into the hundreds of thousands yearly in the U.S. alone.

The Third World War is happening before our eyes, with the military destruction of Yugoslavia, Afghanistan, Iraq and Libya with the future destruction of Syria and Iran and the Ukraine in the works. This is the preferred method rather than all-out war because of the nuclear destruction of the world threat. Other countries not cooperating with the New World Order are also targeted for regime change via the NGOs and CIA intervention. Any country that nationalizes their natural wealth, which rightfully should belong to all the people of that nation, will be targeted for "regime change" so that the multinational corporations can exploit that natural wealth for their own profit.

So, basically the Jesuits gained control of the Vatican and the Freemasons and are behind the planned New World Order, while setting up some Masonic Jews like the Rothschilds, Warburgs and the Schiffs. to place the blame on all Jews if things go wrong. Israel is an important factor in the Jesuit's plan because the planned World War III uses the enmity between Arabs and Israel to promote the war and Jerusalem is the planned capital of the world government.

The unknown wild card is Russia, which has had a resurgence of the Eastern Orthodox Christian Church in spite of the Jesuit's Bolshevik revolution. Putin is a believer of this religion in spite of his KGB past and has countered the New World Order plan to destroy Syria and Iran. Because of the Nuclear Armageddon threat, a direct confrontation with Russia and their ally, China is unthinkable. Only the future will tell!

Another wild card is the Extra-terrestrial presence. Most of their groups have said that according to universe law, they are not allowed to interfere too much in our evolution except in certain situations like a planet wide nuclear war that would destroy all life on the planet. However, not all ET groups obey universal law. Certain ETs helped the Nazis develop their technologies and wonder weapons and some are helping the U.S. with their technologies and wonder weapons. Also, certain groups including the Greys and Onions at S-4 are experimenting with human genetics and claim to be improving them.

Because you are reading this book, you are perhaps now more aware of the world situation than many who rely on the Illuminati controlled news media for their reality picture. For those of you who still doubt the reality presented in this book - do your own research. The internet is a vast source of information (and disinformation) if you know what to look for. Usually sources like the Foreign Affairs Magazine published by the CFR, information from illuminati controlled foundations like the Brookings Institute, the Ford Foundation, NGOs etc. contain a lot of disinformation. The news media, like the New York Times, is controlled but sometimes nuggets of information can even be found there.

Try placing the right word combinations in a Google search engine, for example; CANVAS Arab Spring, Prince Bandar

Chemical Weapons, Vatican CIA, Vatican Bank of England , Jesuits Civil War, Ukraine Gladio, Gladio Kennedy Assassination, Dan Burish S4 or make up your own combinations and see what you come up with. Also, read some of the books mentioned in the bibliography to insure that I am not just making all this up.

Becoming more aware is the first step toward liberation – the truth shall set you free! Further strategies to increase your freedom is to develop self-rule. If you allow your body to rule your spirit, seeking all kinds of sensual pleasures and worldly possessions you are on a sure path to bondage and open yourself to manipulation by others.

Develop self-discernment to understand your own motives for what you are doing. The person that rules his or her own self is much harder to be ruled over by others.

The intellectual mind can also become a tyrant to the spirit. The intellect is an excellent tool to function in the material world, but it is not the end all of existence. The Yogis of India understand this and have developed methods of meditation to still the intellectual chatter box of the mind and perceive deeper realities. Leading a balanced life is usually the best approach.

We are only visitors on the earth, we are born naked and we will one day die and will be unable to take the treasures of the world with us. As Jesus said "it is more difficult for a rich man to go to heaven than a camel to pass through the eye of a needle." He also said that "the kingdom of heaven is within." Does this mean that the rich man is so involved with the outward world in gaining his wealth and power, that he has cut himself off from his inner world where heaven really is?

Jesus's two commandments are "Love thy God with all your

heart and understanding." and "Love thy neighbor as thyself." True Christians are those that try to live by these commandments. Those "Christians" who do not are false Christians. Most of the people of other religions immediately see the wisdom in these two commandments. True Christians do not engage in or promote war, which brings hell on earth and is the work of Satan. Jesuits and the Religious Right take note. "By the fruit of their labors they shall be known."

As I have said, I am not a Christian. But, I have studied Jesus's teaching and I think they are divine wisdom. If his teachings were actually put into practice, we would have heaven on Earth. I am a free thinker and have studied all the major world's religions and have decided to not join any of them because they are man-made. I do love the un-nameable Creator of all there is and have love and respect for all life. I am therefore a pacifist and vegetarian. I am saddened by those destroyers of the Earth who serve Mammon, the money god. I know that, in the ultimate end, they will realize the stupidity and shortsightedness of their actions and will repent and change.

In fact, God has the ultimate conspiracy which may be unfathomable to us mortals. Life has actually, in many ways, improved over the years, in spite of all the bad guys have done. That is because there are a lot more good guys than bad guys. Ultimately, we will need a world government. However, hopefully it will be one of truth and service to mankind - not secretiveness and greed to serve the few at everyone else's expense, like the present New World Order.

The big question is what to do about corporations? What to do about the biggest corporation of all – the Vatican? Large corporations, through their influence, virtually run most governments of the world including the United States. International

Corporations can be outside the control or regulation by governments and become completely autonomous organizations.

Destroyers of the Earth corporations like Monsanto hire their own private armies to defend their destructive chemical and biological technologies. Recently, Monsanto merged with Xe (the old Black Water Co.) corporation founded by former Navy SEAL and Knight of Malta Erik Prince. And, now Xe is changing its name once again to Academi.

The Vatican is an international autonomous organization which, as this book has shown, controls many governments including the U.S. Also, the Corporate "City of London" and United States Inc. in the District of Columbia, (as opposed to the republic of the United States) are international autonomous organizations.

Fascism is the unification of corporations and government. In The U.S., because of the actual control of the corporations over our government, we are a de facto fascist government as is becoming more evident every year.

Corporations provide a service, products and jobs. But when they become too large they also create problems like war, pollution, undue political influence and national debt. Corporations should be limited in size and function to prevent these problems. In the U.S., political campaign financing should be off limits for corporations, foundations and NGO's

Central Banking Corporations should be entirely outlawed. The creation of money rightfully belongs to government - not private banking corporations like the Bank of England or the Federal Reserve Bank. These types of banks create money out of nothing and lend it out for tremendous profit – the ultimate counterfeiting operation which invariably leads to inflation. These Central

Banks probably have the greatest influence over governments of any corporation. Shutting down Central Banks would solve the National debt problems of many nations including the U.S.

The natural resources of any country like timber, mineral and oil wealth should, by strictly enforced law, be distributed to all citizens of that country, after a moderate profit for the extracting company. Imagine what that kind of policy would do for the impoverished people of Africa and Latin America.

Corporations CEOs and other officers should have a cap on their salaries. They should not be able to earn more than the President of the United States period! The present orgy of greed displayed by corporate officers is a disgusting and immoral shame and totally un-necessary for the operation of the company while actually lowering corporate profitability.

The National Security act should be disbanded as unconstitutional. All agencies like the NSA, DIA, CIA, DISC Homeland Security etc. created by this act and others should be dismantled. They have done more harm to the United States than good with their fascist policies while their astronomical costs are heading our country towards bankruptcy. What about the Terrorists? You might ask. Doing away with the CIA, DIA and NATO would eliminate most of the terrorists. If the U.S. would keep its nose out of other countries affairs, there would be little reason for anti U.S. terrorism.

The good guys cannot force the bad guys to change by force - that is a fallacy. Nor can we hate them. Jesus said "Love thine enemy." Nor can we seek justice or revenge. "Vengeance is mine sayeth the Lord." Revenge merely escalates the wrong doing on both sides. One must have faith that God is the real power and that all is part of divine planning. I always try to put myself in the other person position and try to see how I would feel.

We really can only change our selves and, by our living example, show others they way. The New World Order is but the dream - nay nightmare - of insecure idiots who are lost in unreality and their belief that the material world is all there really is. They worship wealth, status and prestige and forget the wisdom of Jesus: "As ye do unto the least so ye do unto me also." Let us pray for these lost souls that they might find their way back to the true living God and away from the Satan of selfishness, pride, cruelty and non-love.

Bibliography

1. *The Two Babylon's* by Alexander Hislop.

2. The documentation of this Vatican strategy lies in the Vatican library. It was studied by Jesuit Cardinal Bea who shared the information with his pupil, Jesuit Priest, Alberto Rivera. Alberto Rivera later quit the Jesuit Order and revealed this information publically. (Chick Publications: www.chick.com)

3. *The Secret History of the Jesuits* by Edmond Paris.

4. *Codeword Barbelon* by P.D. Stewart.

5. *Rulers of Evil* by Tupper Saussy.

6. *America's Secret Establishment* by Anthony Sutton.

7. *The Suppressed Truth about the Assassination of Abraham Lincoln* by Burke McCarty.

8. *From Major Jordan's Diaries* by Racey Jordan.

9. *The Vatican's Holocaust* by Avro Manhattan.

10. *Vietnam, why did we go?* By Avro Manhattan.

11. *Vatican's Assassins* by Eric Jon Phelps.

12. *Marita* by Marita Lorenz.

13. *A Nation Betrayed* by Lieutenant Colonial James Bo Gritz.

14. *October Surprise* by Barbara Honegger.

15. *Dangerous Liaison* by Cockburn.

16. *Wanta! Black Swan, White Hat* by Marilyn MacGruder.

17. *Barry & 'the Boys': The CIA, the Mob and America's Secret History*, by Daniel Hopsicker.

18. *NATO's Secret Armies: Operation Gladio and Terrorism in Western Europe* by Ganser Daniele.

19. *Gladio, NATO's Dagger at the Heart of Europe* by Richard Cottrell

20. *Hillary (and Bill) The Drugs Volume* and *The Murder Volume* by Victor Thorne

21. *Kennedy's Last Stand: Eisenhower, UFOs, MJ-12 & JFK's Assassination* by Michael E. Salla, Ph.D.

22. *Earth an Alien Enterprise* by Timothy Good.

CPSIA information can be obtained
at www.ICGtesting.com
Printed in the USA
BVOW06s1232261016
466050BV00008B/211/P